FIELD-MARSHAL H.R.H. THE DUKE OF CAMBRIDGE

Colonel of the Royal Artillery 10th May, 1861.
Colonel-in-Chief of the Royal Artillery, 1895.

Died 1904.

THE HISTORY

OF

THE ROYAL ARTILLERY

FROM THE INDIAN MUTINY TO THE GREAT WAR

DEDICATED BY
HIS MAJESTY'S GRACIOUS PERMISSION TO
KING GEORGE V.
COLONEL-IN-CHIEF OF THE ROYAL ARTILLERY

VOLUME I
(1860–1899)

MAJOR-GENERAL SIR CHARLES CALLWELL, K.C.B.
AND
MAJOR-GENERAL SIR JOHN HEADLAM, K.B.E., C.B., D.S.O.
COLONEL-COMMANDANT, R.A.

The Naval & Military Press Ltd

published in association with

FIREPOWER
The Royal Artillery Museum
Woolwich

Published by
The Naval & Military Press Ltd
Unit 10 Ridgewood Industrial Park,
Uckfield, East Sussex,
TN22 5QE England
Tel: +44 (0) 1825 749494
Fax: +44 (0) 1825 765701
www.naval-military-press.com

in association with

FIREPOWER
The Royal Artillery Museum, Woolwich
www.firepower.org.uk

The Naval & Military
Press

MILITARY HISTORY AT YOUR
FINGERTIPS

… a unique and expanding series of reference works

Working in collaboration with the foremost
regiments and institutions, as well as acknowledged
experts in their field, N&MP have assembled a
formidable array of titles including technologically
advanced CD-ROMs and facsimile reprints of
impossible-to-find rarities.

*In reprinting in facsimile from the original, any imperfections are inevitably reproduced
and the quality may fall short of modern type and cartographic standards.*

Printed and bound by Antony Rowe Ltd, Eastbourne

PREFACE.

When the Committee of the Royal Artillery Institution entrusted the completion of the pre-War History of the Regiment to Major-General Sir Charles Callwell and myself, it was on the understanding that Sir Charles should be responsible for the period from the close of Colonel Jocelyn's "Mutiny" volume to the commencement of the South African War, while I carried on the story to the outbreak of the Great War. But when we came to the actual planning of our work we both realized that the whole period from 1860 to 1914 was one of continuous development—stimulated and directed rather than interrupted by the South African War; and that if the many diverse influences, both moral and material, which combined to shape the artillery of 1914 were to be represented in their proper proportion and perspective, the period must be treated as a whole. We therefore decided not only to work in the closest co-operation, but also each to take a share in the other's portion. The untimely death of Sir Charles unfortunately prevented the carrying out of this arrangement in its entirety, but he left the Parts which bear his name practically complete as they appear here, and also drafts on other subjects which will be incorporated in subsequent Volumes. More important still, his great experience and sound judgment were available when the plan of the whole work was under discussion.

Regarding this plan, however, some explanation is perhaps called for, especially in connection with the separation of the history of the campaigns from the general narrative.

Between 1860 and 1914 the British Army was engaged in many wars, in all of which the Royal Artillery bore an honourable part. But none of these campaigns—with the possible exception of that in South Africa—affected its development to a degree at all comparable with the influence exerted by the European wars of the period, or by the march of science. To have interspersed accounts of the British campaigns throughout the narrative would therefore only have interrupted the story of tactical and technical development without throwing any light on its causes. It is for this reason that the history of the campaigns has been relegated to separate volumes.

For a somewhat analogous reason it has been thought advisable to defer any reference to the Militia and Volunteers to Volume II, so that the whole story of the gradual drawing closer of the bonds uniting the Auxiliary with the Regular Artillery may be told when dealing with the formation of the Territorial Force. Similarly the accounts of various regimental establishments—such as the School of Gunnery, the Artillery College, the Institution, the Band. the Mess, and such miscellaneous subjects as uniform, personal equipment, etc., have been postponed until they can be dealt with for the whole period 1860-1914 in one place. The story of the Royal Military Academy has been so fully told by Sir Frederick Guggisberg in his book "The Shop" that it has not been thought necessary to refer to its history here.

The digressions into previous periods in the chapters dealing with the training and tactics of mountain and heavy artillery will, it is hoped, be excused in view of the little said about these branches in former volumes of Regimental History.

But the temptation to dip into the future and point a moral by reference to the experiences of the Great War has been sternly resisted. It will be for the historian of the performance of the Regiment in that time of trial to tell how the theories of this period of preparation stood the final test.

In conclusion I would like to take this opportunity of expressing my gratitude to the officials, both civil and military, of the War Office, the India Office, the Ordnance Committee, the Inspection and Design Departments at Woolwich, and of the Royal Artillery and Royal United

Service Institutions, for their assistance; and of acknowledging the debt which I owe to those of my brother officers who have been kind enough to read these pages at various stages of their growth, and to help me with many invaluable suggestions. On the active list they, one and all, rendered yeoman service towards carrying into effect the reforms recorded : in their retirement they have done much to ensure the truth of this presentment to posterity. To name them would be invidious, but I should be singularly wanting in gratitude if I did not make special reference to the assistance received from those who joined the Regiment during the first decade of the period under review. In spite of the burden of their four-score years, and in one case of over four-score years and ten, they have grudged neither time nor trouble to assist me in my endeavour not only to recall events, but to recapture the spirit of that bygone time.

JOHN HEADLAM.

CRUCK MEOLE HOUSE,
 SHROPSHIRE.
  May, 1931.

NOTE.

During the period from 1860 to 1914 there were many changes in the nomenclature employed to denote units of artillery. These changes will be found described in Part I, but to have followed them throughout the narrative generally would have been confusing to the reader. The term "brigade" has therefore been used for the lieut.-colonel's command throughout, and "company" for the major's command in the garrison artillery. These were the terms in use at the beginning and end of the period.

For the same reason the expression "heavy artillery" is used in the sense it bore up till the Great War, that is as meaning "heavy field," or "position" artillery, corresponding to what is now termed "medium" artillery.

Abbreviations have been avoided as a rule, but to save space the words "Royal Artillery" have been omitted when it appeared that this could be done without risk of misunderstanding, as, for instance, when speaking of "the Mess"—"the Institution"—etc.; and the various publications of the latter have been referred to throughout simply as " the Proceedings".

The term 'gun' has been used generally to include all types of ordnance, except where it has been necessary to differentiate.

The diagrams in Part II are taken from the official Handbooks of the guns, and these, as well as the extracts from Regulations and Orders, are published with the kind permission of the Controller of H.M. Stationery Office.

CONTENTS.

INTRODUCTION.

PART I.—ORGANIZATION.
(By Sir Charles Callwell).

PART II.—ARMAMENT.
(By Sir Charles Callwell).

PART III.—TRAINING.
(By Sir John Headlam).

A. Horse and Field Artillery.

B. Mountain, Heavy and Siege Artillery.

C. Coast Artillery.

APPENDICES.

INTRODUCTION.

(By Sir John Headlam).

THE artillery which fought in the Crimea and the Mutiny was little changed from that which had emerged from the long years of war training in the Peninsula. Its guns were still smooth-bores, and its organization and tactics were suited to its armament. But the change was to come quickly. Scarcely had the last Mutineer been hunted down in the jungles of Nepal before French rifled guns were outranging Austrian smooth-bores on the plains of Lombardy. No nation could ignore such a warning, and in the next year—1860—the Royal Artillery received the famous "Armstrong" rifled guns. This first year of the period covered by this Volume is memorable also as having seen the establishment of the School of Gunnery at Shoeburyness and the decision to amalgamate the Artilleries of the three Presidencies in India with the Royal Artillery. These events, so far-reaching in their effect upon every aspect of the life of the Regiment, marked the commencement of an era which was to prove the most momentous in its pre-Great War history; an era that was to close with the advent of the quick-firer, and the separation between the mounted and dismounted branches.[1]

In studying the records of those forty eventful years, and analyzing the causes of the many changes which they brought, the most puzzling enigma is the strange slowness of the generation which first received rifled guns to grasp the potentialities of the new weapons with which science had endowed them. It is a truism that, in the artillery above all, tactical and technical considerations must go hand in hand; and yet for well on to a quarter of a century after the adoption of rifled guns the training of all branches

---

[1] The full text of the orders for the "Amalgamation" and the "Separation" will be found in Appendices A and B.

of the Royal Artillery continued to show that disregard
of service conditions, and that subservience to artificial
standards, which had grown up during the long years of
stagnation after Waterloo.[1] How was it that the Royal
Artillery, alone of European Artilleries, had not changed
its tactics, although the arms in use had been revolu-
tionized.

The national characteristic of caution in accepting new
theories, and the innate conservatism of all regular armies,
may account for much, centralization for more. "The
strictest uniformity is to be observed in the several drills
and exercises for artillery as established and taught at
Woolwich, no deviation from which is to be allowed which
has not previously been sanctioned at Head Quarters"—
so ran the Regimental Standing Orders. Is it any wonder
that precision of drill became the criterion of efficiency?
But a deeper cause must be sought for the persistence in
opposition to the new ideas even after the great object
lesson of the Franco-German War. To understand this
reactionary attitude it is necessary to remember that the
leaders of Regimental opinion had been brought up in the
smooth-bore school, and that the new theories regarding
the employment of artillery demanded the sacrifice of some
of their most cherished traditions. There is little wonder
if the new gunnery in particular was as distasteful to them
as is mechanization to many now. This antagonism was
not overcome until Prince Kraft's famous "Letters"[2] had
opened the eyes of all to what rifled guns could do in the
hands of gunners who knew how to use them. Once convinced however, all ranks devoted themselves to the
recovery of the time lost with a zeal and enthusiasm which
were the admiration of the other arms.

The Field Artillery led the way, followed closely by
the Siege. In the Coast Artillery the awakening came

---

[1] The pitiful tale has been told with admirable restraint and sense of
proportion by Lt.-Colonel H. W. L. Hime in his "History of the
Royal Regiment of Artillery, 1815—1853".

[2] Major Walford's translation appeared in the "Proceedings" in
1887. See chapter IX.

later, for this branch had not only lacked the stimulus which the others had received from the Franco-German War, it had also suffered particularly from the period of depression through which the Garrison Artillery passed previous to the separation of the mounted and dismounted branches. As soon, however, as steps had been taken to restore contentment to the service the response was whole-hearted, and the. progress made by the Coast Artillery during the last decade of the century was at least as great as that of any other branch. Before the century closed it could safely be said that the Regiment at large had fully realized the truth of Major Walford's weighty words, spoken during the first struggles of the Renaissance : words which may well serve to sum up the most important feature of the forty years of Regimental History chronicled in this volume :—

"Outside of the Regiment there is the Army, and the verdict of the Army on the Regiment is that by which we must stand or fall, we must gain or lose prestige. It is not enough that we should be satisfied with regard to ourselves, the Army must also be satisfied with us . . . . and, to put it delicately, the Army is not so fully impressed as we should wish with the efficacy of artillery fire . . . . No test can be found but a War and a European War . . . . we shall then be judged by the *effect of our fire*. The end and object of all our work should be so to train ourselves now in peace that, when the opportunity comes, we may step at once into that position which we feel to be rightly ours, but which a variety of causes combines to prevent our occupying."

PART I.

ORGANIZATION.

By Sir CHARLES CALLWELL.

CHAPTER I.

1860 TO 1862.

General Situation in 1860—The Superior Artillery Staff—The Brigade System—Organization of a 15th Brigade—Lettering of the Field Batteries—The Duke of Cambridge appointed Colonel—The problem of the local European forces in India. G.G.O. 332, (India) of the 10th April 1861—The Amalgamation of the Bengal, Madras and Bombay Regiments of Artillery with the Royal Artillery—The Indian Frontier Batteries—Obstacles hampering amalgamation at first—Advantages accruing from the amalgamation—The " Trent " affair—The Medical and Veterinary Services—Conditions of service in the ranks at this time.

THE year with which this volume of *The History of the Royal Artillery* may be said to commence—1860—synchronises with a stage in the annals of the Regiment presenting features of altogether exceptional interest. The campaign in the Crimea, followed as it had been with such dramatic suddenness by the outbreak of the great Mutiny in India, had thrown an excessive strain upon the administration of the military forces of the Crown. The emergency had severely taxed the limited resources in personnel, in equipment and in armament which the Government had found at its disposal when called upon to despatch troops in large numbers to theatres of war beyond the seas. Difficulties had eventually been largely overcome; but many failures had occurred, and hampering weaknesses had been made manifest—no less in respect to the artillery than in respect to other arms and departments of the service.

The lessons as regards the existence of glaring defects in our military system to be learnt from the experiences of those years of anxiety and stress, had not however been thrown away. The Government, no less than the responsible professional authorities who held high place in connection with the control of the army, perceived that something must be done to secure a condition of greater military efficiency henceforward and in the future. A number of beneficial measures affecting the troops—their organization, their distribution, their recruitment, their weapons, and so forth—had consequently received consideration during the brief period which had elapsed between the closing days of the Indian Mutiny and the commencement of the year 1860. Some of the measures had been already carried into effect, others were in course of introduction, others again were about to be introduced. And no branch of the national fighting forces perhaps was affected by the reforms executed, by the reforms in progress, and by the reforms in contemplation, more appreciably and advantageously than was the Regiment of Royal Artillery.

In his *Crimean Period* of the History of the Regiment, Colonel Jocelyn has depicted the strange state of centralization which, at the time of the contest with the Russian Empire, was so outstanding a feature in its organization and in the method of its control. He has, furthermore, indicated the steps taken shortly afterwards to place matters on a sounder footing. Whatever other consequences may have resulted from the abolition of the time-honoured Board of Control, and from the placing of the Regiment instead under the Commander-in-Chief, that measure did at least transfer the Royal Artillery to a position which was to some extent on all fours with the position occupied by the two other main branches of the army, the cavalry and the infantry.

The expansion which had come to pass in the numbers and the size of the Royal Artillery since the outbreak of the Crimean War—an increase from 103 to 122 in the number of units and from approximately 15,000 to over 22,000 in actual strength in peace time—had rendered this arm of the Service so cumbrous as, in itself, to render a comprehensive reorganization imperative. The introduc-

tion of what was known as the "Brigade System" on
April 1st, 1859, which had got fairly well into working
order by the beginning of the following year, was designed,
among other things, to bring centralization to an end, and
it did reduce centralization to some extent.   Then again,
the adoption of the terms "Brigade" and "Battery" in
place of "Battalion", "Troop" and "Company" constituted
a noteworthy improvement, at least in so far as the field
artillery was concerned.[1]   The separation of the drivers
from the gunners in the units of field artillery, effected in
1858, coupled with the fixing of a limit in respect to the
maximum height of drivers, helped to place the mounted
branch on a sound footing.   The Regiment had in fact
just at this juncture made a distinct advance in efficiency
from the points of view of organization and of administration.   What would amount to a fundamental change in
its constitution was moreover about to take place.   Experience during the Indian Mutiny, and the alterations that
had since the conclusion of that great upheaval been introduced in connection with the government of our Eastern
Empire, had rendered the transformation of the local
European Army into an integral portion of the regular
British Army, and the consequent amalgamation of the
three distinct Presidential Artilleries with the Royal Artillery, desirable.   That amalgamation was not actually
carried into effect until towards the end of the following
year, but in 1860 it had already been virtually decided
upon, and the details affecting its accomplishment were
being assiduously worked out.   The additions of these
three regiments to the Royal Artillery would mean a considerable increase in the number of units composing it,
and a notable swelling of its strength in officers and in
other ranks.   The decision to carry the amalgamation out
afforded additional grounds for ensuring de-centralization

CHAPTER
I.

General
situation
in 1860.

---

[1] The new title "Battery" was popular from the outset alike in
field and garrison artillery units.   But the R.H.A. were loath to
part with their title of "Troop" and they stuck to it, unofficially, for
years afterwards.

CHAPTER
I.

such as those responsible for introducing the Brigade System had hoped to bring about.

General
Situation
in 1860.

But it was not merely in respect to questions of organization and of administration that changes were occurring and were in the air.   The adoption of the Armstrong pattern of gun in the year 1859, followed as it was by energetic steps, promptly taken, to substitute this form of ordnance for the smooth-bores in use, represented the most far-reaching innovation in respect to the armament of the Regiment that had taken place since its creation.   The matter will be dealt with in Part II of this Volume; but the point is one which calls for mention in these introductory remarks.   The very fact moreover of the introduction of this vastly improved armament led, as will be indicated in Part III, to the question of instruction and training being more effectually taken in hand than had been the case in periods antecedent to that of which this Volume of the Regimental History treats.   This development in respect to the weapons with which the Royal Artillery was armed and about to be armed gave, moreover, a signal impetus to technical study and investigation amongst its commissioned ranks.   Men such as Noble, Lefroy and Boxer, who had already made their mark by the year 1860, came to be the forerunners of that host of inventive and scientifically disposed members of the Regiment, who have adorned its lists since those days of awakening.

The
Superior
Artillery
Staff.

On the resignation by Sir Hew Ross in 1858 of his appointment as Adjutant-General of the Royal Artillery, the post had not been filled up.   Colonel C. Bingham became Deputy Adjutant-General R.A., and he was supported by an Assistant Adjutant-General and a Deputy Assistant Adjutant-General—an arrangement which lasted to within a few months of the close of the century.   The Inspector-General of Royal Artillery was Major-General J. Bloomfield, a Peninsular and Waterloo veteran, of fifty years' service in 1860.   Under the provisions of the General Order of 1859, the General Officer commanding the Woolwich District had been relieved of some of his adminis- trative responsibilities with regard to the Regiment; the garrison however remained as before mainly artillery, and Woolwich continued to be the headquarters of the Regiment. The command was in 1860 held by Major- General Sir R. Dacres, who had taken over the command of the artillery in the Crimea on the death of Brig.- General Fox-Strangways at Inkerman.

As result of the new organization (which had been introduced by the General Regimental Order dated the 1st April 1859)[1] under which the old nomenclature of battalions, troops (in the case of the R.H.A.) and com- panies gave place to that of brigades and batteries, the Royal Artillery was re-arranged as "The Horse Brigade", fourteen "Field and Garrison Brigades", the "Riding House Establishment", a "Depot of the Horse Brigade" and a "Depot Brigade." The "Coast Brigade" was estab- lished by another General Regimental Order, dated 1st September, 1859.

The Horse Brigade, which had its headquarters at Woolwich consisted of ten batteries, lettered A to K. The Field and Garrison Brigades consisted of from seven to ten batteries each, the majority however comprising eight batteries; the 4th, 8th, 9th, 11th, 13th and 14th Brigades were Field Brigades, 1st, 2nd, 3rd, 5th, 6th, 7th, 10th and 12th Brigades were Garrison Brigades; the batteries were numbered. The field batteries numbered forty-eight,[2] and the garrison batteries numbered sixty-four. Of the ten

CHAPTER
I.

The
Superior
Artillery
Staff.

The
Brigade
System.

---

[1] As illustrating the extent to which the Regiment was still treated as a service quite apart from cavalry and infantry, it may be mentioned that this very important General Regimental Order was printed on blue paper, foolscap size, and had no number. Certain other General Orders concerned with the R.A. of somewhat later date appeared in the same form. General Orders and Circular Memoranda were at this time (as they or their equivalents have been ever since) ordinarily printed on white paper and they always had their number for the year.

[2] A 9th and 10th Battery were formed in the 4th Brigade at the end of 1859 raising the total number of field batteries to 49 and of garrison batteries to 65.

6 HISTORY OF THE ROYAL ARTILLERY.

CHAPTER
I.

The
Brigade
System.

R.H.A. batteries, six were quartered at home and the remaining four in India. Of the field batteries, twenty-four were stationed at home and the remaining twenty-four in India. Of the garrison batteries, twenty-four were quartered at home, eight were quartered in India, and the remaining thirty-two were quartered at various oversea stations outside India.

Each brigade was commanded by a colonel, with an adjutant as staff officer; he was supposed to administer it, and he did administer it up to a certain point. Of the six field artillery brigades, three were stationed at home and three in India; of the eight garrison artillery brigades three were stationed at home, while the remainder had their headquarters respectively at Gibraltar, in Malta, at Quebec, in India, and in Mauritius. Such a plan might work satisfactorily where the whole brigade was gathered in one single station (as the 5th, Garrison Brigade was at Gibraltar in 1860) or even where the bulk of the brigade was gathered in one single station (as nearly the whole of the 1st, Garrison Brigade and of the 4th, Field Brigade were at Woolwich at that same date). But it did not work equally satisfactorily—and could not be expected to work equally satisfactorily—in the case of a brigade like the 7th, which at this time had its headquarters, its colonel and its brigade staff, planted down in delightful surroundings at Quebec, but which kept three of its batteries at Jamaica, Bermuda and Barbadoes. Nor could it be expected to work quite smoothly in the case of the 12th Brigade, which in 1860 had its headquarters and two of its batteries at Mauritius, whereas its remaining batteries were to be found at St. Helena, at the Cape, in Ceylon, in China and at Sydney in the Antipodes.

The question of promotion of non-commissioned officers was, under the brigade system, vested in the colonels of brigades instead of its resting with the Adjutant-General R.A. at the War Office, as had been the case since 1856: and many returns and reports which the commanders of units had previously submitted to that official were under

the new system furnished instead to brigade headquarters.
But numbers of such documents had on the other hand to
be rendered both to the War Office and to brigade headquarters.   One effect of the introduction of the brigade
system indeed was found to be an enhancement of the
amount of office work with which commanders of units were
thenceforward called upon to wrestle—this in despite of
that decentralization which the adoption of the new organization was supposed to bring in its train.   Such is a not
uncommon sequel to those re-organizations which take
place from time to time in the Royal Artillery, as also in
the re-organizations which successive reformers have
brought about in the British Army as a whole, since the
days of the Crimean War and the Indian Mutiny.   It
should also be mentioned that each brigade had its Colonel
Commandant, in whom was vested the selection of the
adjutant of the brigade, in place of this resting in the
hands of the colonel commanding the brigade.[1]

The General Regimental Order of 1st April 1859 distinctly laid down that brigades and batteries were liable to
be changed at any time from field to garrison, and *vice
versa*.   Such mutations had been of frequent occurrence
only a very few years before.   There had indeed, as has
been indicated in Colonel Jocelyn's record of the Crimean
Period, been no such thing as a permanent field battery;
certain units termed "instructional field batteries" had
been maintained which in reality only represented depots
of horses, guns, and so forth, sufficient for several companies; companies took horses and equipment over and
became field batteries for the time being.   Such companies
reverted after a time to normal garrison artillery work,
often before they had attained any reasonable standard
of efficiency as field batteries.   The difficulties which had

---

[1] Of the Colonels Commandant the seniors were told off to brigades, as there were more than 15 of them. Of the Colonels Commandant appearing on the list in 1860, 4 had served both in the
Peninsula and at Waterloo, 7 had served in the Peninsula only, 5 had
served at Waterloo only.

attended the organization of the field artillery for the Expeditionary Force about to be despatched to the Near East
in 1854, difficulties which had continued and had increased
during the earlier days of the Crimean campaign, had made
manifest the weaknesses inseperable from such haphazard
arrangements. "Drivers" had moreover come to be
separated from "gunners" and to be enlisted as drivers,
as already mentioned, and field batteries (although up to
the 1st April, 1859 they were still designated companies)
had been assured of something at least approaching to
permanency. The brigade system from the date of its
establishment for all practical purposes invested the field
batteries with virtual permanency. But the principle that
a unit of the Regiment could be transformed from a
mounted into a dismounted unit, and *vice versa*, was quite
rightly maintained. Cases of such transformations have
indeed been not infrequent, alike during peace time and
in time of war, since the year 1860, just as cases have also
occurred of batteries of R.H.A. being transformed into
field batteries.[1]

There was no regimental rank of major in the Royal
Artillery it should be remembered at this time. That
grade had been abolished in 1827, although the army rank
in its brevet form existed, just as did the brevet ranks of
lieutenant-colonel and colonel. Units of the Regiment—
troops, companies and (now) batteries—were commanded
by "1st captains," with "2nd captains" to assist them.
The regiment thus differed from the cavalry and the
infantry, not only in having no regimental rank of major,
but also in having a special regimental rank of 2nd captain.
There was also no rank of 2nd lieutenant; it had disappeared in the year 1855.

---

[1] The plan under which garrison artillery units in India used to be
converted for three or four years at a time into "Heavy Batteries",
and afterwards reverted to ordinary garrison duties, a plan which held
good during the period covered by this volume of the Regimental
History, illustrates this, even if the units actually retained their nomenclature while acting in the new capacity.

The intention under the Brigade System was that reliefs were to be carried out by brigades, and this arrangement was in fact put in force during the years that followed. It was furthermore the intention that, before a brigade should proceed abroad, it should spend at least a year at Woolwich. Woolwich was the headquarters of the regiment, and it was the station where—in 1860 at all events—the most advanced instruction was provided for. Sufficient accommodation for very nearly a whole field brigade (as well as some R.H.A. batteries) and for the whole of a garrison artillery brigade was available in its extensive barracks. The brigades first for foreign service were also naturally those first for active service, and the units composing them therefore ought to be, and in fact were, the most efficient in the country. The field batteries which were sent out from home to China in 1860, the field battery despatched to New Zealand in 1861, and the batteries hurriedly shipped to Canada at the end of that same year on the occasion of the "Trent" affair, all belonged to the 4th Brigade, then stationed at Woolwich.

The Riding House Establishment was allowed a captain, a 2nd captain and two subalterns. At this time there were only seven Riding Masters allowed to the Regiment.[1]

The Depot Brigade was organized in eight "Divisions" each under a captain, and was stationed at Woolwich; the title Divisions was almost immediately afterwards changed to "Batteries". Its personnel was composed partly of the employed non-commissioned-officers and men belonging to the Regiment in the garrison (thus including the Band), and partly of recruits who had been enlisted for brigades which were on Indian and Colonial service. (Recruits intended for the brigades stationed at home were enlisted under brigade arrangements by the brigades themselves, and they were trained in the batteries composing the brigades). It was particularly laid down in the General

CHAPTER I.

The Brigade System.

---

[1] The junior was G. Dann, so popular a figure at the Royal Military Tournaments a generation later.

CHAPTER
I.

The
Brigade
System.

Order setting up the brigade system that the instruction of Volunteer Artillery Companies was to be one of the principal duties of the Depot Brigade.   Officers of the Regiment stationed at Woolwich, not on the strength of brigade and batteries, were borne on its strength.   The number of batteries in the Depot Brigade was increased to 11 before the end of 1860.   The functions of the Depot of the Horse Brigade corresponded to those of the Depot Brigade and it was like-wise stationed at Woolwich; it was composed of employed men and of recruits destined for batteries abroad.

The Coast Brigade was a development of the previously existing "Royal Invalid Artillery" which, with an establishment of 654, had consisted of old soldiers employed under the master gunners to look after armament and stores in the fixed defences.   A number of officers risen from the ranks were now added to this organization, and it was laid down that "officers of the Brigade will have entire charge (under the Commanding Officers of Artillery) of the Districts allotted to them, the master gunners in which will be placed under their orders".   The Brigade was to be "distributed amongst the forts, batteries and towers of the United Kingdom".[1]

Organiza-
tion of a
15th
Brigade.

As a result of important additions to coast defences in the United Kingdom taking place just at this time, consequent on the acceptance by the Government of recommendations made by a Royal Commission on the defence of dockyards, etc., an augmentation of the garrison artillery was becoming necessary, and on the 1st May 1860, a 15th Brigade of eight garrison batteries was constituted at Gosport largely for the purpose of manning new works defending the approaches to Portsmouth.   This raised the number of garrison batteries on home service from 24 to 32, as against 40 abroad.

---

[1] Under this system, one which lasted for a good many years, the officers of the garrison batteries which would man the works in time of war had no real responsibility in connection with their armament.

A change of some importance was introduced in respect to the field batteries within eighteen months of the publication of the General Order which established the brigade system.   G.R.O. 454 of the 9th September 1861, laid down that the batteries of the three field brigades which had their headquarters in the United Kingdom, the 4th, 8th and 9th Brigades, were to be distinguished in future by letters instead of by numbers.   Nos. 1, 2, 3, 4, 5, 6, 7 and 8 Batteries in each of the three brigades became A, B, C, D, E, F, G and H Batteries, and there were also a K Battery and an I Battery in the 4th Brigade.   This same alteration of nomenclature was effected at a somewhat later date in the case of the three field brigades which were stationed in India; the reason for the delay was that the amalgamation of the Indian artilleries with the Regiment was just about to be carried out, and that confusion might have arisen had the lettering system been introduced simultaneously.   (As will be seen in a later paragraph, the detailed orders with regard to the future organization of the Indian Regiments of artillery on their absorption into the Royal Artillery appeared in India a month after G.R.O. 454 appeared at home).   This change served to accentuate still further the distinction between the mounted and the dismounted branch of the R.A.

It was moreover ordained by a G.R.O. published in October that Nos. 5, 7 and 11 batteries of the Depot Brigade, which served as depots for the field brigades abroad, should be lettered A, B and C.

H.R.H. The Duke of Cambridge, the General Commanding-in-Chief, was appointed "Colonel of the Royal Artillery" on the 10th May 1861.   Regimental orders had for some time past been worded as being published under his authority in his capacity of general commanding-in-chief; but apart from this he had possessed no direct connection with the Regiment.   He remained at its head until his death in 1904, but his title had been changed to that of "Colonel-in-Chief of the Royal Artillery" in 1895, at the time when he ceased to be Commander-in-Chief.

CHAPTER I.

Lettering of the Field Batteries.

The Duke of Cambridge appointed Colonel.

CHAPTER
I.

The
problem
of the
local
European
forces in
India.

When the fundamental constitutional change in respect
to India, under which the government and administration
was finally transferred from the East India Company to
the Queen, was decided upon, a number of complicated
military questions arose. One of the most important of
them, and one which moreover gave rise to much difference of opinion, military and civilian, was whether the
entirely European portion of the fighting forces which the
East India Company had been maintaining—the units
composed wholly of Europeans[1]—should remain as they
were, part of a local army, or should be absorbed into
the regular British army (the " Queen's Service " as it
used to be called for purposes of distinction), and should
thus become liable to serve anywhere. The troops involved comprised cavalry, artillery and infantry, and the
question was one of particular importance as concerning
the artillery arm because, prior to the Mutiny, the European artillery units in the country had all belonged to the
East India Company's forces. Cavalry and infantry regiments of the Queen's Service had been quartered in the
country in peace time, and some of them had played a
part in historic combats; but units of the Royal Artillery
had not undergone such experience for a century.[2]

The question was furthermore complicated to some
extent by the fact that the three Indian Presidencies each
possessed its distinct army, and its distinct purely European force forming part of that army. Besides their
being administered by distinct governments, these Presidential armies differed from each other in a number of
minor respects—matters of interior economy, equipment,
and so forth. The question at issue therefore came in a

[1] The drivers in the artillery were however in some cases natives.
[2] Units of the Royal Artillery had served for short periods in India
in the middle of the eighteenth century, at a time when the East India
Company was badly found in the artillery arm and fighting had to be
done. A company went out with Admiral Boscawen in 1748 and took
part in the abortive siege of Pondicherry. Four companies were
especially raised in 1755 to go out; one of them was lost in a ship-
wreck on the way out, so another was raised and sent; two of them
took part in the capture of Surat in 1759.

sense to be whether the entirely European portions of three different armies were, or were not, to be incorporated in the regular British army, and it was a question which affected the position and the prospects of the personnel constituting these troops very appreciably—as all ranks, and particularly the rank-and-file, were not slow to perceive.

The problem was not from the outset very judiciously handled. The rank-and-file had enlisted for service under the East India Company, but the Home Government held that they could be transferred to the regular British army whether they liked it or not. Legal opinion was by no means unanimous as to whether such action was lawful or not, the rank-and-file held that they could not be so transferred without their own consent, and large numbers of them insisted that they were entitled to make their choice and that they could not be expected to accept transfer without receiving a bounty. Serious insubordination manifested itself. The situation indeed at one time became so grave that it has been spoken of as "the White Mutiny," and it lost none of its awkwardness from the fact that this insubordination trod so closely on the heels of the Sepoy Mutiny and that it moreover occurred at a time when India had not yet recovered from the strain of that untoward event. Still, the insubordination could from one point of view be accepted as a blessing in disguise, because it provided a not ineffective argument in favour of carrying out a change which H.M. Government had satisfied themselves was necessary.

In bringing their proposal that the local European forces in India should become part of the regular British army before Parliament, Government spokesmen were able to declare that the discipline of the local forces was in an unsatisfactory state and that a change was imperative. The amalgamation was generally opposed by officers of the Indian army, while it was strongly approved of by most officers of the Queen's Service possessing Indian experience. The principle was in due course approved

CHAPTER
I.

The
problem
of the
local
European
forces in
India.

by Parliament, Royal Assent to the Bill dealing with the subject was given on the 20th August 1860, and the working out of the details was thereupon taken in hand by the military authorities at home and in India, acting in conjunction.

In the meantime large numbers of the rank-and-file of the forces concerned had demanded their discharge sooner than accept the contemplated transfer, the grant of a bounty not being decided upon till later. The authorities had finally decided that the discharge must be granted. The result was that some 10,000 malcontents out of a total of 16,000 were actually sent home, where many of them promptly re-enlisted into the "Queen's Service." So it came about that, when the amalgamation actually took place in the latter part of 1861, many of the units transferred represented mere cadres which comprised a full complement of officers and a fairly full complement of non-commissioned-officers, but which were numerically very weak in, and sometimes entirely deficient of, private soldiers.

G.G.O.
332.
(India) of
the 10th
April,
1861.

A General Order issued by the Governor General in India was published on the 10th April 1861, which laid down in detail exactly how the absorption of the local European into the British regular army was to be carried out. The order indicated how the existing European units of each branch of the service in the three Presidencies were to be dealt with. It explained how officers and others, in the case of units ceasing to exist, would be disposed of. It set out full particulars as to future conditions of service of all ranks. It provided for granting a bounty (dependent on the length of time still to elapse before discharge) for such non-commissioned-officers and men as would accept transfer in continuation of their original term of enlistment. It established the Bengal, Madras and Bombay Staff Corps, to which such European officers serving with the non-European corps of the Indian forces as were prepared to accept the arrangement, would henceforward belong, and it provided for the case of those who

should decline to fall in with the plan.   It left some minor CHAPTER
I.
points somewhat obscure, but the difficulties in connec-
tion with these were cleared away by other orders issued
shortly afterwards.

Under the terms of this order, the three European
regiments of Bengal cavalry (they had only been created
during the Mutiny) became the 19th, 20th, and 21st Light
Dragoons (Hussars).   The eleven European regiments of
infantry (five Bengal, three Madras and three Bombay)
became nine regiments of the Line numbered from 101 to
109,[1] two of the Bengal regiments being disbanded.   There
were no all-European Engineer units in the Indian Army;
Engineer units were officered partly by British and partly
by native officers, and they included some European non-
commissioned-officers; but the rank and file was composed
almost entirely of natives.   Under the terms of G.G.O.
332, the European officers and non-commissioned-officers
were however transferred to the Royal Engineers, and it
was arranged that the officers were to remain on three
separate lists for promotion—Bengal, Madras and Bombay
—on the same lines as officers of the three Indian Artilleries, as will be explained in a later paragraph.   The
steps taken with regard to the three Regiments of Artillery
—they were called regiments—require to be dealt with in
considerably greater detail.   It was especially provided in
the G.G.O. that units should on transfer retain their
honorary distinction and battle honours,[2] and in their new
subsidiary titles the infantry regiments moreover retained
their connection with their old Presidencies—e.g., Royal
Bengal Fusiliers, Madras Light Infantry.

The incorporation in the Royal Artillery of the three
regiments of artillery, which had formed part of the Indian
local forces up to the end of 1861, ranks unquestionably
as one of the most important events—if not as the most

G.G.O.
332.
(India) of
the 10th
April,
1861.

The
Amalga-
mation of
the Bengal,
Madras
and
Bombay
Regiments
of Artil-
lery with
the Royal
Artillery.

---

[1] Regiments of the Line were at this time still numbered, it must
be remembered, and, with the exception of the first twenty-five and of
the 60th Rifles and the Rifle Brigade, they consisted of only a single
battalion and depot.

[2] This did not however apply to the artillery absorbed into the R.A.

CHAPTER
I.

The
Amalga-
mation of
the Bengal,
Madras
and
Bombay
Regiments
of Artil-
lery with
the Royal
Artillery.

important event—in the whole history of the Regiment. It should be understood that at the time of the outbreak of the Indian Mutiny the artillery regiment maintained by each of the three Indian Presidencies had been composed partly of European units, and partly of native units which were wholly or party officered by Europeans. Even in the case of European units, however, the drivers forming part of the personnel of horse artillery troops and of such companies as were acting as field batteries, had to a large extent been natives when the crisis arose. A few of the native units mutinied, although in no case did they harm their European officers; some others showed unmistakeable signs of disaffection; some others were promptly disbanded as a precautionary measure. The great emergency satisfied the authorities, before it had finally passed away, that the whole of the artillery maintained in India must in the interests of future security, with the exception of a very few special units, be purely European. So it came about that when the amalgamation was decided upon, the question had for all practical purposes become that of transferring purely European units to the regular British army, just as in the case of the local European cavalry and infantry regiments.

The absorption of the Indian into the Royal Artillery was, it should be observed, greatly facilitated by the fact that so much analogy existed between them in respect to nomenclature, and organization, and armament, and equipment. Horse artillery units of the Indian artilleries were in 1861 called troops, and the rest of the artillery was organized as battalions and companies—the nomenclature that had obtained in the Royal Artillery prior to the introduction of the brigade system in 1859. (The Madras Artillery was however peculiar in that its companies were lettered, instead of being numbered as were those of the two other Presidential artilleries.) The armament of the Indian horse and field artillery units was also practically identical with that of analogous Royal Artillery units, except for the horse and field batteries usually having five guns and one howitzer instead of having four guns and two howitzers. But in the Bengal horse artillery the gun detachments were carried on the off horses while in the Madras and Bombay horse artilleries the detachments were mounted as was the case in the Royal Horse Artillery. Bengal and Madras horse and field batteries, again, employed pole draught, whereas the Bombay horse and field batteries, like those of the Regiment, relied upon shafts. Some other points of difference concerning matters of equipment existed between the regiments which were going to be amalgamated. But they were not points of major importance.

CHAPTER I.

The Amalgamation of the Bengal, Madras and Bombay Regiments of Artillery with the Royal Artillery.

The Indian artilleries had resembled the Regiment in the past in one notable respect. Whereas their horse artillery batteries had for many years been permanently organized units, units which attained a high standard of efficiency as regards work in the field, and mounted drill, and horse management, their field batteries had stood on a less satisfactory footing. Sir C. Napier had, indeed, some twenty years before the question of amalgamation was broached, expressed the opinion that the field artillery service in India was being sacrificed in the interests of the more rapidly moving branch. Non-permanent units such as were the Indian field batteries—companies temporarily acting as field artillery—had furthermore before the time of the Mutiny, and indeed also to some extent during the Mutiny, depended largely upon bullocks for draught purposes. There had been "Light Field Batteries" and "Bullock Batteries". The tactical conditions normally presenting themselves in the course of warlike operations on the Indian plains, invested very rapidly moving guns, just as they invested the cavalry arm, with an exceptional importance. They were conditions which had provided the Indian horse artillery with a glorious record. But just as infantry had played a great part in combats with Mahrattas and Sikhs and in Scinde, so also would those affrays have furnished opportunities for the employment of highly efficient field batteries—

CHAPTER
I.

The
Amalga-
mation of
the Bengal,
Madras
and
Bombay
Regiments
of Artil-
lery with
the Royal
Artillery.

had the highly efficient field batteries existed.   The experiences of the Mutiny, when considerable progress had
already been made in the direction of developing the
Indian field artillery, proved that this was the case.   That
great upheaval had in a measure done for the Indian field
artillery what the Crimean War a year or two earlier had
done for the field artillery of the Queen's Service.

With a view to arriving at uniformity in respect to
equipment, battery organization, and so forth, commissions
on which officers of the three Indian artilleries and of the
Royal Artillery had sat, had been set up in India in 1860.
Agreement had, not without some difficulty, been arrived
at on most points.   The military authorities charged with
framing the instructions for effecting the amalgamation
had the recommendations of these commissions before
them when executing their difficult task.   They decided
that the amalgamation should take the form of organizing
the existing Indian units in brigades, and of adding these
brigades to the one Horse Brigade and the fifteen Artillery
Brigades of which the Royal Artillery was composed at
the time.

The Bengal Artillery to be dealt with consisted of three
brigades of Horse Artillery and six battalions of Foot
Artillery.   One of the two horse brigades comprised five
troops, the other two comprised four troops each, thus
making thirteen troops in all.   The six battalions of Foot
Artillery each consisted of four companies, making twenty-
four in all.

The Madras Artillery consisted of a brigade of Horse
Artillery comprising four troops, and of three battalions of
Foot Artillery, each of four companies, making twelve
companies in all.

The Bombay Artillery was the counterpart of the
Madras Artillery.   It comprised a brigade of Horse Artillery and three battalions of Foot Artillery each of four
companies, making twelve companies in all.

There were thus the cadres of twenty-one troops of
horse artillery altogether and forty-eight companies of foot

artillery. The plan adopted was to reconstitute the horse artillery as four brigades of Royal Horse Artillery—the 2nd, 3rd, 4th and 5th Horse Brigades, the existing brigade of R.H.A. becoming the 1st Horse Brigade. The 2nd and 5th were formed of the Bengal troops, the 3rd of the Madras troops and the 4th of the Bombay troops; the troops became batteries and were denoted by letters. The foot artillery battalions were reconstituted as ten brigades numbered 16 to 25, the companies being called batteries; Nos. 16, 18, 19 and 23 were to be field artillery brigades, Nos. 17, 24 and 25 were to be garrison artillery brigades, Nos. 20, 21 and 22 were to be "mixed" brigades; batteries were distinguished by numbers at the outset, but the field batteries were given letters within a few months.[1] Of the field artillery brigades 16 and 19 were to be formed of Bengal companies, 23 was to be formed of Madras companies, and 18 was to be formed of Bombay companies. Of the garrison artillery brigades 24 and 25 were to be formed of Bengal companies and 17 was to be formed of Madras companies. The 22nd, 20th and 21st "Mixed" Brigades were respectively to be formed of Bengal, Madras and Bombay companies. The companies detailed for the field artillery brigades, and those that were to be field batteries in the mixed brigades, were in most cases already equipped as field batteries at the time. The ten new Royal Artillery brigades were to consist of from four to six batteries each.

The exact composition contemplated for these new brigades which, in a framework corresponding as closely as seemed practicable at the moment to the framework of the Regiment as existing under the brigade system, were being added to it, was formulated in a Governor-General's General Order dated the 12th October, 1861, and the new

CHAPTER I.

The Amalgamation of the Bengal, Madras and Bombay Regiments of Artillery with the Royal Artillery.

---

[1] That the field batteries were not at once distinguished by letters was as already mentioned due to the lettering only having been decided upon at home a very few weeks before the amalgamation order was published in India. A confusion that might have been avoided resulted.

CHAPTER
I.

The
Amalga-
mation of
the Bengal,
Madras
and
Bombay
Regiments
of Artil-
lery with
the Royal
Artillery.
titles were assumed at once in the case of most units.
But the programme as laid down in detail in the General
Order was not completely carried out at the time. This
was owing to lack of the necessary personnel in rank-and-
file, although there were more officers available than were
required, due to so many having before the Mutiny been
serving with Native batteries which had now disappeared.
Actually, only 19 of the new horse artillery batteries,
18 of the new field batteries and 15 of the new garrison
artillery batteries had been added to the Regiment by the
end of 1862, but other batteries were added during 1863
as personnel became available. The G.G.O. of the 12th
October, 1861 was quoted in a General Regimental Order[1]
which was dated the 19th February 1862, and the amalgamation is commonly on that account referred to as
having taken place that year. But it had actually, as
stated above, taken place in India some months before.

Special provisions had to be made with regard to the
officers of the three Indian regiments. The grading of the
commissioned ranks was, as it happened, the same in the
three regiments and was moreover the same as in the
Royal Artillery. There were no regimental majors, and
there were 2nd captains; 1st captains commanded the
troops and companies which were now transformed into
batteries; and the position of lieut.-colonels corresponded
to that which had been occupied by officers of that rank
in the Royal Artillery before the introduction of the brigade
system.[2]

---

[1] The full text of the Order is given in Appendix A.

[2] The regimental rank of major had however only been abolished
in the Indian artilleries in 1858, in which year the rank of 2nd Lieutenant had also disappeared. The rank of 2nd captain had moreover
only been introduced in the year 1858, its creation giving rise to a run
of promotion to which Lord Roberts makes special reference in *Forty-
one Years in India,* as he was one of those benefited. A rank of
"brevet-captain" had existed; it was granted to subalterns after fifteen
years service, if not otherwise promoted; it had for practical purposes
disappeared in the Bengal and the Bombay Artillery for many years
before the amalgamation, owing to promotion being sufficiently rapid
to prevent its application, but it had only disappeared in the Madras
Artillery in 1857. (The existence of such a rank would have been a
great boon to many officers of the Royal Artillery during the period

G.G.O. 332, had laid down that officers of "the exist-ing Regiments of Artillery in the Presidencies of India will remain distinct from each other and from the Royal Artil-lery so long as any officers now in them shall continue to be borne on the rolls". This was not intended to mean that these officers would not belong to the Royal Artillery, but merely that they would continue to be borne on three special lists as heretofore, and that they were to be pro-moted on those lists. The lists came to be quoted in official documents as "Royal (late Bengal, or Madras, or Bombay, as the case might be) Artillery". This system was applied not merely to officers up to the rank of colonel, i.e. to officers performing, or of a rank to perform, regi-mental duties, but also to colonels commandant and general officers—officers removed from the Regiment. For many years to come the Army List, as also the Regimental Seniority Lists prepared by the R.A. Institution, were to show the officers of the Regiment in four separate batches. On the other hand no distinction was to be maintained between the Indian brigades and batteries that were being added to the Royal Artillery, and the brigades and batteries of which the Royal Artillery had before the amalgamation been composed. In that respect the officers of the four lists would be fully interchangeable and would gradually become intermingled. Vacancies caused by pro-motion or retirement or death in the subaltern ranks of one of the Indian artilleries would (normally) be filled by cadets commissioned from the R.M. Academy, and these would appear on the seniority list of the Royal Artillery and not that of the Indian artillery to which the officer who had created the vacancy had belonged. Vacancies in the rank of captain in one of the Indian artilleries would be filled by subalterns of that artillery so long as any remained, but after that they would be filled by promoting subalterns

Marginal note: CHAPTER I.

The Amalga-mation of the Bengal, Madras and Bombay Regiments of Artil-lery with the Royal Artillery.

---

between Waterloo and the Crimean War, when subalterns often had twenty years' service before they were promoted captain—as was the experience of F.M. Sir R. Dacres in the early days of his distinguished career).

The
Amalga-
mation of
the Bengal,
Madras
and
Bombay
Regiments
of Artil-
lery with
the Royal
Artillery.

on the Royal Artillery seniority list.   The same principle
would hold good in the higher ranks.   These conditions
happily proved acceptable to practically all the officers of
the old Indian Regiments of Artillery.[1]

The plan of showing the officers of the old Indian artillery regiments on special lists was adhered to officially
up till 1898, by which time the last officer of rank below
that of major-general had disappeared.   From that time
forward general officers who had originally joined the E.I.
Company's service were included in the Royal Artillery
list acording to their seniority as general officers, but with
"Bengal", "Madras" or "Bombay" (as the case might
be) shown in brackets after their names.

The immediate consequence of the amalgamation was
to increase the number of R.H.A. batteries in the Regiment
from 10 to 29, the number of field batteries from 49 to 73,
and the number of garrison batteries from 73 to 88.   The
following table shows the number of officers (excluding
quartermasters, officers of the Coast Brigade, medical
officers and veterinary surgeons) who were shown on the
Regimental Seniority List respectively on the 1st January
1860 and on the 1st August 1862 :—

	Colonels.	Lieut.-Colonels.	1st Captains.	2nd Captains.	Lieutenants.
1860	35	65	140	155	404
1862	60	135	281	305	760

The
Indian
Frontier[2]
Batteries.

Special reference must be made here to those native
"Mountain Train" and "Light Field" Batteries, having
European officers and forming part of the Bengal Artillery,
which had been raised for work on the North West Frontier
since the annexation of the Punjab had brought the
Government of India into direct contact with the Pathan

---

[1] Only three officers of the Bengal Artillery declined the terms,
according to Stubbs *History of the Bengal Artillery.*

[2] Further details regarding the history of the Indian Frontier Batteries will be found in Chapter XII—Mountain Artillery.

hillmen. They were recent creations and formed part of the " Punjab Frontier Force". Owing to the peculiar nature of their service and to the character of their personnel, these units were retained at the time when the remainder of those troops and companies of the Indian artillery regiments which had native rank and file, were being disbanded. There were two Mountain Trains and three Light Field Batteries, and there was also a Garrison Artillery battery. These frontier batteries were officered by officers of the Bengal Artillery, who in virtue of the amalgamation became officers of the Royal Artillery. But the batteries were not then, nor were they for many years afterwards, acknowledged as units of the Regiment. This may to some extent have been due to their being included in the Punjab Frontier Force, a force which was inclined to be exclusive and distinct.

Be that, however, as it may, these batteries were to perform good and gallant service in many campaigns of the future.[1] They will be referred to in the accounts of those campaigns just as if they were units of the Regiment, and it seems worth mentioning here that two of them, that were in the field against the Waziris in the year 1860, were the last units to be in action against an enemy while actually forming part of the Bengal Regiment of Artillery.[2]

The absorption of the Indian organizations into the Royal Artillery in reality took place gradually. As has been shown above, the units of the Bengal Artillery were collected in brigades that were distinct alike from the brigades in which the units of the Madras Artillery and the Bombay Artillery were being collected, and from the already existing brigades of which the Royal Artillery was composed. It was largely due to this that the amalgama-

CHAPTER I.

The Indian Frontier Batteries.

Obstacles hampering amalgamation at first.

---

[1] These batteries show their battle-honours in the Indian Army Lists—all of which battle honours have been acquired since the amalgamation.

[2] Two companies of the Bombay Artillery, of native personnel with British officers, were also retained with titles of the 1st and 2nd Company Bombay Native Artillery. They are now the 5th (Bombay) and 6th (Jacob's) Mountain Batteries.

CHAPTER
I.

Obstacles
hampering
amalgama-
tion at
first.

tion, as it was called, was effected with little serious friction. Some years were nevertheless to pass before the officers, at least, of the four regiments which had been made one always worked together in perfect harmony.

Jealousies had existed between the three Indian regiments just as they had existed, and as they continued to exist, between the three Presidencies. Jealousies had moreover sprung up between them and the artillery of the Queen's service since the two categories had been brought largely into contact during the Mutiny and immediately subsequent to the Mutiny. This was inevitable, it was natural, and it might even have been in some respects advantageous supposing that no amalgamation had taken place—had the four regiments simply remained, as they had been in the past, friendly rivals. The virtues of *esprit de corps* are universally recognized in the military world. Still, *esprit de corps* finds expression largely, if not indeed mainly, in the conviction that your own corps is worthier than other corps, and so, when two or more corps suddenly find themselves made one, antagonisms and clashings are apt to delay the establishment of absolute concord. Some twenty years after the provisions of G.G.O. 332 of the 10th April 1861 were carried into effect, the organization as Territorial Regiments of the Line was introduced into the British infantry, under which the previously existing single-battalion regiments were joined to each other in pairs; it took several years before the thus united regiments fully accepted the new state of things.

The Bengal Artillery, the Madras Artillery and the Bombay Artillery could all three boast of a fine record of service in peace and war. The war record of the Madras Artillery, while of enviable distinction during the early days of the East India Company's career—the eighteenth century—had however become more common-place of later years owing to units of the regiment having enjoyed fewer opportunities of active service than had formerly been the case. Each of the three Indian regiments (differing in this from the Royal Artillery) had been granted a number of battle honours. These honours always appeared in the half-yearly, official *Civil List*.[1] In the Bengal Artillery and the Bombay Artillery the honours were awarded to, and were shown by, units—the troops and companies possessed their own honours and distinctions. In the Madras Artillery the battle-honours belonged on the contrary to the regiment as a whole and not to troops and companies, except for one troop and three companies which were privileged to bear a Dragon and the word "China" on their appointments in recognition of service performed during the First China War. The amalgamation meant that all these battle-honours necessarily disappeared, to be replaced by the Royal Artillery motto "Ubique", and this was, perhaps not altogether unnaturally, regarded as something of a grievance.

When side by side with the troops and companies of the local artilleries during the strenuous days of the Mutiny, those of the Royal Artillery had at times suffered by comparison. New to the country as they were, ignorant of the language, knowing nothing of the people, fitted out hastily under emergency conditions, the R.A. units had laboured under a distinct handicap. · But, be that as it may, a disposition had existed for a time amongst the personnel of the three Indian regiments to under-value the newcomers, and this disposition had not wholly died away by the end of 1861. Against this, members of the Royal Artillery serving in India were inclined to hold local artillerists cheap on noting how continuous service in tropical climates had sapped the vitality of only too many of them[2]. Added to this there remained the disagreeable

---

[1] This publication included, and indeed consisted mainly of, material corresponding almost exactly to the monthly *Army List* issued then, as now, at home.

[2] Officers of the Indian artilleries had not been in the habit of concerning themselves with niceties of dress to the same extent as had officers of R.A., and when some of them drifted into the Woolwich Mess in the years immediately succeeding the amalgamation, old habitués of that institution were not slow to disparage.

CHAPTER
I.

Obstacles
hampering
amalgama-
tion at
first.

fact that a proportion of the rank and file in the corps that were now being incorporated in the Royal Artillery had shared in the indiscipline which had caused anxiety at the time when the amalgamation of the European troops of the Indian Army with the troops of the Queen's service had first been decided upon—a fact which was common knowledge.   A fear was also undoubtedly entertained amongst officers of the Indian artilleries—just as it was entertained amongst officers of those European infantry and cavalry regiments, formerly included in the Indian Army, which were being transferred to the regular British service—that an absence of influence in high places would, under the new state of things, assuredly prejudice their prospects.   This fear had been freely voiced in Parliament at the time when the general question was being debated in the Legislature.

To suggest that a mutual antipathy existed between those who were being absorbed into the Regiment, and those who were in it, would be to exaggerate.   But a quite natural and indeed inevitable lack of cordiality prevailed for a time.   Neither party perhaps fully realized at the outset what great benefits amalgamation was conferring upon both, and it may not be out of place to indicate briefly what some of those benefits were.

Advant-
ages accru-
ing from
the amal-
gamation.

A result of the amalgamation was the addition of 20 batteries of horse artillery, 21 batteries of field artillery and 19 batteries of garrison artillery, to the total British military forces available for service in any part of the world.   It ensured that the organization, the drill, the training and the personal equipment of these units would correspond to what obtained in the remainder of the regular artillery.   It gave promise that the armament of artillery units in India would likewise correspond to the armament in the hands of the remainder of the regular artillery, although such promise was not in fact fulfilled during a great part of the forty years of the Regiment's History with which this volume is concerned.   Units serv-ing in India (or corresponding to the old Indian artillery

units, although after the first few years not actually the
same) almost always lagged behind in the matter of armament when a new gun was adopted at home—as will
appear in Part II.

CHAPTER
I.

Advant-
ages accru-
ing from
the amal-
gamation.

Its augmentation was far from being the only, or being
even the principal, respect in which the Regiment gained.
Colonel Hime has in his *History of the Royal Artillery
from 1815 to 1853* shown how the Regiment suffered during
that period, owing to the retrenchment brought about by
national exhaustion after the years of war which ushered
in the nineteenth century.   But the Regiment also suffered
from another point of view, a point of view which did not
affect to the same extent our regular cavalry nor yet our
regular infantry.   Apart from some unimportant work at
the Cape, the Royal Artillery had enjoyed no opportunities
of active service from the time of the close of the Waterloo
campaign up to the morning when C and I Troops, R.H.A.
and E Field Battery came into action against Russian guns
on the day before the Alma.   The XVIth Lancers could
boast of Aliwal.   The old 24th Foot could proudly deplore
the losses suffered at Chilianwalla.   But the guns which
had done their share of the work at Bhurtpore, at Meeanee,
at Sobraon and at Gujerat had been manned by gunners in
the East India Company's service, and the little party of
horse artillerymen who had fought it out beside the rem-
nant of the old 44th Foot in the last stand on the rocky
hill above Gandamak during the disastrous retreat from
Kabul, had been borne on the books of the Bengal Regiment of Artillery.   Since the amalgamation no decade
has passed during the course of which some unit of the
Regiment has not been in action in real earnest.

The Royal Artillery also gained greatly in another
respect, at least in so far as its commissioned ranks were
concerned, from the amalgamation and as a result of its
becoming permanently associated with military conditions
existing in India.   The artillery regiments of the old E.I.
Company had, in their relations with the other combatant
branches of that body's fighting forces, stood for years past

CHAPTER
I.

Advant-
ages accru-
ing from
the amal-
gamation.
on a totally different footing from that on which the Royal
Artillery had stood.   There had been no question of a
Board of Ordnance—of those regiments being a service
apart.   The consequence had been that general officers
on the lists of those regiments had normally enjoyed their
fair share of commands of troops of all arms in peace and
in war, and that regimental officers had been given their
fair share of staff appointments unconnected with the
artillery.

Only one single general officer belonging to the Royal
Artillery held a divisional or district command at home at
the time of the amalgamation—that at Woolwich.   Only
one moreover held a district or divisional command outside of the United Kingdom and India—Lieut.-General
Sir W. Fenwick Williams of Kars, who was in charge of
the forces in Canada.   Indian records tell a very different
story.   Two district commands in Madras and one in
Bengal had, for instance, been in the hands of general
officers of the Presidential artilleries at the time of the
outbreak of the Mutiny, and what held good in time of
peace moreover naturally held good in time of war.   The
Royal Artillery lists at the time of the amalgamation displayed at their head the names of a number of veterans
who had gained distinction in the Peninsular and Waterloo
campaigns and of whom the Regiment felt justly proud.
But Sir Hew Ross, Sir R. Gardiner, Sir E. C. Whinyates
and the rest of them, were gunners pure and simple.
Not one of them had held permanent command of troops
of all arms in peace nor yet in war.   And yet at the same
time the most distinguished soldier in the whole Indian
Army by general consent was a Bengal gunner, Sir G.
Pollock, who had been chosen, while actually in charge of
the Agra District, to lead the forces being gathered together
to avenge the disasters of the opening phase of the First
Afghan War, and who had carried out his task with most
signal success.   Another Bengal gunner who had died
some years before the amalgamation, Sir R. Whish, had
at the head of the Lahore Division captured Mooltan, and

had afterwards with his division been present at Gujerat. CHAPTER
Sir Archdale Wilson, yet another Bengal gunner, had been I.
in control of the troops who captured Delhi.

Not for several years however was it to be fully recognized in Pall Mall that general officers of the Royal
Artillery had the same rights and qualifications as had
officers of cavalry and infantry in respect to commands of
troops of all arms.[1]   In India the matter was never in
dispute, and it is worthy of mention here that (as will
be seen in the accompanying Volume) two of the four
divisions organized to take part in the first campaign of
magnitude in which the military forces in India were to
be concerned subsequent to the Mutiny, were to be placed
respectively under a general who had been brought up in
the Regiment and under a general who had won his spurs
as a Bengal artilleryman but who had joined the Regiment
as a result of the amalgamation of 1861-62.

Still, only a very small proportion of the officers who
join the Service can hope to hold high commands.   Nor
can any large proportion of them expect to occupy positions on the staff of the army.   But practically all officers
of the Royal Artillery have enjoyed at least a chance of
serving in India since the amalgamation, and the majority
of them have probably actually done so at some stage of
their military career.   Of these latter, there can be few
who—at least if they have been serving in the horse or

_Advant-
ages accru-
ing from
the amal-
gamation._

---

[1] This was no doubt partly due to the Royal Artillery having till
so very recently been under the Board of Ordnance instead of being
under the Commander-in-Chief.   Two cases of officers of the Regiment
holding mixed commands during hostilities had however occurred at
the time of the American War of Independence :—

General Pattison, whose record is dealt with at length in _Duncan's
History_ held the post of Governor of New York—a mixed command—
but the place was not attacked.

Major and Bt. Lieut.-Colonel W. Phillips was given the local rank
of major-general in 1777; as such he commanded the rear-guard during the retreat from Saratoga and he was Burgoyne's second-in-command at the time of the surrender.   Four years later he was sent with
2,000 picked troops to Rhode Island to prevent the French sailing for
the Chesapeake, but died of disease contracted there.   He had performed a great service to the Regiment in 1762, for he had given
instructions for the formation at Woolwich of the R.A. Band.

CHAPTER
I.

Advant-
ages accru-
ing from
the amal-
gamation.

field or mountain artillery—have not benefited thereby in the professional sense, if in no other. From the time of the Mutiny onwards the numerous mobile batteries which have been included in the Indian military forces have been genuinely efficient units, in the sense that they have been for practical purposes permanently on a war footing. A unit of R.H.A. or of field artillery or of pack artillery, whether stationed in the Punjab or stationed in Mysore or in garrison in the outskirts of Calcutta, has always been in a position to march out of barracks at shortest notice and to take part in more than one day's strenuous combat. Horsed batteries when engaged in their ordinary drill have been accompanied by their first line of ammunition wagons as a matter of course.

Very different conditions had prevailed at home where, unless at the very top of the roster, batteries have been little better than skeletons. The Indian system has, alike for commissioned ranks and for rank and file, rendered ordinary regimental service incomparably more interesting and more instructive than the system necessarily prevailing in the United Kingdom has admitted of. The relatively high rate of pay moreover for many years rendered service in the former country acceptable to officers who were without, or who possessed only restricted, private means. Nor should it be forgotten that, before the Indian Mutiny introduced the Regiment into our great Asiatic Dependency, scarcely any portions of its mounted branches ever served outside of the British Isles in time of peace.

The personnel of the old E.I. Company's artillery regiments also undoubtedly profited by the amalgamation from some points of view. Officers and other ranks were no longer, after it took place, condemned necessarily to spend their days of military service in a land far from their homes, and in a climate that for some months of the year is trying and unhealthy. The very fact that, as a result of the change officers and men even in India were no longer confined to performing duty in one only of the three Presidencies, opened up prospects of variety and of

new experiences. Some officers who had definitely com-
mitted themselves to Indian service on first joining were
actually to pass little of their time in that country subsequent to the amalgamation. The Bengal Artillery, the
Madras Artillery and the Bombay Artillery, no less than
the Royal Artillery, gained appreciably by their becoming one.

Just at the very time when the great amalgamation
was taking place, an appreciable strain was suddenly
thrown upon the Royal Artillery at home, under circumstances to which some reference must here be made. The
struggle between North and South in the United States
had commenced at the beginning of 1861, and on the
7th November the British packet "Trent", which had
taken on board at Havanah, a neutral port, Messrs. Mason
and Slidell and their secretaries, who were proceeding as
envoys from the Confederate States to London and Paris,
was stopped at sea by a United States warship, the "San
Jacinto" under command of Captain Wilkes, and the
gentlemen in question were forcibly removed. On being
informed, the British Government demanded the surrender of the envoys. The public and the press in the
Northern States however showed a strong disposition to
applaud this violation of national rights, the Washington
government procrastinated, and a considerable body of
troops was consequently despatched from our home ports
to Canada to be prepared to act should satisfaction not
be given.

The units of the Regiment quartered in Canada at this
time were one field battery D/4, and Nos. 3, 4, 5 and 6
(Garrison) Batteries of the 7th Brigade. This force of
artillery was reinforced as rapidly as possible by four field
batteries E, F, G and H of the 4th Brigade,[1] and by all
eight batteries of the 10th (Garrison) Brigade. The 4th
Brigade was the first for foreign service; but difficulty

---

[1] A and B Batteries of this brigade (but then numbered 1 and 2)
had been sent out to China in the previous year, and C Battery
had gone out somewhat later to New Zealand. The batteries of the
brigade had been the first to be equipped with the Armstrong gun.

CHAPTER
I.

The
"Trent"
Affair.

was, even so, experienced in making the batteries up to establishment in men and animals, when its units were thus unexpectedly ordered on what at the moment looked like active service. The 10th Brigade likewise had to call on other brigades to reinforce its numbers. The "Trent" affair, regrettable as it undoubtedly was in view of the irritation which the incident caused on both sides of the Atlantic, had at least the advantage that it provided an early test of the newly adopted brigade system in the Regiment, and that it afforded the D.A.G., R.A. and his assistants an illustration of the difficulties attending the despatch of a force of artillery to foreign parts on a sudden emergency. As it happened, President Lincoln's government had realized, even before the bulk of the troops that were hurried off from the United Kingdom had reached Canada, that the removal of the Confederate envoys from the "Trent" had been unwarrantable, and the dispute was settled without an appeal to arms.

The
Medical
and Veterinary
Services.

At the time of the abolition of the Board of Ordnance the officers of the then existing Ordnance Medical Department were for the most part posted to the Royal Artillery. On the introduction of the brigade system they were posted to brigades, and they used to become closely associated as regimental officers with batteries of their brigade, especially so in the case of mounted units.[1] They numbered in 1860 7 surgeons-major, 15 surgeons, and 68 assistant-surgeons, making up a total of 90. This, it may be observed, did not admit of medical officers being told off to each unit, seeing that the number of batteries at that time was 132, and that there moreover were depots and the Riding House Establishment to be provided for. But, inasmuch as there were two or more batteries quartered in many stations, there was no difficulty in so arranging the distribution of the available personnel as to ensure that there should at least be a medical officer told off to every unit quartered in a single-battery station. The arrangement was popular

---

[1] One surgeon-major or surgeon, and two assistant-surgeons was the usual allowance to the brigade.

in the Regiment, it was also popular amongst the medical officers themselves, and it was not without certain advantages in peace time. But it was unsound in principle even then, and it was wholly unsuited to meet the conditions that must arise in the event of a serious war.

Veterinary surgeons belonging to the Ordnance Veterinary Service were posted in like manner to the Regiment on the abolition of the Board of Ordnance. On the introduction of the brigade system they were appointed to brigades, and they were wont to become closely associated with individual batteries in single-battery stations. 26 were borne on the rolls at the beginning of the year 1860, as against 60 horse and field batteries.[1]

The vast majority of the non-commissioned officers and men serving in the Royal Artillery at this period were either fulfilling an original term of enlistment of twelve years, or else were fulfilling a term of re-engagement for a further nine years.

From the year 1829 to the year 1847 all men attested for the service had joined for an unlimited term. In 1847 an Act had been passed, in virtue of which limited enlistment was reintroduced (it had been in force previously to 1829 for more than twenty years), under which recruits for the R.A. were enlisted for twelve years, and could (under safeguards) re-engage for another twelve years on the expiration of their first term. The twelve years term of re-engagement was however altered to nine years a few years later. The consequence was that there were still in 1860 to be found a few non-commissioned officers and men who were serving on unlimited engagement.[2] There were also a certain number serving on limited engagement who had re-engaged for the term of twelve years under the provisions of the Act of 1847.

CHAPTER I.

The Medical and Veterinary Services.

Conditions of service in the ranks at this time.

[1] The medical officers and veterinary surgeons wore artillery uniform with some small differences, as will be described in Vol II.

[2] The writer recollects an old gunner, acting as an orderly, who was serving on unlimited engagement at Plymouth so late as 1894, in which year he died after more than forty years service. The G.O.C. and the whole staff attended the old man's funeral.

CHAPTER
I.

Conditions
of service
in the
ranks at
this time.

Difficulty was being found in securing the necessary number of recruits to keep the Regiment up to its establishment consequent upon its increase of late years. This same difficulty was also being experienced in the other arms of the service, and, as will be seen in the next chapter, the whole question came to a head within a very few years.

THE OFFICERS OF B. BATTERY, 4TH BRIGADE, ROYAL ARTILLERY, IN 1868.

Names reading from left to right: Lieut. A. F. Pickard, V.C., Lieut. G. H. O'Malley, Captain and Brevet Colonel N. O. S. Turner, C.B., H.R.H. Prince Arthur, K.G., Lieut. W. P. Georges, Lieut. F. H. Eardley-Wilmot, 2nd Captain and Brevet Major H. J. F. E. Hickes.

CHAPTER II.

1863 to 1873.

Re-organization of the Royal Horse Artillery in 1864—Corfu given up as a military station—Distinguished conduct of a party of the Coast Brigade—Minor changes of organization between 1864 and 1871—The recruiting problem—Honours and precedence—Prince Arthur in the Regiment—Mr. Cardwell—The Army Enlistment Act of 1870—Reduction in the proportion of the Royal Artillery on foreign service—The abolition of purchase—The block in promotion in the Regiment—Important changes in organization of the Regiment in 1871—The Depots—The 23rd and 24th Brigades in 1872—The Medical and Veterinary services—The localization of the forces—Holders of high appointments at this time—Some distinguished figures in the Regiment.

THE first change in organization of any importance affecting the Regiment, subsequent to the completion of the amalgamation of the Indian Regiments with the R.A., took place in the year 1864. Under the terms of G.R.O. 501 of the 13th April, the Royal Horse Artillery was formed into six instead of five brigades, and its brigades were at the same time given letters A to F to distinguish them, in place of numbers. There had been some little risk of confusion before, inasmuch as there had been both a 4th Brigade of horse artillery and a 4th Brigade of field artillery, the batteries in either case being denoted by letters. There had also been a marked lack of uniformity, seeing that, under the arrangement arrived at at the time of the amalgamation, the ten batteries of the already existing R.H.A. had remained in one single brigade, whereas the four brigades formed out of the Bengal, Madras and Bombay horse artillery troops had in no case comprised more than six batteries.

By the order of the 13th April the 1st Brigade R.H.A.

CHAPTER II.

Re-organization of the Royal Horse Artillery in 1864.

D

was split into two brigades, A and B, each of five batteries; the 2nd and 5th Brigades R.H.A. (comprising the former Bengal horse artillery troops) became C Brigade and F Brigade; the 3rd and 4th Brigades R.H.A. (comprising respectively the former Madras and the former Bombay horse artillery troops) became D Brigade and E Brigade. A and B Brigades remained for the time being stationed at home, while the other four remained stationed in India— 10 batteries at home and 20 in India.

Corfu had for a number of years been one of the most popular of the stations in which British troops were wont to find themselves beyond the seas, as is mentioned by Colonel Jocelyn in his record of the Regiment during the Crimean Period. Since the establishment of the Brigade system four of the batteries of the 6th Brigade (which had its headquarters in Malta and normally kept six of its batteries in that island) had been detached as part garrison of the Ionian Islands. But for some small detachments the four batteries were quartered in and near the town of Corfu. A local parliament was however especially summoned in 1863 to pronounce whether the people of the Ionian Islands wished the British protectorate to continue, or not; and as this assemblage voted unanimously for incorporation in the Kingdom of Greece, H.M. Government relinquished the protectorate at the end of the year. The garrison of British regular troops, including the batteries of garrison artillery, were therefore withdrawn in 1864.

The veterans who constituted the Coast Brigade were— necessarily in view of the nature of their duties and responsibilities—distributed in small parties about the localities of strategical importance to be found along the coast line. One of these localities was the island of Alderney, where defence works and armament were installed and where two garrison batteries were quartered at this time. A party of the Coast Brigade who formed part of its garrison behaved with commendable resource and great gallantry on the night of the 18th-19th October 1865 in

saving the crew of a wrecked French vessel, who had CHAPTER II.
been cast ashore on a rock. So much so, that a special
Regimental Order (No. 4)[1] was published on the 16th Distin-guished conduct of a party of the Coast Brigade.
November in consequence of a report on the subject that
had been furnished to the General Commanding-in-Chief
by Major-General C. R. Scott, commanding in Guernsey.
The Regimental Order concluded with the following
passage :—"Major-General Scott adds that 'the conduct of
these men is the theme of universal praise and admiration'—in which His Royal Highness is convinced that the
whole Regiment will concur". The names of the 17 non-
commissioned-officers and men concerned then follow.

Although up till the beginning of 1871 the distribu- Minor changes of organ-ization be-tween 1864 and 1871.
tion by batteries to brigades underwent no fundamental
alteration subsequent to the amalgamation of the Indian
Artilleries with the Regiment, some minor changes took
place. Batteries were in a few cases transferred from one
brigade to another, and in one or two of these cases field
batteries became garrison batteries, or *vice versa*. Three
garrison batteries, 5/20, 5/23 and 6/23 were reduced in
1868-69. A new garrison battery 6/25, which had only
been formed in 1863 and had taken part in the Bhootan
campaign, was reduced in 1866.[2] But these and similar
changes did not very appreciably increase or reduce the
number of batteries actually borne on the rolls of the
Regiment. These on the 1st January 1871 numbered 30
horse artillery batteries, 66 field batteries and 109 garrison artillery batteries.[3]

---

[1] Regimental Orders had since the beginning of 1865 appeared in
a new guise, in octavo and on white paper, like General Orders and
War Office Circulars. Hitherto, since the the disappearance of the
Board of Ordnance, they had appeared in foolscap size and on blue
paper—a most inconvenient arrangement, as anybody who forages
amongst folios of them in the present day will find.

[2] Another battery which took part in the Bhootan campaign as an
improvised mountain battery, 5/25, retained its 6-pr. Armstrong equipment, and in 1867 it proceeded to Abyssinia. It was the first R.A.
battery to act permanently as a mountain battery in India.

[3] One subaltern was reduced in each garrison battery at home and
also abroad except in India, and these units for several years were
allowed only 4 instead of 5 officers.

CHAPTER
II.

Minor
changes
of organ-
ization be-
tween 1864
and 1871.

An important reorganization and rearrangement by batteries took place at the beginning of this year, but, before
indicating what then took place, some reference seems to
be called for to the important questions in connection with
recruiting for the army as a whole that were arising and
in which the Royal Artillery was concerned, to some other
very important measures introduced about the same time,
and also to interesting points in connection with precedence
which were settled in the year 1869.

The re-
cruiting
problem.

The difficulty of securing an adequate supply of recruits
had already been engaging the attention of the military
authorities during the 1860-62 period, and it continued to
do so in the immediately succeeding years.   The great War
Minister, Lord Herbert of Lee (Mr. Sidney Herbert) who
was in office in 1860, died in harness in 1861.   He was
succeeded by Sir George Cornwall Lewis, who, like his
predecessor, died in harness in 1863.   He was succeeded
by Earl de Grey and Ripon, who held office till early in
1866 when he gave way to Lord Hartington.   Lord
Hartington's tenure of the position on this occasion was
comparatively brief, but during it a Royal Commission was
appointed on recruiting under the chairmanship of the
Earl of Dalhousie (formerly Lord Panmure, Secretary of
State for War from 1855 to 1858).   The Commission sat
during the summer and autumn of 1866—a period during
which the campaign of Sadowa was fought—and it reported
early in 1867.   The sudden breaking out of war on the
Continent in 1859, in 1864 and again in 1866 was dis-
closing the precarious character of international relations.
The contests which on each occasion ensued served moreover as striking illustrations of the extreme rapidity with
which the neighbours of the United Kingdom were able
to expand comparatively modest peace effectives into formidable hosts ready to take the field.   Lord Dalhousie and
his colleagues did not fail to realize the need of adequate
reserves, but their report refrained from grappling effectually with the problem.   Impressed with the importance
of keeping the ranks full of old and experienced soldiers,

the military witnesses who were examined urged the maintenance of the existing terms of service—enlistment for
12 years, followed by re-engagement for a further 9 years.
Nor did the Commission take the fact adequately into
account that the length of the existing term of colour service was acting as a deterrent on men of good class from
joining the ranks. The Report confined itself to putting
forward certain proposals on matters of detail which were
calculated somewhat to popularize the army.

Earl Grey alone amongst those giving evidence appeared
to recognize that some system of shorter service with the
colours would not only tend to bring in more recruits, but
would also render the creation of a really effective reserve
possible. It was admitted on all hands that one of the
difficulties in the way of keeping the ranks full was the
amount of foreign service which the existing distribution
of the forces of necessity entailed upon the troops, and the
evidence given before the Commission, as also some of the
documents and returns laid before it and quoted in its
Report, helped to draw general attention to the expediency
of reducing the overseas garrisons if such reductions could
be carried into effect without imperilling security. Circumstances—the awakening conscience of the inhabitants
of the oversea dominions, for instance, and the abandonment of the Ionian Islands—were already helping towards
easing the difficulties in connection with foreign service.
But it was reserved for Mr. Cardwell some three years
later to introduce the principle of comparatively short
service with the colours, to be followed by some years in
the army reserve.

Before giving consideration to the great reforms introduced during the Cardwell era, however, a reference must
be made to an important change affecting the precedence
of the Royal Horse Artillery, which came into force towards
the end of the year 1869.

The question of the precedence of the Regiment in connection with other regiments and corps forming part of the
Regular Army had been clearly established by custom and

by official ordinances for many years past. *Queen's Regulations* of 1837, of 1844 and of 1859, successively had been
perfectly clear on this point.   In these volumes it was laid
down that the Royal Horse Artillery "whether mounted
or dismounted" had precedence of all other corps on
parade, and that the rest of the Regiment took precedence
of all other corps except the Household Cavalry and the
Cavalry of the line.   It was also by General Order 832 of
August 1863 laid down that "a Battery of Royal Artillery
with its guns is to be saluted like a regiment with its
colours".

   The precedence of the horse artillery over all other
troops on parade was pronounced afresh in the issue of
Queen's Regulations which appeared in 1868.   Some doubts
upon the point would however appear to have arisen on
the subject shortly after The Duke of Cambridge had
become General Commanding-in-Chief in the year 1856,
as is suggested by the following document :—

   " Most humbly submitted to Your Majesty
" by
   " His Royal Highness the General Commanding-in-
" Chief with the concurrence of Your Majesty's Secre-
" tary of State for War.
   " That in the year 1756 precedence was given to the
" Royal Artillery before all Infantry, including the
" Regiments of Foot Guards.
   " The Regiments now designated the Life Guards
" and the Royal Horse Guards were formed in 1660 and
" 1661, at which period there was no Horse Artillery.
   "As therefore the Foot Artillery have precedence of
" all Infantry, including the Regiments of Foot Guards
" and dismounted Cavalry, it is submitted to Your
" Majesty that it would be consistent with the regula-
" tions that the Royal Horse Artillery should take pre-
" cedence of all Cavalry, including Your Majesty's
" Regiments of Life Guards and Royal Horse Guards.
   " It is therefore most humbly submitted for Your
" Majesty's approval : That the Royal Horse Artillery

" shall take precedence accordingly of all Cavalry, in-
" cluding Your Majesty's Regiments of Life Guards and
" Royal Horse Guards."

" Horse Guards,
    " 22nd June 1857.   'Approved'.
                             VICTORIA REG."

In so far as the Royal Horse Artillery were concerned,
this decision merely reaffirmed what was already distinctly
laid down in the published regulations. But it also raises
an interesting question as to the Regiment as a whole.
The Duke here wrote that the Foot Artillery had precedence not only of the infantry in general, including the
Foot Guards, but also of dismounted cavalry. But that
was not so in the year 1857. Precedence had been given
to the Royal Artillery over infantry and "dismounted
dragoons" in the year 1756—dragoons at that time being
synonymous with cavalry other than Household Cavalry,
inasmuch as our cavalry regiments of the line in those
days were either "Dragoon Guards", or "Dragoons" or
"Light Dragoons".[1] This held good up to the end of the
eighteenth century; for, on the 15th May, 1799, the
Adjutant-General wrote :— "The Commander-in-Chief is
pleased to confirm the order relative to the rank of the
Artillery, issued in the year 1756."
    The Commander-in-Chief at that time was the Duke
of York, and he was still Commander-in-Chief in 1804,
when a volume entitled *General Regulations and Orders*
appeared, which can be accepted as the fore-runner of the
King's Regulations of to-day. In this the question of the

---

[1] In the first volume of Duncan's *History of the Royal Artillery*
we read the following quotation from a letter of the 2nd April, 1756 :—
"It is the Duke of Marlborough's orders that Colonel Belford writes
to Captain Pattison to acquaint General Bland that it is His Royal
Highness' command that the Artillery takes the right of all Foot on all
parades, and likewise of dragoons when dismounted." (Charles, Duke
of Marlborough was Master-General of the Ordnance. His Royal
Highness, here referred to, was the Duke of Cumberland the Commander-in-Chief).

Royal Artillery having precedence of cavalry of the line
when dismounted was finally disposed of; for it was laid
down (after giving the Royal Horse Artillery the precedence over all other services) that "cavalry whether
mounted or dismounted, take the right of the line." That
moreover was repeated, if not always in exactly the same
words, in all the successive editions of *King's Regulations*
and *Queen's Regulations* which appeared on different dates
between 1804 and 1857. Be that, however, as it may,
the question of the precedence of the Royal Horse Artillery
cropped up afresh eleven years after Her Majesty had
approved by sign manual of the Duke of Cambridge's proposals of the 22nd June 1857—as is indicated by the
following document :—

> " It is humbly submitted to Your Majesty by
> " Your Majesty's dutiful cousin and servant
> " George
> " That Your Majesty command that the sign manual
> " of 22nd June be cancelled;
> " And that, as was formerly the case, Your Majesty's
> " Regiments of Life Guards and the Royal Horse
> " Guards, as part of the Body Guard of the Sovereign,
> " have precedence of all other Corps whatsoever. But
> " that the Royal Horse Artillery when on parade with
> " their guns take the right and march past at the head
> " of the Household Cavalry."

" 28th October, 1868.

'Approved'.
VICTORIA REG."

In his reference to what "was formerly the case" the
Duke evidently had in mind the position of affairs before
the creation of the Horse Artillery in the year 1793. Ever
since that creation, and up to this decision of 28th October,
1868, the Royal Horse Artillery had enjoyed precedence
over the Household Cavalry whether mounted or dismounted. Duncan in his History of the Regiment up to

Waterloo quotes a letter from the Master-General of the
Ordnance (the Earl of Chatham) on the 9th June, 1804,
which shows clearly that this was the case in the early
days of the R.H.A.   Moreover the decision of the 28th
October, 1868, was not communicated officially in the
usual manner to the Regiment at the time—and thereby
hangs a tale.   This can however best be told when touch-
ing on another matter of historical interest to the Royal
Artillery, the period spent by H.R.H. Prince Arthur,
afterwards Duke of Connaught, as a subaltern in the
Regiment.

Prince Arthur had passed the entrance examination for
Woolwich at the beginning of 1867, and he joined the
R.M. Academy in February of that year as a cadet.
During his year and a half at the Academy he lived in the
Ranger's House, Greenwich Park, but was present at all
drills and classes like the rest of the cadets; Lieut. A. F.
Pickard, **VC.**, R.A.[1] acted as his Orderly Officer.   The
Prince was commissioned a lieutenant in the Royal Engineers in the summer of 1868, and on the 2nd November
of that same year he was transferred by *Gazette* to the
Royal Artillery.   In this he was posted to B/4, commanded
by Bt. Lieut.-Colonel N. O. S. Turner and stationed at
Woolwich.   He served as a subaltern in this field battery
for nine months and was then, under date the 3rd August
1869, transferred to the Rifle Brigade.   During the months
spent as an artillery officer, he lived in a house on Woolwich Common with Lieut. Pickard in attendance.

Shortly before his term in the Regiment came to a
close, his battery, B/4, marched over from Woolwich to
Windsor Great Park one Friday, to take part in a review
which H.M. the Queen was holding on the following day
in honour of the Khedive of Egypt.   The troops to parade
for this review consisted (besides B/4) of C/C R.H.A., the
Household Cavalry, and several battalions of Foot Guards
and infantry of the line.

---

[1] Lieut. Pickard's services in New Zealand will be referred to in
the accompanying "Campaigns" volume.

CHAPTER
II.

Prince
Arthur
in the
Regiment.

The review was marked by one unusual occurrence. When C/C and the Household Cavalry moved off to gallop past, surprise was created when it was observed that B/4 were following them round. B/4 moreover galloped past too; and this is the only occasion, it is believed, on which a field battery of R.A. has done so at a Royal—or indeed any other sort of—Review. A staff officer had ridden up to the commanding officer of B/4, Colonel Turner, to ask if the battery could gallop past, and on the reply being in the affirmative, the necessary order had been given.[1] The force was for the most part encamped in the Great Park, and it had been arranged that a church parade should be held on the Sunday, at which Her Majesty would be present. When the officer acting as adjutant of the artillery, Lieut. (afterwards Major-General) M. H. Saward, R.H.A., met the staff officer who was posting the markers for the church parade, he was instructed to place the markers for C/C on the left of those of the Household Cavalry. He objected, claiming that the R.H.A. took the right of the line. When the staff officer insisted, Saward summoned Lieut.-Colonel A. Light, his commanding officer. A document was thereupon produced, signed under authority of General the Earl of Lucan who was in command of the parade (and who was also Gold Stick), in which it was laid down that the Household Cavalry took the right; and the parade was in due course so formed up. Officers and men of C/C were highly indignant, and the men gave vent to their feelings in unmistakable fashion before they quitted Windsor. It was only a few days later, on the 17th August, that a Regimental Order was published indicating that the Household Cavalry had pre-

---

[1] The field artillery, needless to say, do not admit that they are not well able to gallop when the occasion arises, and they do often gallop at manœuvres and on active service. There used in the "eighties" to be a field battery commander in India, a former Madras gunner, who galloped his battery all over the country around the station where they had their being. Damage was occasionally sustained by horses, or by material, or by detachments as a result of these spirited manœuvres; but the gunners forgot their hurts in their appreciation of the major's profuse expenditure of forcible figures of speech.

cedence of all other troops, but that the R.H.A., when on parade with their guns, took the right of the line and marched past at the head of the troops—the rule that has held good ever since, and which was embodied in the next edition of *Queen's Regulations*, that of 1873.[1]

Lord Hartington had been succeeded in the summer of 1866 by Major-General J. Peel, who a year later gave place to Sir J. Pakington. Pakington remained Secretary of State till the end of 1868, when Mr. Gladstone's government replaced that of Mr. Disraeli. Mr. Cardwell then became War Minister, and he held that position for over five years—memorable years in the history of the British Army. Under his auspices four great measures were carried out, the effect of which, in spite of later changes and reorganizations and modifications, remains to this day. These four measures were : (1) The unification of the War Office. (2) The introduction of so-called short service. (3) The abolition of purchase. (4) The localization of the forces. During the Cardwell era much moreover was effected in the direction of reducing the strength of the forces on foreign service, as also towards increasing the actual peace establishment of the army—in achieving which later development the famous War Minister was undoubtedly assisted by the accident of the Franco-German War of 1870-71 taking place during his term of office. In what he accomplished, he was aided by a small band of progressive officers, and by none more devotedly than by a still comparatively junior member of the Regiment, Captain and Bt. Lieut.-Colonel (afterwards General Sir R.) Biddulph, who was his Private Secretary from 1871 to 1873.

The first two of Cardwell's great measures were put into force in 1870, and they were decided upon before

CHAPTER
II.

Prince
Arthur
in the
Regiment.

Mr.
Cardwell.

---

[1] In the annual Army Estimates the R.H.A. were, at this time and for another dozen years, shown at the head of the various tables and before the cavalry, including the Household Cavalry. In the Estimates for 1883-84 the R.H.A. were for the first time shown with the rest of the R.A., and after the cavalry—obviously a more convenient plan.

CHAPTER
II.

Mr.
Cardwell.
some of the progressive officers—Sir G. Wolseley (who
conducted the Red River Expedition during that year)
for instance—had joined the War Office. Brig.-General
(afterwards General Sir J. M.) Adye, R.A., was, under the
unification arrangements which were being introduced into
the central administration of the army, appointed Director
of Artillery and Stores in 1870, and he assisted the
Secretary of State in connection with certain later reforms.
The unification of the War Office which was effected by
the War Office Act of 1870, however affected the manufacturing and experimental side of the Royal Artillery
rather than its fighting units, and it will be touched upon
later in Chapter VII. The details of another reform,
one of special interest to the commissioned ranks of the
Regiment, which was introduced in 1870 and which dealt
with a very serious block in promotion amongst officers
of the rank of Captain in the R.A. and R.E., will be dealt
with in a later paragraph of this chapter.

The Army
Enlist-
ment Act
of 1870.
Under the provisions of the Army Enlistment Act the
first term of engagement was fixed at twelve years (as had
been the case before); but only a portion of these twelve
years were to be passed with the colours, the residue being
spent in the Army Reserve. The act provided for the
Secretary of State being empowered to fix the relative
periods from time to time; but at the outset the period
with the colours in the case of infantry was fixed at six
years, and in the case of the artillery was fixed at nine
years. The terms of service have varied on occasion since
1870, and a distinction has often existed in this respect
between men serving abroad and those serving at home.
But the broad principle that in time of peace the standing
army feeds the reserve, while in time of war the reserve
feeds the standing army, has governed the procedure in
connection with terms of service ever since, while re-
engagement for a further period beyond the original twelve
years has not been much encouraged except for non-
commissioned officers and in special cases. It may be
mentioned that before the Army Enlistment Act received

the Royal Assent the war between France and Germany had broken out.[1]

It so happened that Mr. Cardwell had been Colonial Secretary from 1864 to 1866, and that he had been impressed then with the importance of the colonists contributing towards the support of the troops stationed in their territory, and of their furthermore providing troops of their own for purposes of security where this was practicable. Some steps had already been taken before his becoming War Minister to reduce the forces on foreign service. The abandonment of the protectorate over the Ionian Islands had, as has been mentioned in an earlier paragraph, permitted the withdrawal of the British garrison from Corfu, including four garrison batteries. In the year 1866, a considerable force, including two field batteries and one garrison battery, was withdrawn from New Zealand, where it had been intermittently carrying on a war with the Maories for several years past—the services of the R.A. in these hostilities are narrated in the Volume dealing with the campaigns during this period. We have seen in the last chapter how the garrison of Canada was appreciably increased at the end of 1861 owing to the "Trent" affair; the protracted nature of the War of Secession in the United States prevented any considerable withdrawal of regular troops from this quarter before 1867. But a reduction was carried out in 1867, and a further large reduction was effected in 1869; so that by the beginning of 1871 there were only 3 garrison batteries left in the country, whereas in 1864 there had been 10 field batteries

CHAPTER II.

Reduction in the proportion of the Royal Artillery on foreign service.

---

[1] " The fact was that the system of recruiting up to 1870 was, and always had been unpopular. The service was a hard one. Regiments were kept abroad for upwards of twenty years; and of the thousands who enlisted yearly but few ever returned, and even then were often prematurely aged and broken down. It is no wonder that the poor people of the country looked upon enlistment of their sons with dread, and almost as equivalent to a sentence of banishment and of death. So great was the difficulty, that between 1861 and 1869—although the men were then better paid, fed and clothed than in former years—the average number of recruits obtained was only 12,546 per annum." *Recollections of a Military Life* by General Sir J. M. Adye.

and 12 garrison batteries. At the beginning of 1864 there
had been 62 field batteries and 73 garrison batteries abroad;
at the beginning of 1871 the figures were 46 field batteries
and 65 garrison batteries.

None of the measures affecting the army, brought forward by Mr. Cardwell, aroused such opposition as did that
by which the system of buying and selling commissions in
the cavalry and the infantry was brought to an end. The
matter was one which did not perhaps affect the Royal
Artillery directly; but it very appreciably affected the
Regiment indirectly. The adoption of a system of entrance
for officers into the cavalry and infantry analogous to that
already prevailing for entrance into the Royal Artillery
was bound to act as a deterrent on candidates presenting
themselves for admission to the R.M. Academy, unless the
prospects of young gentlemen entering the two "scientific
corps" were to be at least as promising as the prospects
of those entering the other arms. At the time when the
purchase question came up for decision this was by no
means the case, in so far as the Regiment was concerned,
owing to the stagnation in respect to promotion that prevailed in it. The higher pay and the openings of a non-
military kind which the Royal Engineers enjoyed placed
that corps in a relatively more favourable position; but it
likewise suffered from this depressing stagnation in respect
to promotion. This question of promotion in the two
scientific corps was bound to have come to a head in any
case before long, but the abolition of purchase caused the
problem to be grappled with effectually.

It is unnecessary to relate at length here the well-
known story of how the abolition of purchase was carried
out. Suffice it to say that the Bill dealing with the matter
was brought before the House of Commons at the same
time as the Army Estimates for 1871-72, and that it in due
course passed its third reading. When introduced in the
House of Lords immediately afterwards, it was met by the
passing of an amendment which virtually shelved the bill.
The Government thereupon took the unusual step of pro-

CHAPTER
II.

The
abolition
of
purchase.

The block
in promo-
tion in the
Regiment.

ceeding by Royal Warrant, this was signed by the Queen
on the 20th July 1871, and it brought the purchase system
to an end on the following 1st November.   The Royal
Warrant dealing with the stagnation in promotion in the
Royal Artillery and the Royal Engineers had, as it happened, been signed by Her Majesty a fortnight before.

Complaints had been frequent of late years that promotion in the Royal Artillery and in the Royal Engineers
was not sufficiently rapid to keep them in a condition of
efficiency.   A House of Commons committee under chairmanship of Mr. Childers considered the matter in 1867;
but the proposals for meeting the difficulty put forward
by this body took the form of plans for bringing about
retirement.   Such plans would have been costly to the
tax-payer, and they would have had the effect of depriving
the country of the services of a number of comparatively
young officers, just when these were likely to be at their
best.   Differences as it happened existed between the four
separate lists on which officers of the R.A. (as also those
of the R.E.) stood for promotion.   The lengths of service
in years of the senior captain, 2nd captain and lieutenant
on the four artillery lists at the beginning of 1866 had
stood as follows :—

	1st Captain.	2nd Captain.	Lieutenant.
R.A. List	22	16	10
R.A. (late Bengal) List	24	18	9
R.A. (late Madras) List	25	16	9
R.A. (late Bombay) List	21	17	8

Acturial calculations had shown that the situation
would grow worse, and at the beginning of 1871, when Mr.
Cardwell after long consideration took steps to improve
matters, the four artillery lists showed the following
figures :—[1]

[1] Steps had been taken during 1869, by limiting the number of
Lieutenants commissioned from the R.M. Academy, to reduce the total
number of subalterns by about 50. During the following year the
number of subalterns allowed 8 garrison batteries at home and in the
colonies (but not in India) was reduced from 3 to 2.

CHAPTER
II.

The block
in promo-
tion in the
Regiment.

	Senior 1st Captain.	Senior 2nd Captain.	Senior Lieutenant.
R.A. List	24	17	14
R.A. (late Bengal) List	27	18	13
R.A. (late Madras) List	26	16	12
R.A. (late Bombay) List	26	17	12

One or two captains showing 18 years' service and upwards had usually been found in line regiments of late years, but that this was so was due to the purchase system. These veteran company officers had been left behind, while juniors in the same regiments had bought the commission of major over their heads. The existence of the purchase system, with the extraordinary anomalies to which it gave rise, indeed rendered any unimpeachable statistical comparison between the position of officers of the line and officers of the Royal Artillery almost impossible. But there could be no question as to the prospects of the latter in the matter of promotion being, on the average, far less promising than the prospects of the former. Mr. Cardwell came to the conclusion that what was needed in the R.A. and the R.E. was a better proportion between the ranks in the two corps, and he grappled with the problem in uncompromising fashion.

" He now proposed a change of organization, viz. : " that a battery of Artillery should be commanded not " by a captain but by a field officer. The battery is the " tactical unit of Artillery, and is a far more important " and responsible command than is allotted to a captain " in the other branches of the service. This had always " been recognized, especially in the Peninsula and in " the Crimea, when officers commanding field batteries " were classed with officers commanding regiments for " appointment to the Order of the Bath, which was given " to them in addition to brevet promotion. It was there- " fore proposed to substitute the rank of major for that " of first captain, while, in order to keep batteries " effective, all majors, captains and lieutenants holding

" extra-regimental appointments were to be supernumer- CHAPTER II.
" ary. An equivalent promotion was proposed for the
" Royal Engineers, and provision was made accordingly The block in promotion in the Regiment.
" in the estimates of 1872-73 at a cost of £19,000
" for the Royal Artillery and £10,000 for the Royal
" Engineers." [1]

Strong opposition was raised in certain quarters to the plan of promoting the 1st captains of the R.A. and the R.E. to the rank of major, on the grounds that some of the senior captains of the line would be superseded as a consequence. The figures given above, for instance, show that the senior 2nd captain on the Madras List in 1871 had only 16 years' service; the junior 1st captain on that list would naturally only have about the same length of service, and a number of senior captains in the line had more service. Still, this grievance was as nothing as compared to the fact that scores of 1st captains on all four lists of the Regiment were, under the existing system, being superseded every time that a captain of the cavalry or of the line was promoted major. Supersession was moreover an inevitable feature of the purchase system. That system had been tolerated in the cavalry and infantry for two hundred years, and it was only now being put an end to. The matter was taken up in the House of Lords, where a motion was actually carried which would have had the effect of delaying the introduction of the proposed measure.[2] This motion the Government ignored, and a Royal Warrant was duly signed on the 5th July 1871, restoring the rank of major in the two scientific corps, and promoting all first captains in them to that rank.[3] [4]

---

[1] From *Lord Cardwell at the War Office* by Gen. Sir R. Biddulph.

[2] The motion was brought forward by a peer who had become a lieut.-colonel by purchase after nine years' service, thereby superseding swarms of officers in every branch of the service.

[3] The system under which lieutenants and captains of the Foot Guards at this time held the rank respectively of captain and lieut.-colonel in the army was abolished just at this time, although not retrospectively.

[4] Promotion was accelerated in 1872 by 36 field officers and 21 captains on the Indian lists of R.A. being retired on special annuities so as to dispose of certain surplus officers.

CHAPTER II.

The block in promotion in the Regiment.

Important changes in organization of the Regiment in 1871.

The efficiency of the Regiment was soon afterwards appreciably increased by the seconding of most of the majors, captains and lieutenants who were extra-regimentally employed. Hitherto all such officers had been borne on the strength of batteries, except in a few special cases where they were borne on the strength of the depôts. The consequence had been that it had been rare for batteries to have their full complement of officers with them, even during the drill season.

The question of increasing the available fighting strength of the army at home had been engaging the attention of Mr. Cardwell and his professional advisers even before the outbreak of the Franco-German War, and something had, as we have seen, been effected in this direction by the bringing home of certain of the troops that had hitherto been normally quartered in foreign parts. The sudden outbreak of hostilities on the Continent, coupled as it was with the publication of a draft treaty between France and Prussia on the subject of Belgium, caused H.M. Government promptly to obtain a vote of credit for £2,000,000, and to secure sanction from Parliament for an additional 20,000 men for the army. Of these 20,000 men, 5,317 were to be allotted to the Royal Artillery, and steps were shortly afterwards taken to effect a considerable increase in the number of mobile batteries on the home establishment. The full detail of what was intended was published in a Regimental Order dated the 1st February, 1871, some of the provisions of which however had already been, or were already in process of being, carried out.

Under the terms of this order E. Brigade R.H.A. was broken up, six batteries were added to B and C Brigades stationed at home, 5 of them being transferred from the Indian establishment; a new battery H/B, was also raised. So that after the order had been carried into effect there were 16 batteries at home and 15 batteries in India, instead of 10 at home and 20 in India as had been the case immediately after the amalgamation.

20 field batteries were added to the number already existing at home. This was carried out under the following arrangements:— The 1st Brigade (Garrison) of 8 batteries was converted into a field brigade, and two batteries (I and K) were raised and added to it. Two new batteries (C and I) were added to the 4th Brigade.[1] Two batteries, I and K, were raised and added to the 11th Brigade. 4 of the existing batteries in the 14th Brigade, E, F, G and H, which were on garrison establishment, were transformed into field batteries, and two batteries, I and K were raised and added to it. Besides the reductions above mentioned being carried out in the garrison artillery in consequence of a number of its batteries becoming field batteries, one garrison battery in each of eight brigades (the 3rd, 7th, 10th, 12th, 13th, 15th, and 17th Brigades) was broken up. The batteries of the 25th (Garrison) Brigade, stationed in India, were moreover distributed amongst other brigades.

The net result of these changes, as affecting the Regiment as a whole, was that one battery R.H.A. and 20 field batteries were added to it, whereas the total number of garrison batteries in it was reduced by 20. The figures after the changes had been put in execution were 31 batteries of horse artillery, 83 field batteries and 91 garrison batteries.

Certain minor changes were carried out at the same time in respect to the depôts. The organization of these had undergone modifications at various times during the previous eight years, and one of these modifications had been to remove some of the depôt batteries from Woolwich —a step which was to be carried further in the near future, with the idea of creating territorial connections. At the end of 1871 the depôts had the following organization:—

There was a central staff at Woolwich; but the whole

CHAPTER II.

Important changes in organiza- tion of the Regiment in 1871.

The Depôts.

---

[1] There had been batteries C/4 and I/4, which had been sent to New Zealand in 1861 and 1863, but these had been transferred to other brigades at the end of the war out there.

was broken up into two divisions, each with its staff.   The
1st Division comprised 5 batteries numbered 1 to 5, of
which 4 were stationed at Sheerness (which was the headquarters of the division) and 1 was quartered at Shoeburyness.   The 2nd Division was stationed at Woolwich and
consisted of 7 batteries; of these 2 (A h.a. and B h.a.)
were horse artillery batteries, 3 (A. B and C) were field
batteries, and the two remaining ones (6 and 7) were garrison batteries.

A yet further change of organization, one affecting the
23rd and 24th Brigades, was carried out in the summer
of 1872.   The 23rd Brigade, as such, was broken up and
its batteries were transferred to other brigades.   The 24th
Brigade thereupon became the 23rd Brigade.

"Mixed" brigades had now been wholly eliminated.
The 1st, 4th, 8th, 9th, 11th, 14th, 16th, 18th, 19th and
20th were field brigades, the 2nd, 3rd, 5th, 6th, 7th, 10th,
12th, 13th, 15th, 17th, 21st, 22nd and 23rd were garrison
brigades.   Of these the 1st, 4th, 7th, 11th, 12th, 14th,
17th, 21st and 22nd Brigades were stationed at home, the
2nd, 3rd, 5th, 6th, 8th, 9th, 10th, 15th, 16th, 18th, 19th,
20th and 23rd Brigades were stationed in the Colonies and
India.   Thus three of those constituted at the time of the
amalgamation of the Indian artilleries had found their way
to the United Kingdom, the 17th, 21st and 22nd Brigades,
while five, the 16th, 18th, 19th, 21st and 22nd Brigades
were still stationed in India; two, the original 23rd and
25th, had disappeared.

Lessons taught by the Franco-German War had
directed the attention of our military authorities to the
importance of drawing up tables showing what brigades
and divisions and army corps were to consist of in time of
war.   Those charged with these investigations speedily
perceived that no organization existed for mobile ammunition reserves in the field nor for ensuring an efficient
medical service in case of serious hostilities.   Such
decisions as were come to did not in respect to ammunition

supply go beyond plans on paper.   But, as regards the medical and hospital services, the decisions that were arrived at led to a change which was of practical interest to the Royal Artillery.   For the regimental system, under which medical officers formed an integral part of cavalry and infantry regiments and of the R.A., was found to be incompatible with the proper development of an efficient medical and hospital service for purposes of war.

A Royal Warrant consequently appeared on the 1st March 1873, which abolished the regimental system and transferred all the medical officers belonging to regiments to the Army Medical Department.   Such officers were however allowed to continue wearing the regimental uniforms for some time to come, and those who had formerly belonged to the R.A. were as far as possible kept doing duty with their old corps.   Their names moreover remained on the R.A. lists for some years subsequent to the appearance of the Royal Warrant.

Veterinary surgeons, on the other hand, continued to be posted to cavalry regiments and to the Royal Artillery for some years to come.[1]

What constituted the most important part of the last of Mr. Cardwell's great measures of reform, was not introduced until the year 1873.   The localization of the forces, as this was carried into effect in that year, dealt almost entirely with the infantry arm.   It consisted, in the first place, of setting up the linked battalion system and associating the regiments of the line definitely with territorial districts of the United Kingdom.   It consisted, in the second place, of affiliating the infantry militia and volunteer corps, that were already associated with the territorial districts, to the regiments of the line which were now becoming associated with those districts.

---

[1] The Royal Horse Infirmary at Woolwich, afterwards an R.A remount depot, served for a number of years about this time as virtually the headquarters of the military veterinary service.   Newly commissioned officers joined there to receive instruction, and the buildings were used as a centre of veterinary research.

But the introduction of this system was in reality to no small extent facilitated by the fact that the principle of localization had already been applied after a fashion to the artillery two years before. The British Isles had in the year 1871, in so far as the artillery was concerned, been divided into 12 sub-districts. These sub-districts had been so mapped out as to be co-terminous with the existing military districts, each such military district henceforward comprising one or two artillery sub-districts. Each of these artillery sub-districts had been placed under command of a lieutenant-colonel R.A., in whom was vested the administrative control of all the artillery militia corps and of all artillery volunteer corps within its borders. The advantages of this system soon became apparent, the plan worked satisfactorily from the outset, and its success helped to point the way for the localization of the infantry of the line and for the establishing of close association between the infantry of the auxiliary forces and that of the regulars.

Mr. Cardwell's highly productive career as War Minister came to an end towards the close of 1873, on the fall of Mr. Gladstone's government and Mr. Disraeli's accession to office.

Officers belonging to the Regiment, who during this period held important positions in the army were, with few exceptions, occupying what may be called regimental appointments, except in India. Sir W. Fenwick Williams was one of the exceptions, for, after completing his term as commanding the troops in Canada, and then spending five years as Lieut.-Governor of Nova Scotia, he became Governor and Commander-in-Chief at Gibraltar. Major-General B. Cuppage, a Peninsula and Waterloo veteran, was in command in Jersey from 1863 to 1868. Sir Richard Dacres was succeeded at the head of the Woolwich District in 1864 by Major-General E. C. Warde, who was in his turn followed by Major-General Sir D. E. Wood in 1869. Colonel E. B. Hamley became Commandant of the Staff College in 1870.

CHAPTER
II.

Holders
of high
appoint-
ments at
this time.

In India, Major-General J. Fordyce had command of
the Presidency District from 1868 to 1873, and Major-
General Sir H. Tombs assumed command of the Allahabad
Division in 1871 and was transferred shortly afterwards to
the Oudh Division. A large number of R.A. colonels held
brigade commands at different times, with troops of all
arms under their charge. The following may be named :—
H. Tombs, G. J. L. Buchanan, E. Kaye, G. P. Sealy,
G. Bourchier, G. Selby, A. W. Macintyre, G. B. Shake-
spear, J. Turner, W. Olpherts and J. D. Woolcombe.
They in most cases belonged to the former Indian lists.
Brigadier-General Tombs commanded one of the two columns operating in the second phase of the Bhootan campaign in 1865, and Brigadier-General Bourchier commanded one of the two columns in the Lushai campaign
of 1871-72.

As regards purely regimental appointments, General
Bloomfield, Inspector-General, had been replaced by Major-
General A. C. Taylor in 1864, and General Taylor was
followed by Major-General Sir C. Dickson in 1870. Colonel
G. Gambier became D.A.G., R.A., at the War Office in
1864, vice Colonel Bingham; he held the appointment
until 1870, when he was succeeded by Colonel W. A.
Middleton.[1] Up till 1871 there were separate Inspectors
R.A. to each Presidency in India, but an Inspector-General,
Major-General A. Huyshe, was appointed in 1871; he was
succeeded by Brig.-General D. Gaye in 1873. Colonel
J. M. Adye was D.A.G., R.A., in India from 1863 to 1866,
when he was succeeded by Colonel W. A. Middleton who
held the appointment for two years, being then followed
by Major-General M. A. S. Biddulph. General Biddulph
was succeeded by Colonel C. G. Arbuthnot in 1873.

Several of the Colonels Commandant whose names
appeared at the head of lists of Royal Artillery officers in
1860, had taken part in the' great wars of the beginning
of the century. Whether they had served in the Peninsula

---

[1] Superior appointments in connection with armaments are touched
upon in Part II.

CHAPTER
II.

Some dis-
tinguished
figures
in the
Regiment.

or at Waterloo was shown by the letter "P" or the letter
"W" before their names. Before the end of the period
1863 to 1873, with which this chapter deals, most of these
veterans had passed over. Although many references to
what they accomplished have appeared in earlier volumes
of this History of the Regiment, a brief record of the
careers of the most distinguished amongst them would seem
to be appropriate.

General Sir R. W. Gardiner, G.C.B., K.C.H., died in the
year 1864. He was born in the year 1781, obtained his
commission in 1797 and was almost at once in the field,
the occasion being the capture of Minorca. He was in the
Peninsula between 1808 and 1809 being present at Roleia,
Vimiero and the retreat to Corunna. He then took part in
the Walcheren Expedition, but returned to the Peninsula,
to be present at Barossa, the siege of Badajoz, Salamanca,
Vittoria, the Pyrenees, Orthez and Toulouse. He was also
present at Waterloo. He reached the rank of major-general
in 1841 and was Governor of Gibraltar from 1848 to 1855.
He prepared a number of valuable papers on professional
subjects during the years before the Crimean War.

Lieutenant-General Sir E. C. Whinyates, K.C.B., K.H.,
died in 1866. Born in 1782 and commissioned in 1798, he
took part in the expedition to the Helder, and he also took
part in the expedition to Copenhagen in 1807. He served
in the Peninsula from 1811 to 1813 and was present at
Busaco and at Albuera. He commanded the 2nd Rocket
Troop at Waterloo. He was in command at Woolwich from
1852 to 1856 and he reached the rank of lieutenant-general
in the latter year.

Field-Marshal Sir Hew Ross, G.C.B., died in 1868. He
was born in 1779 and was commissioned in 1795. He obtained the command of the Chestnut Troop in 1805 and he
remained at its head until the year 1825 when he was promoted to the rank of regimental lieutenant-colonel. He
took the troop out to the Peninsula in 1811, and by means
of a forced march he contrived to take part in the battle of

CHAPTER
II.

Some dis-
tinguished
figures
in the
Regiment.

Talavera. On the formation of the Light Division the Chestnut Troop was included, and with this Division he was afterwards present at the Coa, at Busaco, at Fuentes d'Onoro, at the sieges of Ciudad Rodrigo and of Badajoz, at Salamanca, at Vittoria, at the battles of the Pyrenees, at the Nivelle and at St. Pierre; but owing to returning home on leave he missed Orthez and Toulouse. He took the troop over to Belgium in 1815 and was present at Waterloo. He had been promoted brevet lieut.-colonel in 1813, and he was given the K.C.B. for Waterloo. He was appointed D.A.G., R.A., in the year 1840 and he became major-general in the following year. He took Lord Raglan's place at the head of the Ordnance Board in 1854, and on the abolition of the board he became A.G., R.A., in 1855, retiring in 1858. He had been given the G.C.B., in 1855, and he was promoted Field-Marshal in 1868, very shortly before his death—the first officer brought up in the Regiment to receive the baton.

Lieutenant-General A. C. Mercer also died in 1868. He had obtained his commission in 1799 and before the Waterloo campaign had seen no service, except at Monte-video in 1807. His battery, "G", R.H.A., was present at Quatre Bras, and at Waterloo it greatly distinguished itself by saving two squares of Brunswick infantry, between which it was posted, when, already in confusion owing to the enemy's artillery fire, these were assailed by a strong force of French Horse Grenadiers and Cuirassiers. Wellington's orders had been that, when a battery was charged by cavalry, the detachments were to retire into the nearest square. Mercer ignored these and he beat the hostile horse off by his fire. No brevets nor distinctions came his way, but the name of no artilleryman of those days, except possibly that of Norman Ramsay, is better remembered in the Regiment to-day than is that of Mercer.

Field-Marshal Sir George Pollock, G.C.B., was born in 1786. He passed through the R.M. Academy—some cadets preparing for service under the East India Company were

CHAPTER
II.

Some dis-
tinguished
figures
in the
Regiment.

being educated at Woolwich just at that time—and joined
the Bengal Artillery in the year 1803.   Within a few
months he found himself in the field, engaged in Lake's
victorious campaigns against Holkar, and he was present
at Deeg and at the siege of Bhurtpore.   He served in the
Nepal operations in 1814 and he took part in the 1st
Burmah War ten years later.

He was in command, as a brigadier-general, first of the
Dinapur and then of the Agra District from 1838 to 1842,
and was then, having been promoted major-general,
selected to take command of the force which was being got
together to relieve Sale's garrison at Jellalabad.   He fought
his way to the beleagured city a few days after the garrison
had broken out.   Then, as a result of his own persistent
representations, he was permitted by the Indian Government to advance on Kabul so as to avenge the disasters
of the previous year.   At the head of divisions commanded
by Generals Sale and McGaskill he made his way to the
Afghan capital after severe fighting, arriving there just
before General Nott (who was advancing from Kandahar)
reached the place.   Then, as senior in the theatre of war,
he assumed command of all the forces in Afghanistan,
effected a satisfactory settlement, and evacuated the
country.   For these services he received the thanks of
Parliament, was awarded the G.C.B., and was granted a
special pension of £1000 a year by the E.I. Company.
The "Pollock Medal" to be awarded at the end of each
term to the cadet passing out of Addiscombe at the head
of the list, was moreover instituted by the Company at the
same time as a memorial to him.

After this Sir G. Pollock was for two years Military
Member of the Council in India, but he was obliged to
leave the country in 1846 owing to ill-health, and he never
returned.   From 1854 to 1856 he was one of the then
Directors of the E.I. Company especially appointed by
H.M. Government.   This was his last public service until,
in 1871, he was appointed Constable of the Tower.   He
had been promoted Field-Marshal in 1870; but he only

enjoyed the honour for two years for he died in 1872. He was buried in Westminster Abbey.

General F. R. Chesney, the greatest explorer whom the Regiment has produced, was born in 1789; he joined at the age of 16 in 1805, but was fated to take no part in the great wars of the beginning of the 19th century. A keen soldier, he made his way out as a captain to Constantinople towards the close of the Russo-Turkish war in 1829, hoping to join the Ottoman armies, but he only arrived immediately after the peace of Adrianople. He then obtained leave to travel in Egypt and Syria, and while in Egypt he surveyed the desert north of Suez and came to the conclusion that a canal across it was perfectly feasible. M. de Lesseps some years later admitted that reading Chesney's report on the subject first caused him to turn his attention to the great project which he ultimately carried through. After going up the Nile to the 2nd cataract and crossing the desert from Keneh to Kosseir, Chesney proceeded to Palestine and Syria, and, reaching the Euphrates, travelled down the river by raft to Baghdad, satisfying himself that the channel was navigable. He then visited the lower Tigris and the Karun and afterwards travelled through Persia and Armenia and back to Aleppo, before returning home to urge the desirability of opening up the Euphrates valley route to India.

As a result of his reports Parliament voted a sum of money, and in 1835 he proceeded at the head of an expedition to the Gulf of Alexandretta, taking 13 brother officers of the Regiment as well as rank and file with him, together with two steamers in parts. These were conveyed across the hills to where the Euphrates reaches the plain and put together; one was wrecked, the other reached Baghdad, and Chesney returned to England with his reports in 1837. But he could not induce the Government to proceed further in the matter. He served in China from 1843 to 1847, and in 1856, at the age of 67, joined in a party which surveyed the country between the Gulf of Alexandretta and the Euphrates with view to a railway.

He was promoted major-general in 1855 and general in 1868 and died in 1872.   He had received the gold medal of the Royal Geographical Society in 1837, and was made honorary D.C.L. in 1860.

CHAPTER III.

1874 TO 1881.

THE army was at the end of 1873 to some extent in a transition stage, for the full effect of some of Mr. Cardwell's great reforms was not yet felt. This held good particularly in respect to the conditions of service for the rank and file; for many private soldiers, still to be found with the colours, had enlisted for the full period of twelve years, and there were moreover many others on the rolls who had extended their service up to twenty-one years. Those who had enlisted under the new system of twelve years service, of which the latter part would be spent in the Army Reserve, were moreover practically all still with the colours. But the terms of service under the new system, as they had been originally decided upon with regard to the Royal Artillery, had already undergone modification. The conditions for this arm had at the outset been fixed as nine years with the colours followed by three years in the Army Reserve. But certain investigations, following on lessons derived from the Franco-German War, had satisfied the military authorities that these conditions would not meet requirements.

Muzzle-loading guns had during the years 1871 and 1872 been substituted for the Armstrong breech-loading guns in the horse artillery and the field batteries on the home establishment, and it had at the same time been decided that provision ought to exist for conveying in a mobile form a total of 500 rounds per gun in the field in the event of war. The question of laying down an appropriate war organization for brigades, divisions and army corps was being examined into at the same time, and these investigations at once made apparent that special ammunition columns in some form or other would have to be created on mobilization. The authorities decided that the personnel for such columns must be provided by the Royal Artillery, and they came to realize that this arm of the service consequently stood in need of reserves quite as large as did the infantry. That the conditions as regards colour service and reserve service had in the first instance been laid down for the artillery as nine years and three years, instead of the periods of seven years and five years (eight and four in the case of men serving abroad) determined upon for the infantry, was largely due to the prevalent idea that it took several years to make an efficient gunner or driver. It had however been due also to the realization that the rank-and-file personnel of batteries in India would in due course be providing reservists, but that, owing to their being virtually at war establishment in peace time, those batteries would not need reservists to bring them to a war footing in case of emergency, and that the reservists sent home from that country would consequently be available to feed the batteries on the home establishment in the event of mobilization. But by the year 1874 the importance of possessing an ample reserve of trained gunners and drivers was understood, and the conditions of service in the Regiment had therefore been made the same as those obtaining in the infantry—seven years with the colours and five in the reserve, but with the liability of an eighth year with the colours for men serving abroad.

The establishment as regards officers was that each battery was now commanded by a major, and that each had a captain; batteries were moreover supposed to have three

subalterns each, except in the case of garrison batteries at
home and in the colonies, which had only two.   A certain
number of lieutenant-colonels were told off to each brigade,
but their position was wont to be somewhat ill-defined and
anomalous.   The problem of the higher organization of the
Royal Artillery was however under the serious consideration of the War Office, where it was fully recognized—as it
was within the Regiment itself—that, outside of the interior
economy of the battery, the whole system left much to be
desired.

Horse artillery batteries and field batteries were at this
time organized in three "divisions" and six "sub-divisions", the sub-division representing the personnel, horses
and equipment for one gun.   Garrison batteries were
organized as two "sub-divisions", each nominally in charge
of a subaltern, except those in India where the battery
unit comprised three sub-divisions.   The terms "section"
and "sub-section" were not adopted till some years later.

The distribution of the batteries at home and abroad
was as follows at the beginning of 1874 :—16 horse artillery, 47 field artillery and 34 garrison artillery batteries
were quartered at home, and there was also one garrison
battery which was properly on the home establishment but
was temporarily on the Gold Coast on account of the
Ashanti War.   15 horse artillery, 36 field artillery and 26
garrison artillery batteries were stationed in India; of the
garrison batteries 3 were mountain batteries and 4 were
heavy batteries.   30 garrison batteries were moreover distributed in the colonies; 1 was in St. Helena, 1 at Hong
Kong, 1 at Mauritius, 1 at Cape Town, 2 in Ceylon, 1 at
Singapore, 2 at Aden, 3 at Halifax, 2 in Bermuda, 1 in
Jamaica, 1 in Barbadoes, 7 in Malta and 7 at Gibraltar.
Thus, while the number of horse artillery batteries at
home and abroad was practically the same, and while there
were considerably more field batteries stationed in the
United Kingdom than oversea, 57 garrison batteries were
serving abroad (including the one on the Gold Coast) as
compared to only 34 at home.

CHAPTER
III.

The
situation
in 1874.

Field batteries on the home establishment were for the most part quartered in single battery stations, although 6 of them, besides depôts, were to be found at Woolwich. Although the advantages of Aldershot for training purposes were beginning to be understood, there was only barrack accommodation available for 7 batteries at the Hampshire cantonment, and the usual arrangement was for this number to be made up by 2 horse artillery and 5 field batteries—an arrangement that was to hold good for a number of years later.

The de-
partment
of the
D.A.G.,
R.A., at
Army
Head-
quarters.
During the greater part of the stage in the history of the Regiment with which this volume is concerned, the administration of the Royal Artillery at Army Headquarters in Pall Mall rested in the hands of the Deputy Adjutant-General, R.A., who was assisted by an Assistant Adjutant-General, R.A., and by a Deputy Assistant Adjutant-General, R.A. An analogous staff of three was maintained at Army Headquarters in India, to administer the Regiment in that country. The appointment of D.A.G., R.A., had however, it should be mentioned, been abolished before 1899, as will appear in a later chapter. These staff officers changed every five years in accordance with the normal practice (the term became four years later). But a more or less permanent staff of clerks were housed in Pall Mall as part of the branch of which the D.A.G., R.A., was the head, and the senior member of this permanent staff in 1874 was Lieutenant J. Ritchie, who was to occupy that position for many years. His work throughout was especially concerned with the posting, and so forth, of the commissioned ranks, it was largely of a confidential character, and for some thirty years his name was one of the best-known names in the Regiment.[1]

---

[1] Ritchie had put in several years in Pall Mall as a non-commissioned-officer before he was given a commission in the Coast Brigade in 1872. He became successively captain, major and lieutenant-colonel, occupying the same position, and he only quitted the War Office on his retirement from the service in the year 1898—as described in Chapter V.

The brigade system, under which a colonel was supposed to command and administer the brigade, had never
worked wholly satisfactorily, and the Indian military
authorities in particular had found it inconvenient and
inappropriate. It was however only, as we shall see, to
last two years longer when, on the 3rd March 1875, a
Regimental Order appeared which introduced several modifications, particularly in regard to this question of the
command of the brigades.[1] Under the terms of the order,
Regimental colonels were thenceforward to be dissociated
from brigades, and work was to be found for them instead
by appointing one to command the Royal Artillery in each
military district at home and at each of the more important
stations oversea. The order especially laid down that, in
view of Woolwich being the headquarters of the Regiment
and of so large a number of batteries always being quartered there, a colonel would in future command each
branch—R.H.A., field artillery and garrison artillery.
The Regimental Order furthermore prescribed that the
senior lieutenant-colonel in each brigade was in future if
possible to be stationed at the headquarters of the brigade,
and was to be responsible for the correspondence of the

CHAPTER
III.

Changes
in organi-
zation in
1875.

---

[1] "From this year (1865) up to 1871, the military authorities in
India supported by the government of that country, persistently wrote
against the brigade system, which they condemned as being totally
unsuited to the exigencies of Indian service, in which it was a necessity
for batteries to be widely detached at isolated stations, where they lost
all touch with their brigade headquarters, had to be administered at
distances varying from 100 to over 1000 miles at great expense and
delay, and the connection of the battery unit with its headquarters
for all purposes only existed in theory. In 1871 the Indian Government, being very desirous to carry out great reductions, again pressed
the occasion as one on which the question of brigade organization
should be reconsidered, as saddling the government with great expense
and totally unsuited to Indian requirements. This representation led
to the formation of a committee, which sat in 1872, to enquire into
the brigade system, the result of which was a rearrangement so as to
render reliefs and administration more suited to foreign conditions.
The changes recommended by the committee were not, however,
carried out until 1875." (From a paper on changes in artillery organization from 1857 to 1895 prepared in the War Office by Lieut.-Colonel
J. Ritchie. The 1872 committee was under the presidency of Sir R.
Airey, the Adjutant-General).

CHAPTER
III.

Changes
in organi-
zation in
1875.

brigade with the War Office and for preparing brigade returns.

Another change introduced by the order was that all employed men at Woolwich were in future to be attached to the 9th Division of the Coast Brigade, which was stationed there, instead of their being attached to the Depôt Brigade as heretofore. The headquarters staff of the Depôt Brigade was moreover abolished, so that the two divisions composing the brigade were rendered independent.

Three new brigades were also formed at home— E Brigade, R.H.A., and a 24th and a 25th Brigade, both of the latter field artillery. But this meant no increase in the number of service batteries; the units to form the new brigades were simply taken from other brigades, those to constitute the two field artillery brigades being for the most part the I and K Batteries of those brigades which, as one result of the reorganization of the year 1871, numbered ten batteries instead of the normal eight. The new E Brigade, R.H.A., was to consist of five batteries, and each of the six brigades of horse artillery would now comprise that number. It will be remembered that an E Brigade, a 24th Brigade and a 25th Brigade had been in existence only five years before. The frequent changes that were taking place in the designation of units—changes which were in reality due to efforts to bolster up the brigade system—caused irritation, not altogether unnaturally, in the Regiment, and they helped to make the brigade system unpopular.[1]

---

[1] As an example of such changes in designation may be cited the experience of the " Dragon Troop" of the old Madras Horse Artillery, which had at the time of the amalgamation in 1861 received the title of C/3. Two years later this title had been altered to C/D. In 1871 the battery had become F/B, and now, under this new Regimental Order the designation was transformed into A/E. It may be added that two years later the battery was to become A/C, and that, four years after that it found itself to be L/A. Not until the year 1889 did the " Dragon Troop " at last gain a haven of rest as simply "P" Battery and it remains "P" Battery still after a lapse of nearly forty years, although since the Great War it has been transformed into a field battery.

One result of the abolition of purchase had been that
a system had been introduced in 1870 under which young
gentlemen obtained their commissions in the cavalry and
infantry direct, after passing a competitive examination;
the R.M. College was at the same time closed as a cadet
college. This created somewhat anomalous conditions in
the matter of the relative standing of young officers of
those arms, as compared with that of young officers in
the R.A. and the R.E. The course at the R.M. Academy
normally lasted $2\frac{1}{2}$ years at this time, and, although the
age limit in the case of candidates for Woolwich was
generally lower than the age limit in the case of young
gentlemen presenting themselves for examination for
direct commissions, the fact remained that the young
gunner or sapper officer ordinarily obtained his commission
somewhat later than did the young cavalry or infantry
officer. Against this it could be contended that the young
gunner or sapper officer joined his corps as a lieutenant,
whereas the young cavalry or infantry officer up to 1871
joined it as a cornet or an ensign and, subsequently to
that, as a sub-lieutenant.[1] If the gunners and sappers
had to wait longer for their commissions, those commissions ordinarily pushed them over the heads of their
cavalry and Infantry rivals, who often took quite three
years to reach the rank of lieutenant.[2]

It was however adjudged that the young officers of R.A.
and R.E. were getting the worst of the transaction, and
so it became customary for a number of years to antedate

Chapter III.

*1st Com-
missions at
this time.*

---

[1] The title "sub-lieutenant" gave place to "2nd lieutenant" in 1877.

[2] The famous defence of Rorke's Drift supplied an interesting example of this. Lieut. Chard, R.E., had obtained his commission from
Woolwich as a lieutenant in 1870. Lieutenant Bromhead of the 24th
had obtained his commission as an ensign some eighteen months earlier,
but had not reached the rank of lieutenant till late in 1871. Chard
was consequently the senior and in command, although Bromhead had
about $1\frac{1}{2}$ years more service to his credit. Both officers however
received the same reward—special promotion to rank of captain and a
brevet-majority—for their conduct in the dire emergency.

CHAPTER III.

1st Commissions at this time.

their commissions six months when they passed out of Woolwich. Arrangements as to officering the cavalry and infantry were in the meantime in a transition stage. The direct commission plan led to the successful candidates at the competitive examination remaining for considerable periods unposted, and therefore on the hands of their parents or guardians—to the dissatisfaction of all concerned. Sandhurst was therefore reopened and a scheme was put in force under which these embryo, and temporarily unwanted, warriors spent a given time at that institution as officers; but it did not prove an unqualified success, even after various modifications had been introduced into the course. So the cadet system was reverted to in 1877, and thereafter successful candidates at the entrance examination went to the R.M. College for a year as cadets. This placed the two great military colleges on an analogous footing, except that the course at Woolwich was 1½ years the longer. It was however reduced to 2 years in 1878, and the batch of cadets passing out in the summer of that year was the last one to be granted the six months antedate. The military authorities considered that the fact of their joining as lieutenants, and not as 2nd lieutenants, fully compensated them for the additional year which they had to spend as cadets.

The re-organization of the year 1877.

A much more important and sweeping re-organization of the Regiment than that of 1875 took place at the beginning of 1877. Under the provisions of G.O. 22 of that year, supplemented by Regimental Order No. 88, the brigade system, as such, was finally abandoned. The term "Brigade" was preserved—for lack of a better one—but the idea that the brigade of artillery, as it had been constituted in the year 1859, could be worked like a regiment of cavalry or infantry had long since been shown to be impracticable "It having been found advisable, for purposes of better administration and relief, to make certain alterations in the existing organization of the Royal Regiment of Artillery"—so commenced G.O. 22—"the arrangements herein set forth will take effect from the 1st July

next." The order went on to declare that, although each
brigade would under the new plan have its own headquarters, "Woolwich, for so many years the seat of all
the scientific and professional institutions of the Corps is
still to be looked upon as the headquarters of the whole
Regiment and its centre of instruction." The old brigade
staffs in India and abroad were to be broken up, as were
some of those at home. The Regimental Order moreover
prescribed that reliefs were in future to be carried out by
batteries instead of by brigades, and it went on to indicate
in detail how exactly the batteries were to be grouped in
future.

There were to be three brigades of horse artillery A,
B and C, each consisting of 10 service batteries, lettered
A to K, and a depôt battery. Their headquarters were to
be respectively at Woolwich, Dublin and Aldershot.

There were to be six brigades of field artillery, each
consisting of 14 batteries and a depôt battery. Each of
the six brigades was constituted by joining together two
of the twelve former brigades. Thus the 1st Brigade, with
headquarters at Woolwich, was composed of the former 1st
and 9th Brigades; the 2nd Brigade, with headquarters at
Sheffield, was composed of the former 4th and 18th
Brigades; the 3rd Brigade, with headquarters at New-
bridge, was composed of the old 8th and 14th Brigades;
the 4th Brigade, with headquarters at Leith Fort, was
composed of the old 11th and 16th Brigades; the 5th
Brigade, with headquarters at Woolwich, was composed of
the old 19th Brigade and the recently formed 24th Brigade;
the 6th Brigade, with headquarters at Colchester, was composed of the old 20th Brigade and the recently formed 25th
Brigade. The batteries remained distinguished by letters,
running from A to O, but omitting J, in each of the new
brigades; but while those batteries which belonged to the
senior of the old brigades were generally able to retain
their former letters, the batteries belonging to the junior
of the old brigades in almost all cases had to adopt new
letters—for instance, the former A/1 remained A/1, but

CHAPTER
III.

The re-
organiza-
tion of the
year 1877.

CHAPTER III.

The reorganization of the year 1877.

the former A/9 and the former B/9 became respectively H/1 and I/1.

There were to be five brigades of Garrison Artillery, numbered 7 to 11, and each was to consist of 18 batteries (except the 8th Brigade which was to consist of 19 batteries), together with a depôt battery. Their headquarters and the stations of their depôt batteries were respectively:—7th Brigade at Portsmouth, 8th Brigade at Devonport, 9th Brigade at Dover, 10th Brigade at Cork, 11th Brigade at Sheerness. The batteries were to be distinguished by numbers as before; but as thirteen of the old garrison artillery brigades were now being grouped to form five brigades, and as only two of the old brigades (the 7th and the 10th Brigades) had been distinguished by numbers between 7 and 11, only a few of the batteries could retain their old designations.

The Depôt Brigade was broken up, the depôt batteries which were to form part of the new brigade organization taking its place. The Regimental Order laid down that these depôt batteries were to be responsible for the training of recruits, that they would furnish the drafts for abroad, and that they were to receive invalids and men for discharge, or men who were passing to the reserve, as they came home from abroad. No reference, it may be observed, was made to whether the depôts would receive and equip reservists called up in case of mobilization—an important point which would seem to have been overlooked. A "District Staff" was also set on foot at Woolwich for the reception of the many employed men not directly concerned with the batteries in garrison, e.g., the R.A. Band.

The Regimental Order provided that there should be a Brigade-Major R.A. to each of the more important military districts, under the Regimental Colonel, who would deal with the admistration both of the batteries within the district and also with certain matters in connection with the administration of the artillery brigade which had its headquarters within the district. Especial arrangements were prescribed with regard to Woolwich; this was owing to

there being three regimental colonels stationed there, one
to each branch, whereas two field artillery brigade headquarters and no garrison artillery brigade headquarters
existed within the district.   The organization, as sketched
out above, held good up to the year 1882—organizations
of the regiment did not last long in those days.   But those
five years were years which tested it effectually.   The
short service system introduced under the Cardwell régime
was for the first time, put to the proof in the year 1878,
and the occurrence of the Afghan and the Zulu Wars
served as additional trials of the existing organization of
the regular army as a whole, as also the Royal Artillery in
particular.

In 1871 and during the early seventies the understanding had been that a division should be composed of 7
battalions together with 2 field batteries and a reserve
ammunition column.   An army corps was at that time to
consist of three divisions, a cavalry brigade and reserve
artillery; the cavalry brigade would include a horse artillery
battery in addition to its three regiments of cavalry; the
reserve artillery would consist of 3 horse artillery batteries,
3 field artillery batteries and a reserve ammunition column.
The artillery of the army corps would therefore comprise
4 horse artillery and 9 field batteries, making 78 guns in
all, together with 4 reserve ammunition columns.   It was
understood that the ammunition columns would be created
somehow by the Regiment, but, although figures as to
vehicles, horses and personnel existed on paper, it was not
very clear how either the horses or the personnel would
be produced.[1]   Arrangements as to hospital services, transport etc., remained in a very vague condition.

Some modifications were introduced in 1877, especially
in connection with the artillery and with the non-combat-

Marginal notes:

CHAPTER III.

The re-organization of the year 1877.

War organization of a division and an army corps at this time.

---

[1] How this was to be managed, had been the subject of an exhaustive memorandum prepared by Lieut.-Colonel W. E. M. Reilly, then
Assistant Director of Artillery and Stores.   But such arrangements as
were arrived at were purely paper arrangements.

CHAPTER
III.

War
organiza-
tion of a
division
and an
army
corps at
this time.

ant services. It was laid down that there were to be 3
field batteries to each division. The expression "corps
artillery" was moreover substituted for "reserve artillery"
in an army corps; this corps artillery was to comprise 3
horse artillery batteries, as before, but was only to include
2 instead of 3 field batteries; so that there would altogether
be 4 horse artillery batteries and 11 field batteries, making
90 guns instead of 78.[1] The organization of the ammunition
columns also underwent a great expansion on paper at that
time; the establishment of divisional ammunition columns
was almost doubled, while the corps reserve ammunition
column was now to consist of three sections, and it represented an organization more than three times as strong
in personnel, horses and vehicles as that contemplated for
the army corps in 1871. This, it should be noted, was
the organization laid down at the time when mobilization
actually took place in the early part of 1878.

That the modern need for abundance of ammunition
and much transport was coming to be recognized by our
military authorities is shown by the fact that, whereas the
army corps of 1871 was supposed to have an establishment
of 31,768 of all ranks with 7,598 horses, the army corps
of 1877 was supposed to have an establishment of 34,526
of all ranks with 12,934 horses—this although the number
of battalions and of cavalry regiments remained the same,
and although there was only an increase of two batteries.
("War Establishments" were not published officially at this
time, and the figures given respectively in *The Handbook
for Field Service* published by the R.A. Institution, and
in *Wolseley's Pocket Book* are not identical; those given
above are taken from the latter work).

Following upon the uprising of the Serbs and the Mon-
tenegrins against Ottoman rule in the years 1875 and 1876,
war had broken out between Russia and Turkey in 1877.
There followed the passage of the Danube by the forces of

---

[1] It was not customary to include horse artillery units in the corps
artillery in Continental armies.

the Tsar, the embittered struggles around Plevna, the
eventual fall of that improvised place of arms, and the
advance of the Russians during the winter over the Balkans
and practically up to the gates of Constantinople.[1] In
consequence of the situation which had thus arisen, our
Mediterranean Fleet steamed up the Dardanelles at the
beginning of February, a vote of credit for £6,000,000
was passed by Parliament, and an acute crisis then arose
owing to the drastic terms of the Treaty of Stefano which
was being imposed upon the Sultan.   The Army Reserve
were called out at the end of March, large numbers of
horses were purchased in haste, the utmost activity prevailed in the manufacturing departments of the army, and
especial attention was paid to the amplification of the existing siege-train equipment.   A contingent of 7,000 troops
of all arms was furthermore organized in India, including
two field batteries, M/1 and F/2; this proceeded to Malta,
where it arrived early in May.

The reservists, on this the first occasion of their being
called up, responded most satisfactorily, only a few failing
to appear.   Woolwich, which was now under command of
Sir C. D'Aguilar, became for the time an especially busy
centre owing to the number of batteries in garrison that
were being brought up to their war establishment as such,
and also owing to the special connection of the place with
the transport service, as this was then organized.   But the
lack of adequate preparation for creating ammunition
columns hampered effective mobilization.   For while the
equipment for such units was available, there were not

CHAPTER
III.

The
mobiliza-
tion of the
year 1878.

---

[1] Sir Collingwood Dickson was especially sent out to Constantinople
in May 1877 to act as principal military attaché there, and he remained
until nearly the end of 1879. Major-General Sir Arnold Kemball on
the Bombay list was at the same time sent out to accompany the
Turkish forces in Armenia.   It is interesting to note that three artillery
subalterns, who in later years became well known in the Regiment as
Major-General Sir F. Eustace, Major-General Sir W. Knox and
Brigadier-General Lord Playfair, found themselves in Constantinople
just as the war had well started, and, having a friend in high places in
the person of Sir C. Dickson, obtained leave to go to the front, where
Eustace earned the name of "the Pasha", which stuck to him for the
remainder of his life.

CHAPTER
III.

The
mobiliza-
tion of the
year 1878.
even cadres to which it could be issued, let alone properly organized bodies of officers and men and horses such as were essential if the material was to be turned to proper account.   Many useful lessons were learnt by administrative authorities and staffs, and these were to prove of considerable value when the expeditionary force for Egypt was being got together in 1882.   But the Berlin Congress, coupled at it was with the adjustment of a special compact between H.M. Government and that of the Emperor Alexander II, had put an end to all idea of hostilities by the end of July.

Owing to the fact that batteries serving in India were always virtually at a war establishment even in time of peace, the outbreak of war with Afghanistan in the autumn of 1878 did not at the outset throw any excessive strain upon the artillery forces quartered in that country.   The batteries detailed to take part in the campaign only numbered in the first instance 3 of horse artillery, 6 of field artillery and 7 of garrison artillery, besides 5 native mountain batteries.   To complete these units for active service, others that were not included in the order of battle nor quartered near the north-west frontier were called upon to supply some officers, non-commissioned-officers and men, as well as some horses; but the numbers needed were not large, so that these replenishments could be easly arranged. The conditions of the struggles were such that the creation of ammunition columns on the European model was unnecessary.   Some drafts, over and above normal requirements, had naturally to be sent out from home.   But such inconvenience as was caused to batteries in India that were taking no direct part in the struggle, and to batteries at home, was only felt very gradually, so that steps could be taken to reduce it to a minimum.

Hostilities directed against the Zulus commenced at the beginning of 1879, and the ill-success which attended the early operations of the forces detailed for the purpose— they included a field battery and a garrison battery, already

on the spot—necessitated the hasty despatch of reinforcements from home to the theatre of war in the month of
April.   These reinforcements consisted of cavalry and
infantry, besides three field batteries of which one was to
act as an ammunition column.   The batteries were brought
up to their war establishment by drafts which were supplied
by other batteries at home.

CHAPTER
III.

The
Afghan
and Zulu
Wars.

But for a brief suspension of belligerency consequent on
the signing of the Treaty of Gandamak, the Afghan War
lasted for nearly two years.   Much wastage in personnel
and horses, mainly owing to disease, occurred at the front,
and during the greater part of 1879 and 1880 those batteries on the Indian establishment which were not on
service or told off as reserve units, were being called upon
from time to time to find drafts in officers and men and
horses in the interests of the batteries taking part in the
campaign.   Inasmuch moreover as a considerable number
of officers of the Regiment were being taken temporarily
for special duties in connection with the Ordnance Department, with the transport service, or on the staff, those
batteries which did not enjoy the good fortune of being
sent to the front or of being detailed as reserve near the
front, were generally short of their establishment in commissioned ranks during the whole period that the war
lasted.

We have seen in the last chapter how the medical
officers belonging to the Regiment were removed from it
and transferred to the Army Medical Department in the
year 1873.   Veterinary officers continued to be borne on
the strength of the Royal Artillery and to wear its uniform
up to 1879, when the Army Veterinary Department was
established by Royal Warrant.   The veterinary surgeons
belonging to the various cavalry regiments and to the R.A.
were then, under the provisions of the warrant, transferred
to the new department.

With-
drawal
of its Vet-
erinary
Surgeons
from the
Regiment.

CHAPTER III.

Variations introduced as regards the peace establishment of horse artillery and field batteries at home.

Up till the year 1879 the peace establishments of all service batteries of R.H.A. and of all service field batteries on the home establishment, respectively, were the same. The military authorities had however come to the conclusion that in the event of war two army corps and a cavalry division could be placed in the field, and in the Army Estimates for the financial year 1879-80 provision was made for the 13 field batteries told off to the 1st Army Corps and the 13 field batteries told off to the 2nd Army Corps to have the same establishments as regards personnel, 155, but for those of the 1st Army Corps to have an additional 12 horses each, 84 instead of 72. The 10 field batteries on the home establishment that remained over were to have lower establishment, viz., 145 officers and other ranks and 60 horses, and they were to be 4-gun batteries in peace time. All the horse artillery batteries at home were, however, to have an identical establishment.

The field batteries sent out to Zululand went at the establishment laid down for a battery belonging to the 1st Army Corps, with 10 additional horses. That was also the establishment at which the field battery already in the theatre of war was standing at. The principle of batteries first for service at home having a higher strength[1] than others had been recognized for some years, but it had been a matter of arrangement within the Regiment. Only the total establishment of horse and field artillery at home had been laid down in Army Estimates. In future years the establishments of batteries on the various footings were always laid down in this document.[2]

The mountain artillery.

Mountain batteries had played so prominent and so effective a role during the Afghan war that, under the provisions of a Regimental Order published in April 1880,

---

[1] Strength must not of course be confused with establishment. The establishment is a fixed paper affair with which in practice the strength seldom coincides.

[2] It had been decided in 1877 to allow three subalterns to each garrison artillery battery in the colonies, but the establishment was not made up abroad for two or three years, completing the establishment in the garrison batteries at home had not begun at the end of 1881.

mountain artillery was in reality constituted a special branch of the Regiment, although it continued to form part of the garrison artillery. Service in mountain batteries in India was by the R.O. made permanent for officers serving in the branch, up to their promotion or to their resignation. Garrison batteries converted into mountain batteries only retained the special equipment, native personnel and animals, for a time and they then reverted to ordinary garrison service; but under the terms of this order the officers could in case of such a reversion claim posting to other mountain batteries. The R.O. laid down that special lists of candidates for mountain batteries were to be maintained, and the service was in this respect put on a footing somewhat analogous to that enjoyed by the Royal Horse Artillery.

Garrison batteries organized as mountain batteries however maintained their nomenclature as units of the garrison artillery. 6/8 for instance, a battery which had been fitted out with mountain artillery equipment and the new "screw" gun in 1879 and had gone up to Kabul, remained 6/8. In the following year it was however directed by Regimental Order that a mountain battery should in future show "Mountain" in a bracket after its number.

A notable step in the direction of grouping batteries for disciplinary, administrative and (in the case of mounted branches) tactical purposes was taken in May 1881. It was then laid down by Regimental Order that if more than three horse artillery or field batteries were quartered in one station or command, they were to be grouped as two or more "Divisions". Fortified places of the requisite importance and manned by the requisite personnel were to be divided into "Artillery Districts". Divisions and Artillery Districts were to be under command of lieutenant-colonels, who were under this arrangement furnished with a definite object, and the adoption of the plan connoted, in the case of the horse artillery and the field artillery, a significant advance from the tactical point of view.

But the question of appropriate nomenclature in re-

Chapter III.

The mountian artillery.

Introduction of 'Divisions' and 'Artillery Districts.'

CHAPTER III.

Introduction of 'Divisions' and 'Artillery Districts.' spect to the artillery arm has always proved a stumbling block to reformers and administrators in this, as in other, lands, and the particular titles hit upon on this occasion were not wholly felicitious. Under the system now ordained there would be the "division" in the mounted branch of the Regiment comprising two or three batteries; but each battery was also, in virtue of long standing custom approved by regulations, split up into three "divisions". A "division" might thus, in the horse and field artillery sense, signify either a group of two or three batteries, or else two guns. Moreover an infantry division of all arms would now include as one of its component parts an artillery division. Then again, as affecting the dismounted branch of the Regiment, there were now to be "artillery districts" in all the more important fortresses at home and abroad; but the expression rather clashed with that of "artillery sub-districts", the territorial organization in vogue for recruiting purposes.

The grouping of units which was provided for in this Regimental Order of 1881 was only of a temporary and fortuitous nature. There was no intention of linking together such batteries as would be included in one of the divisions or artillery districts except for the time being. Reliefs and changes of stations would continue to take place by batteries, and not by groups of batteries. A committee was however sitting during 1881 under presidency of Lord Morley, which was charged with the duty of examining into the whole problem of artillery organization. Important measures of reform were shortly to be introduced as a result of its labours, and under these the system of grouping units under command of lieutenant-colonels was to be carried a step further—as will appear in the succeeding chapter.[1]

---

[1] Although the change only affected the Royal Artillery very indirectly some mention of the territorialization of the infantry, which took place in this year, 1881, would seem to be not out of place. Mr. Cardwell had been succeeded in Pall Mall by Mr. Gathorne-Hardy, who had in 1876, during his term of office, appointed a committee under presidency of Colonel Stanley to consider afresh the question

Some years were still to pass before senior officers of the
Regiment were to receive a fair share of high appointments
outside of India.   Sir Fenwick Williams retained the
Governorship of Gibraltar until 1875.   Major-General R.
Biddulph succeeded Sir G. Wolseley as High Commissioner
and Brigadier-General in Cyprus in 1879, and he retained
the position for seven years.   Major-General C. L.
D'Aguilar succeeded Sir D. Wood as commander at Woolwich in 1874; he was followed by Major-General J. Turner,
who only occupied the appointment for two years, being
succeeded by Major-General the Hon. E. T. Gage in 1881.
The important military appointments held by Sir C.
Dickson and Sir A. Kemball during the Russo-Turkish war
have already been referred to in this chapter.   Apart from
the purely regimental posts, the above represent the sum
total of superior appointments held by senior officers of
the Royal Artillery outside of India during the eight years
1874-1881.   But in India they fared better.

The future Commander-in-Chief both in India and at
home, Lord Roberts, was, as a brevet-colonel appointed
Quarter-Master-General in India in 1875 with the temporary rank of major-general.   On the outbreak of war with
Afghanistan in 1878 he, and also Major-General M. A. S.
Biddulph, who was holding a brigade appointment at the
time, were given command of divisions.   Major-General J.
Hills commanded a division for some time during the second
phase of the war.   Lord Roberts' record during the two
phases of the Afghan campaign is well-known, and after

CHAPTER
III.

Holders
of high
appoint-
ments at
this time.

of localization of the forces. This committee had recommended the
joining together of the single-battalion infantry regiments to form two-
battalion territorial regiments.   Colonel Stanley had succeeded Mr.
Gathorne-Hardy as War Minister in 1878; but he had not taken steps
to give practical effect to the recommendations of his committee.
When, however, a change of Government took place in 1880, Mr.
Childers was brought into the War Office as Secretary-of-State, and he
in the following year put in force the plan which had been proposed
by the Stanley Committee. Those who were serving in the army at
the time will well remember the outcry which arose and for which
there was much excuse, but before many years had passed the advantages arising from the new organization which had been imposed on
the main arm of the service were realised on all hands.

Chapter
III.

Holders
of high
appoint-
ments at
this time.
their conclusion and a year on leave he was, at the end of
1881, appointed Commander-in-Chief in Madras with the
local rank of lieutenant-general.   General Biddulph on the
conclusion of the first phase of the Afghan struggle was
given a divisional command in Bengal.   Colonel C. G.
Arbuthnot commanded a brigade on the Khyber line during
the second phase.   General Sir E. B. Johnson was Military
Member of Council from 1877 to 1880.   Major-General Sir
J. Brind held command of a division in Bengal from 1874
to 1879, and Major-General A. W. Macintire was for some
time in command of the Hyderabad Subsidiary Force.
Besides some of those whose names are mentioned in the
last chapter and whose period had not expired by the beginning of 1874, the following held brigade commands in India
between that date and the end of 1881; Brigadier-Generals
M. A. S. Biddulph, A. T. Cadell, W. W. Barry, J. E.
Michell and C. R. O. Evans.

As regards the purely regimental appointments, it has
to be recorded that Sir C. Dickson was succeeded in 1875 as
Inspector-General by Major-General Sir J. W. Fitzmayer,
who however only held the position for two years, giving
way in 1877 to Major-General A. T. Phillpotts; General
Phillpotts was followed by Major-General R. P. Radcliffe
in 1880.   Colonel Middleton died as D.A.G., R.A., in the
year 1875, shortly before the date of the expiration of his
term in office, and was succeeded by Colonel R. P. Radcliffe.
On his taking over the appointment of Inspector-General,
General Radcliffe was followed at army headquarters by
Major-General Sir C. G. Arbuthnot.   As regards India,
Major-General Gage had been succeeded as Inspector-
General R.A., by Colonel C. G. Arbuthnot in 1878.
Major-General G. Leslie had taken up the appointment in
1880.   Colonel Arbuthnot had been succeeded as D.A.G.,
R.A., by Lieut.-Colonel A. H. Murray in 1878.

The names of only five veterans of the Peninsular War
and Waterloo remained graven on the lists of Colonels
Commandant, R.A., at the beginning of the year 1874.
The letters "P" and "W" had finally disappeared from

those lists by the close of the year 1881. It so happens, however, that the first exceptionally distinguished gunner to pass away during the period with which this chapter has to do, belonged to a generation which did not see the light till nearly a decade had passed subsequent to the triumph of Waterloo.

Major-General Sir Henry Tombs, **V.C.**, k.c.b., was born at sea in 1824 and was appointed to the Bengal Artillery from Addiscombe in the year 1841. Arriving in India at a date immediately antecedent to Sir J. Gough's operations against the Mahrattas, he found himself in the field within two years of joining, and he was present at the victory of Panniar in 1843. He saw plenty of active service while still a subaltern, for he took part in both the Sikh Wars and was present at nearly all the more important combats that took place during their progress. These included Moodkee, Ferozeshah and Aliwal during the Sutlej campaign, and Ramnagar, Chilianwalla and Gujerat during the final struggle to secure British supremacy in the Punjab. He had reached the rank of 1st captain by the year 1857, and Colonel Jocelyn, in the volume of the *History of the Regiment* that records the events of the Mutiny, tells the tale of Tombs' brilliant services during the course of that great contest. Suffice it to say here that he emerged from it a **V.C.**, a brevet-colonel and a c.b., and that a special reference to his exploits was made by Lord Panmure, the Secretary of State, in Parliament. Given command of the Gwalior Brigade in 1864, he was shortly afterwards in charge of the force which recaptured Dewangiri in Bhootan, resuming the Gwalior appointment on the conclusion of the campaign. He was promoted major-general in 1867 and was, as mentioned in the last chapter, given command of a division in India in 1871. But his health was already failing, he had to resign the appointment before many months had expired and he died, still a comparatively young man, in the year 1874. The Tombs Memorial Scholarship, awarded at the end of each term to the Woolwich cadet at the top of the list of those joining the Regiment, serves to perpetuate the memory of one of its finest soldiers.

Lieutenant-General Sir Archdale Wilson, Bart., G.C.B., was born in 1803 and joined the Bengal Artillery in 1819. He took part in the siege and capture of Bhurtpore in 1825-26 and commanded the artillery in General Wheeler's force in the Jullunder Doab during the Punjab campaign of 1848-49. As commandant of the Bengal Artillery, he was present at the action of Badli-ke-Serai, and, on General Reed's health breaking down, succeeded to the command of the forces before Delhi at the time of the siege and storming of the city. Although this, the first decisive stroke dealt the mutineers, was largely due to Wilson having resolute advisers surrounding him, the responsibility for sanctioning the bold measures that were urged upon him rested on his shoulders. For his services he was promoted major-general, was created a baronet, was awarded the K.C.B., and was granted a pension of £1,000 a year by the East India Company. He afterwards commanded the artillery during Sir Colin Campbell's operations against Lucknow.

General Sir J. E. Dupuis, K.C.B., was born in 1800 and entered the R.M. Academy in 1815, but did not receive his commission until the year 1825. In the year 1836, while still a subaltern, he joined the British Legion formed under command of Colonel de Lacy Evans, to aid the Spanish government in its contests with Don Carlos, and he was present at several actions during the following two years after which the legion was broken up. Going out to the Crimea as a lieutenant-colonel, he was present at the Alma, Balaclava, Inkerman, the siege of Sebastopol and the action of the Tchernaya; he commanded the siege-train for some months, and, having reached the rank of full colonel while in the field, was promoted major-general for distinguished service at the end of 1855. In 1857 he was sent out to command the R.A. in India at the time of the Mutiny, and was present at the battles round Cawnpore at the end of that year. This was his last active

service.   He was promoted general in 1868 and he died
in 1876.

Major-General F. M. Eardley-Wilmot, F.R.S., was in
1838, while a subaltern, appointed member of a committee
to establish a society for scientific improvement in the
Regiment. This became the R.A. Institution.   In 1839
he was one of the officers selected by Colonel Sabine to
establish and conduct magnetic observatories in various
parts of the world; his station was the Cape of Good Hope,
and whilst there he saw active service in the Kaffir War of
1846.   In January 1847 he became Captain of the Cadet
Company and was seven years at the R.M.A.   During
these years he acted as Secretary of the R.A.I.   In July
1855 as a lieutenant-colonel he was appointed Superintendent of the Gun factories at the Royal Arsenal, and
held the position until Mr. Armstrong was brought in in
1859; the Crimean War brought him great increases of
work and responsibility.   He was afterwards successively
C.R.A. in Canada, and Commandant at Shoeburyness,
and in 1875 was president of the committee which initiated
the system of Practice Camps.   He died in 1877.

General Sir J. Bloomfield G.C.B., was the last of the
Peninsula and Waterloo veterans whose names were borne
as colonels-commandants on the lists of the Regiment.
He was born in 1790 and joined in 1810.   He served in the
Peninsula and France during 1813 and 1814, and was
present at Vittoria, the siege of San Sebastian, the crossing
of the Bidassoa, the Nivelle, the Nive, Orthes and Toulouse,
receiving the silver medal with six clasps.   At Waterloo he
was acting as orderly officer to Sir George Wood, commanding the artillery.   As already mentioned, he was Inspector-
General of Artillery from 1860 to 1865.   He died in 1880.

CHAPTER IV.

1882 to 1890.

The re-organization of 1882—The Egyptian Expedition—Unsatisfactory condition of the garrison artillery—Reversion to the plan of field artillery depôt batteries—Distribution of the Regiment in 1884 —Demand for additional garrison artillery—Mobilization problems—Reduction of the horse artillery at home—The grade of 2nd lieutenant—Re-arrangement of the superior artillery staff in India—Mountain batteries and heavy batteries in India—Lord Harris' committee—"Brigade-Divisions" and "Sections"—The re-organization of 1889—Holders of high appointments at this time—Some distinguished members of the Regiment.

Chapter
IV.

The
re-organ-
ization of
1882.
A far-reaching re-organization of the Regiment, which was carried into effect under the provisions of General Order 72 of 1882, and of a special Regimental Order appearing at the same time, was based on the recommendations of Lord Morley's committee, on which Sir J. Adye, Sir C. G. Arbuthnot and Colonel W. E. M. Reilly had sat as artillery members. The changes thereby introduced gave the finishing stroke to the brigade system as originally designed in 1859, the former brigade staffs being converted into district staffs. Although the term bridage was preserved, it from now forward merely served to distinguish groups of batteries connected with prescribed recruiting districts and agencies.

The General Order laid down that the Royal Horse

Artillery was henceforward to be organized as two brigades, each consisting of 13 service batteries, lettered A to N (without J), and of a depôt; both the depôts were to be stationed at Woolwich. Two service batteries were reduced at the same time. (One battery had been broken up in 1879 and another in 1881 owing to decrease in the number of batteries adjudged necessary for India, two batteries had also been joined to make one in 1875; the disappearance of these three, together with the reduction of two in 1882, accounts for the number of batteries falling from 31, the figure that held good in 1871, to 26).

The field artillery was reconstituted as four brigades in place of six, and its six depôt batteries were transformed into garrison artillery depôt batteries. The 1st Brigade was to consist of 24 batteries (A to X), and the 2nd Brigade was to consist of 19 batteries (A to S); the 3rd and 4th Brigades were each to consist of 18 batteries (A to R). By the device of abolishing the six depôts it was proposed to find sufficient guns and horses to raise a number of the service batteries at home from the 4-gun to the 6-gun establishment. The intention was that recruiting for the field artillery should be carried out by the garrison artillery depôts and that, after a very brief preliminary training, the recruits were to be transferred to service batteries at home. Instead of young soldiers for oversea being trained in field artillery depôt batteries, and of drafts for India being found by these units, service batteries at home were now to provide the necessary men for abroad. The special Regimental Order carried the grouping of field batteries on the home establishment a step further by providing for subaltern acting-adjutants for divisions, but it laid down that these must be borne on the strength of batteries.

Thus from being organized in five brigades—7th to 11th—the garrison artillery was now transformed into eleven brigades, each consisting of either 8 or 9 batteries and forming part of one out of eleven "Territorial Divisions". These Territorial Divisions were to be distinguished as follows :—

CHAPTER
IV.

The
re-organ-
ization of
1882.

Title.	Headquarters.
1st Northern	Newcastle
2nd Lancashire	Liverpool
3rd Eastern	Yarmouth
4th Cinque Ports	Dover
5th London	Woolwich
6th Southern	Portsmouth
7th Western	Plymouth
8th Scottish	Leith
9th Welsh	Pembroke Dock
10th North Irish	Carrickfergus
11th South Irish	Cork

There were thus altogether 11 depôts, serving the field
and garrison artillery, the same number as there had been
under the organization laid down in 1877 which provided
six field artillery and five garrison artillery depôts. Of
the former field artillery depôts the 1st became Depôt
London, the 2nd became Depôt Northern, the 3rd became
Depôt North Irish, the 4th became Depôt Scottish, the 5th
became Depôt Lancashire, and the 6th became Depôt
Eastern. Of the former garrison artillery depôts the 7th
became Depôt Southern, the 8th became Depôt Western,
the 9th became Depôt Cinque Ports the 10th became Depôt
South Irish and the 11th became Depôt Welsh.   The
special Regimental Order provided for lieut.-colonels of
garrison artillery in command of Artillery Districts being
allowed adjutants.

The
Egyptian
Expedi-
tion.
       Within three months of the appearance of the instruc-
tions dealing with this far-reaching re-organization of the
Royal Artillery, serious trouble arose in Egypt.   The
trouble speedily led to British diplomatic intervention and
to a decision being taken by H.M. Government to prepare
in certain eventualities for despatching a military force to
the scene of unrest.   Alexandria was bombarded on the
11th July, and on the 21st those reservists who had quitted
the colours within the previous eighteen months were
called out.   The War Office decided to place an army corps

of somewhat special composition—the troops to be provided
from home and from the Mediterranean garrisons—in the
field, as well as an Indian Contingent. The artillery
detailed for the force to be despatched from home comprised two horse artillery batteries and six field batteries,
besides a field battery converted into an ammunition
column. Four garrison batteries from home and the
Mediterranean were added, for the purpose of forming a
siege train. The Indian Contingent included a field battery and a mountain battery. The proportion of horse
and field artillery accompanying the force fell considerably
short of that contemplated for an army corps as laid down
on paper; for the two infantry divisions were only to
include two field batteries each instead of three, and the
corps artillery was only to consist of one horse artillery
battery and two field batteries, instead of its consisting of
three horse artillery and two field batteries.[1]

As all the batteries selected from those at home were on
the highest establishment, and as only two horse artillery
and seven field batteries were mobilized in the United
Kingdom at home at the outset, no difficulty was experienced in bringing them up to war establishment as regards
non-commissioned-officers and men. The few hundred
artillery reservists called out were amply sufficient to meet
all requirements, but the situation was less satisfactory as
regards horses. "In the R.A. the number of horses which
were embarked for Egypt in excess of the peace establishment came to 541. The artillery, besides providing extra
horses for its horse and field batteries and ammunition
reserve, had to find 20 horses for the cavalry regimental
transport, 260 for infantry regimental transport, and 12
riding horses for the Royal Engineers. A very heavy call

CHAPTER
IV.

The
Egyptian
Expedi-
tion.

[1] Another field battery was placed under orders for Egypt when
the campaign was in full swing, and it marched down the hill from
Woolwich barracks amidst stirring scenes two days before news came
to hand of the victory of Tel-el-Kebir. It was played back up the hill
to barracks by the R.A. Band two days later to the consolatory strains
of "Slap bang! Here we are again! Here we are again! Here we are
again! What jolly dogs are we!"—a music hall ditty much in vogue
just at that time.

CHAPTER
IV.

The
Egyptian
Expedi-
tion.

was made on the corps, and altogether the R.A. at home
(including 101 which were sent to Cyprus for remount
purposes and which were sent back from Malta) was
denuded of 934 serviceable horses".[1]   Finding these 934
horses proved for the time being a somewhat serious drain
on the batteries at home.   Some of them were temporarily
reduced almost to skeletons in respect to teams; the gaps
were filled by remounts within a few weeks.

Unsatis-
factory
condition
of the
garrison
artillery.

Sir C. G. Arbuthnot, who before taking up command
of a brigade on the Khyber line towards the close of the
Afghan War had been Inspector-General of Artillery in
India, and who, as mentioned on p. 82, had come to the
War Office as D.A.G., R.A., in 1880, had become impressed soon after his taking up the appointment with the
unsatisfactory trend of reports on the garrison artillery
which passed through his hands.   Service in the dismounted branch of the Regiment had been becoming less
and less attractive to the commissioned ranks ever since
the field artillery had been established on a permanent
basis some five-and-twenty years earlier.   This was partly
due to most officers finding life in field batteries preferable
to duty in connection with fortresses, and it was also partly
due to the former offering the better prospects of taking
part in campaigns and therefore of possibly earning special
promotion.   It was also due to the relatively greater
amount of foreign service which fell to the lot of the
garrison artillery, and to the fact that such service was
largely carried out in stations oversea which had little to
recommend them.   The recent Zulu and Afghan Wars
had made plain that the field gunner was apt to enjoy
better openings when the enemy was in the gate than was
the garrison gunner.   The number of units of the dismounted branch normally abroad had, it is true, been
appreciably reduced some ten to twelve years earlier.
There seemed however to be no likelihood of such reduc-

---

[1] From *Mobilization and Embarkation of an Army Corps* by Lieut.-
Colonel G. A. Furse.

tions being carried further—the portents indeed rather pointed the other way.

The unpopularity of the garrison artillery was manifesting itself not only amongst the officers of the Regiment but also in other ranks. By the end of 1882 General Arbuthnot was experiencing great difficulty in keeping the dismounted branch up to its peace establishment. The excess of foreign service was believed to be one cause of the disinclination of recruits to come forward. But the fact that the non-commissioned-officers and men manning the armament of the modern type of fortress were, even at home, wont to find themselves relegated to lonely fastnesses, such as those at the mouth of Cork Harbour and the structures planted down in the sea in the Spithead water-area, tended to render service in the garrison artillery repellent The state of inefficiency into which that branch would necessarily drift without some modifications of existing regulations, became a matter for serious and immediate consideration, and it was proposed that a proportion of gunners in each battery should be granted increased pay, should be regarded as artificers, and should be allowed to extend their colour service to 12 years. To this it was objected that any soldier of ordinary intellect could be made a good gunner in three years, and furthermore that it would tend to decrease flow into the army reserve. Matters however grew worse, by the end of the year a considerable shortage of the establishment in the garrison artillery had arisen, and so a committee consisting of Sir C. G. Arbuthnot, Major-General H. A. Smyth and Colonel R. Hay was assembled to examine into and report on the matter.

The committee considered the problem both from the point of view of the non-commissioned-officers and men, and from that of the officers. They in due course recommended some increase to pay to a proportion of the gunners; and they also proposed that special "armament pay" should be granted to officers, with the object of rendering service in the dismounted branch more popular

CHAPTER
IV.

Unsatis-
factory
condition
of the
garrison
artillery.

CHAPTER
IV.

Unsatis-
factory
condition
of the
garrison
artillery.
in the commissioned ranks.[1]   Of the preference that was
being unmistakably displayed amongst officers of the Regiment for service in the field artillery, as compared with the
garrison artillery they wrote :—"The result is that service
in the garrison artillery, the most scientific branch of the
arm and which should command the services of the best
officers, instead of being sought after, is shunned, and if
priority of choice were given to young officers on joining
the Regiment according to their places in the batch, the
best would select the field artillery, and the garrison artillery, which requires the most scientific officers, would only
get those who, from idleness or want of ability, had failed
to obtain a good place in their batch".   No immediate
result crowned the labours of the committee, but the
matter was not allowed to drop altogether and, as will be
seen in a later paragraph, the recommendations put forward in 1883 were, with modifications, adopted at a later
date.

Reversion
to the plan
of field
artillery
depôt
batteries.
The system introduced in 1882 under which garrison
artillery depôts dealt in the first instance with recruits for
the field artillery, but under which service field batteries
at home were to all intents and purposes charged with the
whole training of the recruits for that branch, and under

---

[1] One cause of a certain repugnance with which service in the
garrison artillery was looked upon amongst officers of the Regiment
ought not to be concealed. This was that the higher authorities had
in the past been to some extent making a practice of correcting slack-
ness, or even misconduct, on the part of an officer serving in the
mounted branches, by transferring the delinquent to the dismounted
branch—generally to some station situated in the uttermost parts of
the earth. The glaring case might, for instance, be quoted of a very
smart horse artillery subaltern who had carried theories of " spit and
polish" so far as to drive his division to mutiny. The limit had been
attained when he ordered the metal work of spades and gun buckets
to be polished ! The authorities met the situation by transferring the
subaltern to the garrison artillery in the Far East. (He was a good
officer, lived to be a brigadier-general, and is long since deceased).
By the year 1882 such procedure had come to be honoured in the
breach rather than in the observance; but some of its effects remained.
One does not select a penal settlement for place of residence if there
is accommodation available elsewhere. The officer who had not, at
one stage of his career, been thought good enough for the mounted
branches generally remained in the dismounted branch for good and
all and his presence tended to lower the average.

which the service batteries were furthermore made responsible for finding the drafts for India and abroad, had
speedily led to an outcry.   Majors commanding field batteries complained forcibly of the dislocation which this
system caused, and of the additional work which was
thrown upon their non-commissioned-officers, their officers
and themselves in training the recruits.   Their lamenta-
tions were endorsed by lieutenant-colonels and colonels,
and the consequence was that orders were issued early in
1884 for transforming one battery on the lowest peace
establishment in three of the four field artillery brigades
(X/1, H/3 and N/4) into a depôt field battery, and also
one battery of R.H.A. (L/B) into a depôt field battery,
thus providing a depôt battery for each of the four field
artillery brigades.

Of these depôt batteries, that for the 1st Brigade was
to be located at Newcastle (the garrison artillery depôt
belonging to the Northern Division being transferred from
Newcastle to Sunderland) and it was affiliated to the
Northern, Lancashire and Scottish Territorial Divisions
for recruiting purposes.   The 2nd Brigade depôt battery
was to be located at Colchester, and it was affiliated for
recruiting purposes to the Cinque Ports and London Territorial Divisions.   The 3rd Brigade depôt battery was to be
located at Hilsea, and it was affiliated to the Southern,
Western and Welsh Territorial Divisions.   The 4th
Brigade depôt battery was to be located at Fermoy, and
it was affiliated to the two Irish Territorial Divisions for
recruiting purposes.   These field artillery depôt batteries
were to be training batteries, preparing recruits and young
soldiers for joining service units, and they were also to
be charged with furnishing drafts for batteries oversea;
actual recruiting for the field artillery was mainly to be
carried out by the affiliated garrison artillery depôts.   By,
in 1882, transforming the six, then existing, field artillery
depôt batteries into garrison artillery depôt batteries, the
guns and horses needed to bring several service field batteries from the lower to the higher peace establishment

CHAPTER
IV.-

Reversion
to the plan
of field
artillery
depôt
batteries.
had been made available. By in 1884 re-creating four
field artillery depôt batteries, the army was deprived of
one horse artillery and three field artillery service batteries. It was a case of robbing Peter to pay Paul. If
the new plan had a good deal to commend it, that plan
also had its disadvantages.

But for temporary disturbances caused by the Zulu
and Egyptian campaigns the distribution of batteries forming the Regiment had not varied greatly during the dozen
years preceding 1884. British commitments in Egypt
had however led to a battery of horse artillery being
quartered at Cairo permanently, and two garrison batteries
were also normally stationed in the country; the outbreak
of troubles in the Sudan moreover brought about the despatch of an additional garrison battery to Egypt in this
year, and a field battery was landed temporarily on the
Red Sea Littoral during operations near Suakin. A field
battery had been kept in Natal since the close of the conflict
with the Transvaal in 1881. The normal number of horse
artillery batteries in India was 10, and of field batteries
was 43; 27 garrison batteries were on the Indian establishment in 1884, of which 6 were mountain batteries and
6 others were heavy batteries. The remainder of the
garrison batteries on foreign service were (apart from those
stationed in Egypt) distributed as follows :—1 at Cape
Town, 1 at St. Helena, 1 in Mauritius, 2 in Ceylon, 2 at
Hong Kong, 1 at Singapore, 3 at Halifax, 2 in Bermuda,
1 in Barbadoes, 1 in Jamaica and 15 in the Mediterranean—8 at Malta and 7 at Gibraltar.

The figures as to batteries on the home establishment
in 1884, subsequent to the restoration of field artillery
depôt batteries were :—15 service batteries R.H.A., 34
service field batteries and 37 service garrison batteries,
together with 2 depôt batteries R.H.A., 4 depôt field
batteries and 11 depôt garrison batteries. The Riding
Establishment at Woolwich and the "Shoeburyness
Detachment" represented additional units.

A demand for an addition of eight batteries to the existing force of garrison artillery was put forward from the military side of the War Office in 1885. The main grounds for this demand lay in the fact that garrison artillery batteries were now needed in Egypt (4 were actually employed in Egypt and the Sudan during the Nile Campaign of 1884-85), that the Indian military authorities wished to increase their force of mountain artillery, and that two additional batteries were required for the Far East in view of the growing importance of Singapore and Hong Kong. But misconceptions concerning the higher policy of Imperial Defence had for years past tended to invest maritime fortresses with an undue importance in the eyes of the Government's professional advisers. They had, as in the notorious case of the Royal Commission of 1860, caused great sums of money to be expended on fixed defences which ought to have been devoted to expansions of fighting resources afloat. Still, some justification existed for anxiety as to the condition of our protected havens at home and abroad just at this time, for the relative strength of the Royal Navy, as compared to that of certain foreign navies, was coming to be looked upon in service quarters as wholly inadequate.[1]

As is not unusual when any proposal for military expansion is put forward, financial objections proved to be a stumbling block, even if an increase of three garrison batteries was eventually sanctioned. And in the course of the somewhat prolonged discussions concerning the matter which took place the possibility of providing some of the requisite funds for the proposed augmentation of the garrison artillery by reducing the number of horse artillery batteries on the home establishment was raised. Although no action in this direction was taken at the time, the fact that the suggestion had been put forward and discussed, was not without its influence when the scheme for ensur-

CHAPTER IV.

Demand for additional garrison artillery.

---

[1] Lord George Hamilton's great building programme was not agreed to until 1887.

ing the existence of a striking force of two army corps and a cavalry division in the United Kingdom came up for consideration a few months later.

Lord Wolseley, who had been absent from the War Office for a year, engaged on the Nile Campaign, returned to it to resume his position as Adjutant-General in the latter part of 1885, and Major-General H. Brackenbury, who had been serving under him in the Sudan, took up charge of the Intelligence Department at Headquarters shortly afterwards. The Intelligence Department at that time included a section which dealt with problems of mobilization and war-organization, and Brackenbury was not long in perceiving that these problems stood in need of special attention. A Mobilization Committee was constituted, and by the end of 1886 this had laid down certain lines as to the composition of the force which the United Kingdom was in a position to place in the field on the outbreak of a serious war, and had ascertained that the bringing of such a force up to its war footing would be most seriously hampered by the lack of the field artillery units requisite to create the ammunition columns regarded as essential if the force was to be properly constituted for a serious campaign. The Committee aimed at ensuring the existence, when the forces were brought to a war footing, of a striking force consisting of a cavalry division and two army corps, together with some line of communications troops.[1] The number of service batteries required for this force was 8 horse artillery batteries (2 for the cavalry division and 3 for each army corps) and 22 field batteries, but a further 16 field batteries were needed for transformation into ammunition columns. The actual number of horse artillery batteries and of field batteries on the establishment at home was respectively 13 and 35, so that there was a surplus of 5 horse artillery batteries and a shortage of 3 field batteries. Examination of the

---

[1] The cavalry brigade no longer formed part of an army corps as now contemplated.

figures of European armies moreover served to indicate CHAPTER
that the cavalry division and two army corps contemplated IV.
as the field army of the United Kingdom would be un- Mobiliza-
usually well endowed with horse artillery. The Mobiliza- problems.
tion Committee consequently recommended that 3 horse
artillery batteries should be converted into field batteries
and that 2 more should be broken up, also that field batteries not on the establishment of the two army corps as
service batteries in peace time should be reduced to the
4-gun basis, the financial saving effected under these
arrangements being utilized in connection with other
items in the scheme.

Mr. Childers had been succeeded as Secretary of State
for War by Lord Hartington at the end of 1881, who held
that position till June 1885. He then gave place to
Mr. W. H. Smith; but after only a very few months
that statesman was followed by Mr. Campbell-Bannerman,
under whose directions the Army Estimates for the
financial year 1887-88 were drawn up.

These Army Estimates provided for the transforma- Reduction
tion of 3 of the horse artillery batteries at home into field of the
batteries and for the reduction of two others, and their horse
appearance aroused a storm of opposition in Parliament artillery
and in the Regiment on this account. Major-General Sir at home.
C. Fraser, VC., a distinguished cavalry officer with a seat
in the House, secured the signature of 116 other Members
of Parliament who had served in the regular or the
auxiliary forces to a petition, and this was forwarded to
Mr. Stanhope (who was now Secretary of State) protesting
against the contemplated diminution in the number of
horse artillery batteries.[1] The Secretary of State, how-

---

[1] "The undersigned members of the House of Commons, now
serving, or who have served in Her Majesty's Forces, having heard
with great regret of the intention of the Secretary of State for War
to reduce the Royal Horse Artillery by four batteries, wish respect-
fully to record their strong sense of the inadvisability of this course,
and their hope that the Secretary of State may see grounds to recon-
sider a step which in their opinion is detrimental to the interests of
the Service and of the country."

CHAPTER
IV.

Reduction
of the
horse
artillery
at home.
ever, accepted the view held by the high military authorities at the War Office that, with the funds at his disposal,
the mobilization of a cavalry division and two army corps
of the accepted composition could not be regarded as a
practical proposition unless the reduction was carried out.
He had however already bowed to the storm to the extent
of limiting the reduction of the horse artillery to 4 batteries instead of 5. The one horse artillery battery was
saved by effecting a reduction of 4 gunners in each of the
38 batteries of garrison artillery at home, the Treasury
agreeing to this plan after they had approved the Army
Estimates as originally drawn up.

The substantial reduction in the number of horse
artillery batteries maintained in the United Kingdom was
strongly resented on the mounted side of the Regiment.
But most military authorities of the present day would
agree that the War Office acted rightly in this matter—
certainly so, as regards transforming 3 of the horse artillery batteries into field batteries. The breaking up of the
other battery was perhaps more questionable. This meant
the loss of a service cadre (even if that cadre was not
actually required under the mobilization scheme), and it
is easier to destroy service cadres than it is to create them
afresh. But this country was, relatively speaking, richer
in this form of artillery before the disappearance of the
4 horse artillery batteries, and even after it, than any
other of the great military Powers of the Continent—as
is made manifest in the tables given below as a foot-note.[1]

That young officers on being commissioned joined the
Regiment as lieutenants, the grade below that of lieutenant having been abolished some years before 1860 as far
as the R.A. was concerned, has already been mentioned.
The grade of second-lieutenant was however revived for

---

[1] The first of these tables gives the figures of peace establishments
in the various armies. The second table gives the figures in reference
to the armies which the various Powers contemplated placing in the
field on the outbreak of war, and for which they maintained the requisite organization in peace time.

young officers on quitting the R.M. Academy in the year
1887.   There had always been an equivalent grade in the
case of the cavalry and infantry under different titles—
cornet, ensign, sub-lieutenant and second-lieutenant.

CHAPTER
IV.

The
grade of
second-
lieutenant.

PEACE ESTABLISHMENTS.

	United Kingdom	Germany	France	Russia	Austria	Italy
No. of H.A. Batteries ...	9	47	57	50	16	6
No. of H.A. guns per 1,000 cavalry	3·7	3·1	4·9	2·4	2·3	1·5
No. of H.A. guns to 100 field guns	23	15	14	21	15	5

FIELD ARMIES.

	United Kingdom	Germany	France	Russia	Austria	Italy
No. of army corps	2	19	18	24	14	12
No. of cavalry divisions...	1	9	6	18	8	3
No. of H.A. guns per 1,000 cavalry	7	4·5	6	2·9	2·2	1·9
No. of H.A. guns to 100 field guns	36	15	15	9·5	8	3·6

Germany and France alone, besides the United Kingdom, contemplated including horse artillery batteries in their corps artillery and in
neither country was it proposed to include more than two batteries
per corps under this category.

H

CHAPTER
IV.

Re-
arrange-
ment of
the
superior
artillery
staff in
India.

In a reference made in Chapter I to the superior artillery staff at home in 1860, it was explained that the arrangement holding good at headquarters at that time, and which was to hold good for several years to come, was that administration rested in the hands of a D.A.G., R.A., who was assisted by an A.A.G. and a D.A.A.G., and that there was furthermore an Inspector-General R.A. A very similar arrangement to this had been maintained in India since the amalgamation of 1861, except that there was no A.A.G. to assist the D.A.G., R.A. There were, on the other hand, A.A.G's, R.A., in the Madras and Bombay Presidencies.

An important change took place in this respect in the year 1887 in India, on Colonel C. E. Nairne taking up the appointment of Inspector-General of Artillery with the rank of brigadier-general. For the post of D.A.G., R.A., was abolished, and Nairne became responsible for much of the duty which had previously been performed by that official, in addition to carrying out his own inspectional functions; he was allowed an A.A.G. (at first Colonel G. T. Pretyman and afterwards Colonel M. H. Saward) to assist him. This, be it observed, connoted a measure of centralization—the result indeed was to develop the Inspector-General into something uncommonly like a C.R.A., and the point is of interest, for whereas the system adopted in India in 1887 took the direction undisguisedly of centralization, the system which was to be adopted some years later at home on the abolition of the post of D.A.G., R.A., was (as will be seen in the ensuing chapter) to take the direction of decentralization, in so far as decentralization was practicable considering the peculiar conditions that exist in the Regiment as compared with other branches of the service. Sir F. Roberts had satisfied himself that the system of Presidential Armies had become unworkable and was out of date, and the centralization of administrative responsibility for the Royal Artillery was to prove very helpful to him during the reorganization of the army system in India which was to be carried into effect within the immediately ensuing years.

A Regimental Order of the year 1884 had laid down that garrison batteries in India which were fitted out with heavy artillery equipment were to be distinguished by the word "Heavy", following the number of the battery. It had quoted as an example "No. 8 (Heavy) 1st Brigade, Cinque Ports Division".[1] In the year following, a Regimental Order issued instructions that garrison batteries which were to become mountain batteries were in future to receive the equipment on arrival in the country and were to retain it for the first eight years of their service in India. This same principle was extended in 1887 to the case of garrison batteries becoming heavy batteries; they, like mountain batteries were to be mobile units for the first eight years of their stay in the country and would then revert to the position of normal garrison batteries.

Discussion as to the garrison artillery had been intermittently in progress at the War Office, since 1885, but little had been effected towards improving the position of the branch. A Committee of eight members was however set up during 1887, under the chairmanship of Lord Harris, which ostensibly was charged with examining into the whole question of artillery organization, but which was in reality intended to consider what could be done to increase the efficiency of the dismounted branch and to ascertain the opinion of officers of the Regiment in general as to the expediency, or otherwise, of effecting a definite separation between its mounted and its dismounted side. The members of the Committee, representing the Regiment, were Lieutenant-General Sir R. Biddulph and Major-Generals R. Hay, W. Stirling and H. Brackenbury, and a large number of witnesses, including prominent officers of all arms of the service besides those belonging to the artillery, were examined. The Committee issued its report early in 1888. The document consisted of three portions :—(1) points on which there was common agreement and which was subscribed to by the whole of the

Chapter IV.

Mountain batteries and heavy batteries in India.

Lord Harris' Committee.

---

[1] A curt, convenient style, supposing that you wanted to send the unit a message in a hurry on the battlefield !

CHAPTER
IV.

Lord
Harris'
Com-
mittee. members; (2) signed by four members (including Generals
Biddulph, Hay and Stirling), which was opposed to the
Regiment being separated into two branches; and another
(3) signed by the remaining four members, including
Lord Harris and General Brackenbury, which advocated
separation.[1]

In its reference to the crucial question of separation,
a notable passage in (2) read as follows :—"On the subject
of a division of the Royal Artillery into two corps, the
evidence taken by the Committee shows a very general
desire on the part of the officers of the Royal Artillery at
regimental duty to have a separation between field and
garrison artillery.   The main cause of this desire arise from
personal motives; and if it is admitted on the one hand that
the *majority* of voices are in favour of separation, it must
be allowed on the other hand that the *weight* of evidence
is undoubtedly in favour of the existing system."   In a
special reference to the Crimean War (the last continental
war in which the United Kingdom had been engaged) the
following passage also appeared :—"Whilst other branches
of the Service were reduced to filling up their ranks with
hastily raised and untrained recruits, so inefficient that the
Commander-in-Chief wrote that he would prefer to have no
men sent out at all rather than these, the Royal Artillery
was kept well supplied with trained artillerymen drawn
from every garrison of the Empire."

As was natural the opinions of the higher military
authorities differed widely, and, as might be expected,
those of the Duke of Cambridge and Lord Wolseley represented the opposite poles.   While Lord Wolseley felt con-

---

[1] As to the field artillery the committee wrote :—"With respect to
the field artillery the evidence given as to its efficiency appears to
show that there is no necessity for any change in its administration,
while such change in organization as is desired by some officers is
based principally upon tactical requirements, and is thus so intimately
connected with the general organization of the army as a whole that
the committee do not feel themselves in a position to offer any recommendation regarding it."

vinced that, with an army all over the world, separation was certain in future, the Colonel-in-Chief deprecated making "any such great organic change in the organization of the Regiment, as likely to impair its present adaptability to the varied and varying requirements of the British service". There was general agreement however that, seeing how contradictory were the conclusions arrived at by the members of the Committee concerning this matter, no step of a drastic character ought to be undertaken in the immediate future, but that means of popularizing the garrison artillery must be devised. "The only plan which recommends itself to the Committee," appears in the agreed portion of the report "as offering any hope of success, is permanently (subject to certain restrictions hereinafter mentioned) to increase the pay of officers of the Garrison Artillery, and also to reserve to them certain appointments for which their training and occupation specially fit them".

Chapter IV.

Lord Harris' Committee.

An appropriate change in nomenclature of the groups of field batteries under lieutenant-colonels had taken place in the year 1885, for it had then been decided to substitute the term "brigade-division" for "division". The new title, if somewhat clumsy, had the virtue of distinctiveness, and it was adhered to for a number of years. The term "division" for two guns with their detachments, etc., in a horse artillery, or field, or mountain battery, and for a half battery of garrison artillery, was in the year 1889 changed into "section"; "sub-section" was at the same time substituted for "sub-division" as designating the single gun with its detachment, etc. But it was at the same time provided that, when the horse artillery or field or mountain battery was holding a foot parade, the "section" was to be called a "division" for fear of drill confusion.

"Brigade-Divisions" and "Sections."

Certain proposals tending to effect a partial separation of the officers in the mounted branch from those in the dismounted branch were put forward by Colonel E. Markham, who was now D.A.G., R.A., during the early part

The reorganization of 1889.

CHAPTER
IV.

The re-
organiza-
tion of
1889.

or 1889.[1]   But although these were welcomed in some departments of the War Office they failed to find favour in others, and Mr. Stanhope consequently decided that nothing could be effected in this direction for the present.[2] But plans were drawn up for a reorganization of the Regiment, and although in framing them especial attention was devoted to the garrison artillery, it was in respect to the R.H.A. and to the field artillery that the changes which were eventually decided upon were to prove the most lasting.   Instructions with regard to this reorganization were contained in an Army Order (No. 367), and in a complementary Regimental Order, which appeared on the 1st July, 1889.   By the terms of these ordinances the expression "brigade" disappeared as an administrative appelation under which a number of batteries were grouped together.

The Royal Horse Artillery batteries were now to be lettered A to T, and the two previously existing depôt batteries were to be amalgamated as one.   The depôt battery was to train recruits and to furnish the drafts for batteries beyond the sea.

The field artillery batteries were now to be numbered from 1 upwards to 80.   The four previously existing depôt batteries were to be concentrated at Woolwich and were to be administered as two divisions of two batteries each. No. 1 Battery, 1st Division, was to feed the service batteries numbered 1 to 20, No. 2 Battery, 1st Division, was to feed the service batteries 21 to 40, and so on.   The 1st Depôt Division was to be affiliated for recruiting purposes to the Eastern and Western Garrison Artillery Divisions (the organization and scope of these garrison artillery divisions is explained below) while the 2nd Depôt Division

---

[1] Colonel Markham was given the temporary rank of major-general at the end of this year—a recognition of the importance of the appointment.

[2] The appointment of Inspector-General of Artillery was, however, abolished in this year on the grounds that the work of the mounted branch differed too widely from that of the dismounted branch, for an officer, however experienced, to be capable of profitably inspecting both.

was to be affiliated to the Southern Garrison Artillery Division.

The mountain artillery was now constituted a special branch of the Regiment, with its batteries numbered from 1 to 10. One battery, which was quartered at home, at Newport (Mon.), was to act as a depôt and was to supply the necessary drafts to the 8 batteries that were quartered in India and to the one that was at this time quartered in Natal.

The garrison artillery was now to be organized as three divisions, Eastern, Southern and Western, the previously existing system of 11 Territorial Divisions being abolished. The Eastern Division was to consist of 29 batteries and was to have its depôt at Dover, the Southern Division was to consist of 42 batteries and was to have its depôt at Gosport and the Western Division was to consist of 25 batteries and was to have its depôt at Devonport; these three depôts were the former depôts of the Eastern, Southern and Western Territorial Divisions. The existing depôts at Woolwich and Yarmouth were to become "auxiliary depôts" for the Eastern Division, the existing depôts at Seaforth,[1] Dunbar[2] and Cork were to become auxiliary depôts for the Southern Division, and the existing depôt at Sunderland was to become an auxiliary depôt for the Western Division; the existing depôts at Pembroke Dock and Carrickfergus disappeared. The Militia Artillery and also the Volunteer Artillery were told off to the three Divisions, together with the lieut.-colonels holding the position of Officer Commanding Auxiliary Artillery.

The Colonels on the Staff, C.R.A. at Dover, Portsmouth and Devonport were to exercise administrative command over the three garrison artillery divisions which had their quarters at those three stations. They were to carry out a number of specified administrative duties in connection with the batteries included in the divisions, both at home

CHAPTER IV.

The re-organiza-tion of 1889.

---

[1] Liverpool in 1882.
[2] Leith in 1882.

CHAPTER
IV.

The re-
organiza-
tion of
1889.

and abroad.   They were in fact to act in a dual capacity—
besides their responsibilities in connection with the divisions, they commanded the batteries that were actually
quartered within the military districts of which Dover,
Portsmouth and Devonport were the respective headquarters.   It was moreover laid down by the Regimental
Order that the stations at home and abroad allotted to each
division in a table inserted at the end of the Order would
remain fixed; each division would thus become identified
with certain stations, its batteries changing places with
each other in relief.[1]

The Regimental Order made no alteration with respect
to the "Miscellaneous Establishments", i.e., the Riding
Establishment, the Coast Brigade, the District Staff and
the Shoeburyness Detachment.

Holders
of high
appoint-
ments at
this time.

The Egyptian Expedition of 1882 was signalized, in
so far as the Royal Artillery was concerned, by two very
high positions in the expeditionary force being entrusted
to officers of the Regiment—the first occasion on which
such a thing had occurred outside of India.   General Sir
J. M. Adye was appointed Chief of the Staff to Sir G.
Wolseley, and he moreover, in virtue of his standing in
the army, occupied the position of second-in-command;
Lieutenant-General Sir E. B. Hamley was given command
of the second of the two divisions despatched from home.
Brigadier-General H. Brackenbury commanded the River
Column up the Nile in 1885, after the death of General
Earle at Kirbekan.   Shortly after the Egyptian campaign
Sir J. Adye became Governor and Commander-in-Chief at
Gibraltar, and he occupied that position from 1883 to 1886.
General Sir E. B. Johnson was Director-General of Military
Education at the War Office from 1884 to 1888; he was
then succeeded by Lieutenant-General Sir R. Biddulph.
Major-General H. A. Smyth took over the command at
Woolwich in 1883 and was followed by Major-General
G. le M. Tupper in 1887 for a year, after which Major-

---

[1] This rule was not strictly adhered to except at first.

General A. H. Williams took over charge. Major-General
H. Brackenbury, as already mentioned, became head of the
Intelligence Department at the War Office as D.Q.M.G. in
1887; the title shortly afterwards was changed to Director
of Military Intelligence. Lieutenant-General H. A. Smyth
went out to take command at the Cape in 1888 and he
was transferred from South Africa to the Governorship of
Malta in 1890. Major-General W. H. Goodenough was
appointed to command the North-Western District in 1889.

In India, Lieutenant-General Sir F. Roberts became
Commander-in-Chief in 1885 with the rank of General,
while Lieutenant-General Sir C. G. Arbuthnot took over
the command in Madras in the year following. Major-
General E. F. Chapman was Quarter-Master General from
1885 to 1889. Major-General D. Macfarlane took up command of a division in 1885 and Major-General B. L. Gordon
of another in 1886. Some of the holders of brigadier-
general's appointments mentioned in the last chapter completed their term between 1882 and 1890; officers of the
Regiment to be newly posted to such commands during
those years were Brigadier-Generals A. H. Murray, A. C.
Johnson, H. M. G. Purvis, B. L. Gordon, B. H. Pottinger,
G. J. Smart, W. T. Budgen, G. T. Pretyman and
T. Graham.

As regards purely Regimental appointments, it should
be noted that a decision was arrived at in the year 1886
to make the command of the artillery at Aldershot one of
those appointments the holder of which was ordinarily a
major-general who however only got brigadier-general's
pay and allowances;[1] Major-General W. J. Williams was
the first to occupy the position. The plan was extended
to the Southern District in the following year, and Major-
General W. Stirling took up the command. Gibraltar and
Malta were similarly made general-officers commands in
1889, and Major-Generals B. L. Forster and A. H. King

---

[1] General officers had been holding the command of the cavalry
brigade and of the three infantry brigades at the camp for several
years past.

CHAPTER
IV.

Holders
of high
appoint-
ments at
this time.
respectively were selected to fill them.   Finally Major-
General H. le Cocq was appointed to command the artillery
in Ireland in 1890.   The creation of these five generals'
appointments went a long way towards meeting the
grievance which had been entertained hitherto by the
senior officers in the Regiment in that fewer openings
existed for them to look forward to than was the case in
the cavalry and the infantry.

Major-General Sir C. G. Arbuthnot succeeded General
Radcliffe as Inspector-General in 1883; he was however
moved on to the higher appointment of President of the
Ordnance Committee within two years.   He was followed
as Inspector-General by Major-General W. E. M. Reilly,
who however died within a few months; the vacancy was
thereupon filled by Major-General W. H. Goodenough,
who however only held the appointment until 1889 when
it was abolished.   Major-General R. Hay succeeded General
Arbuthnot as D.A.G., R.A., in 1883 and he was followed
by Colonel E. Markham (to whom reference has already
been made in this chapter) in 1887.   Brig.-General C. E.
Nairne succeeded Major-General Leslie as Inspector-General in India in 1887.   Colonel M. Elliot took over the
appointment of D.A.G., R.A., in India from Colonel
Murray in 1884 and occupied it till 1887, when, as already
mentioned, it was abolished.

The Royal Artillery in the year 1883 had to deplore
the loss of two of the most distinguished officers whose
names have been borne upon the rolls of the Regiment
since its creation in 1716—Sir E. Sabine and Sir Fenwick
Williams of Kars.   If Shrapnel early in the nineteenth
century had won a European reputation by his invention
of the form of projectile known by his name, and if
Chesney had—abroad as well as at home—been acknowledged as one of the very foremost explorers of his time,
Sabine was unquestionably the most famous scientist whom
the Regiment has produced and Fenwick Williams was the
first gunner ever to win renown outside of the British
Empire as a fighting leader and a modern paladin.   Another

veteran, Sir G. Brooke, who had seen an exceptional amount of service in India, had died a few weeks earlier in the same year.

General Sir George Brooke, K.C.B., was born in 1791 and joined the Bengal Artillery in 1808, to find himself almost immediately in the field in Bundelkund during 1809 and 1810. He served through the campaign in Nepal in 1815-16, took part in the siege of Hattras in 1817, and went through the Mahratta war in the following year. He was in the siege and capture of Bhurtpore by Lord Combermere in 1825-26, and was then to see no more active service for twenty years. In 1845-46 he took part, now a lieutenant-colonel, in the Sutlej Campaign, commanding the artillery at Moodkee and Ferozeshah as a brigadier, and being also on the field of Sobraon. Two years later he went through the Punjab Campaign, holding the position of brigadier in command of the horse artillery, and he was present at Ramnagar, Chilianwalla and Gujerat. He became commandant of the Bengal Artillery in 1852, was promoted major-general in 1854, and handed over the command to Brigadier-General Archdale Wilson very shortly before the outbreak of the Indian Mutiny. He reached the rank of general in 1870 and died early in 1883.

General Sir E. Sabine, K.C.B., F.R.S., was born in 1788 and joined the Regiment in 1803 at the age of fifteen, but he saw no active service in the various campaigns in Europe during the succeeding ten years. He was crossing the Atlantic in a transport to take part in the struggle in America in 1813 when the ship was captured by an enemy privateer; but the vessel was recaptured by a British frigate, and Sabine then took the field in the Niagara campaign. He returned to England in 1816 and, recognized as a keen scientist, was made F.R.S. in 1818. He had at an early age taken up the question of terrestial magnetism and astronomy, and in the year 1818 and 1819 he was allowed to accompany the expeditions of Ross and of Parry to the Arctic seas, in the capacity of astronomer.

CHAPTER
IV.

Some dis-
tinguished
members
of the
Regiment.

He was engaged on observations in connection with magnetic inclination from 1821 to 1823, and he had by that time come to be regarded as one of the greatest living authorities on this subject. For the next seven years he was, with the sanction of the Duke of Wellington, engaged on scientific pursuits and was practically permanently on leave; but in 1830 he was recalled to regimental duty and he served till 1837 in Ireland. From 1840 to 1861 he filled the position of superintendent over the work of setting up observatories for studying magnetic variation and terrestial magnetism, and in the year 1849 he received the gold medal of the Royal Society; he had reached the rank of major-general in 1856. He was President of the Royal Society from 1861 to 1871, and he had held the position of general secretary to the British Association from 1839 to 1859. He became colonel commandant of the Regiment in 1865, full general in 1870, and retired on full pay in 1877. He died at the age of 94 in 1883. He was a D.C.L. and LL.D., a K.C.B., and the author of a whole library of scientific works.

General Sir W. Fenwick Williams, Bart., of Kars, G.C.B., D.C.L., was born in Nova Scotia in 1800 and entered the R.M. Academy in 1815; but owing to the reduction of establishments after Waterloo, he did not receive his commission in the R.A. until 1825. In the year 1841 he went out as a captain to Constantinople to be employed under the Ottoman government in the arsenal there, and he remained in Turkey for the next thirteen years. He acted as British Commissioner for the settlement of the Turko-Persian frontier in 1848, and, for his services on this and other occasions in connection with problems concerning the Sultan's dominions he was promoted brevet lieutenant-colonel and colonel, which latter rank he held in 1854 at the commencement of the Crimean War, when he was appointed British Commissioner with the Ottoman forces in Anatolia.

The Turkish troops told off to guard the Armenian frontier against the Russian invading forces were in a disorganized condition, they were demoralized owing to pay being in arrears, to lack of clothing, and to the breakdown of commissariat arrangements, and their superior officers tacitly permitted Colonel Williams to become virtually commander-in-chief. Defence works had been completely neglected since the end of the previous Russo-Turkish War in 1829, but Williams at once set himself to render Erzerum secure and he converted the city into an efficient fortress during the winter of 1854-55. Then, on learning in June that the Russians under General Mouravieff were approaching Kars, he proceeded thither and on arrival took over command of the place. A Russian attack delivered on June 16th was beaten off with loss; but the enemy thereupon established a strict blockade, and for four months to come the Turkish garrison, inspired by the presence and by the example of their British commander, not only kept the enemy at bay but maintained an active defence. Williams, however, eventually found himself compelled to capitulate owing to famine, and on the 28th November terms of surrender were agreed upon with Mouravieff, who wrote : "You have made yourself a name in history, and posterity will stand amazed at the endurance, the courage and the discipline which this siege has called forth in the remains of an army." For his services Colonel Williams was promoted major-general, was given a baronetcy "of Kars" and the K.C.B. and was awarded a pension of £1,000 a year. He was also made a D.C.L.

On returning home he commanded at Woolwich from 1856 to 1859, and was afterwards, as already mentioned in earlier chapters, successively in command of the troops in Canada, Governor of Nova Scotia and Governor of Gibraltar. He was appointed Constable of the Tower in 1881, and he died a few weeks after Sir E. Sabine in 1883.

Field-Marshal Sir Richard Dacres was born in 1799 and, luckier than his junior, Sabine, obtained his commission in 1817 soon after leaving the R.M. Academy; but he did not reach the rank of 2nd captain until 1837. On the out-

CHAPTER
IV.

Some dis-
tinguished
members
of the
Regiment.

break of war with Russia in 1854, he went out to Turkey
as lieut.-colonel in command of three troops of horse artillery forming part of the cavalry division under Lord Lucan.
He was present at the affairs of Bulganak and McKenzie's
Farm, at the Alma, Balaklava and Inkerman, and, on the
death of Brigadier-General Fox-Strangways in the latter
battle, succeeded to the command of the whole of the
artillery in the Crimea, which position he occupied during
the siege of Sebastopol. For his services he was promoted
major-general and was given the K.C.B. He was, as already
mentioned, in command at Woolwich from 1859 to 1865.
He became full general in 1868 and G.C.B. in 1869. He
succeeded Sir F. Williams as Constable of the Tower in
1881 and was promoted Field-Marshal in 1886, but he died
a very few months later.

CHAPTER V.

1891 TO 1899.

Number of batteries and establishment of the Regiment in 1891—The separation question—The special Regimental Order of the 28th July, 1891—Local garrison artillery units in certain oversea stations—Changes in garrison artillery organization in 1894—Augmentation of the number of service units in 1895—Progress of the garrison artillery—Decision to increase the garrison artillery in 1897-98—War establishments of horse and field artillery at home—Increase of the field artillery in 1898-99—Disturbed conditions in the years 1897 and 1898—Siege artillery—The question of field artillery depôts—Progress of the separation question—The splitting up of the Regiment in 1899—Abolition of the appointment of D.A.G., R.A.—Changes in India—Holders of high appointments at this time—Some distinguished figures in the Regiment—The distribution of the Royal Artillery at the beginning of September, 1899.

As a notable increase in the number of units, and also in the total establishment and strength of the Regiment was to take place within the next few years, the figures at the beginning of the year 1891 as laid down in the Army Estimates for 1891-92 may appropriately be given. The number of units constituting the garrison artillery was (as will be shown in a later paragraph), to be reduced within a few months owing to the introduction of the "double company" system, but the total figures of officers and other ranks were not appreciably affected by this.

The Royal Horse Artillery comprised at this time 9 service batteries and 2 depôt batteries stationed at home, together with 11 service batteries stationed in India. Of the 9 service batteries in the United Kingdom 5 were on the "higher" establishment and the remaining 4 were on the "lower" establishment. The total establishment at

CHAPTER
V.

Number
of batteries
and estab-
lishment
of the
Regiment
in 1891.

CHAPTER V.

Number of batteries and establishment of the Regiment in 1891.

home amounted to 1,911 of all ranks, while that in India came to 1,799 of all ranks.

The field artillery at home consisted of 38 service batteries and 4 depôt batteries. Of the service batteries 13 were on the "higher" establishment, 11 were on the "2nd army corps" establishment, and the remaining 14 were on the "lower" (4-gun) establishment. There were also 42 service batteries in India. This made the total of 80 service field batteries. Their establishment at home came to 7,139 of all ranks, and in India it came to 6,838 of all ranks.

The mountain artillery comprised 10 service batteries, of which one was at home, another was in Natal, and the remaining 8 were in India; the total establishment of the branch came to 1,232 of all ranks.[1]

The garrison artillery consisted of 38 service batteries at home, 31 service batteries abroad, exclusive of India, and 27 service batteries in India, together with 9 depôts at home. There were also the St. Helena Detachment and the Sierra Leone Detachment at home.[2] The total establishment of all ranks at home and in the colonies (including one service battery in Egypt) was shown as 13,939[3] in the Army Estimates; the figure for India was 3,200.

Although important changes were to take place at home within the next eight years, the number of service units in India—11 of horse artillery, 42 of field artillery, 8 of mountain artillery and 27 of garrison artillery—was to remain the same up to the date when the Indian Contingent sailed for Natal a few days before the outbreak of the South African war in the year 1899. The above given figures show that the total establishment of the Regiment

---

[1] There were at this time 8 native mountain batteries in India, as described in Chapter XII. But these native batteries were not considered part of the Regiment until several years later.

[2] These were approximately the equivalent of half batteries, and they were supposed to be hurried out to their foreign stations on the first threat of war.

[3] This does not include the permanent staff of Militia and Volunteer Artillery—1,148 of all ranks.

at home and abroad at this time mounted up to 36,058
of all ranks.

The organization as laid down for the home army in
War establishments was to be modified in the year 1898
and the ratio of artillery to the other arms was then to be
considerably increased. But the war organization differed
little in the year 1891 from that which had been in force
ten years earlier, before the Egyptian Campaign of 1882;
the army corps however, no longer included a cavalry
brigade, as had then been the case. The artillery to be
included in an army corps consisted of three "divisions"
of field artillery, one to each of the infantry divisions,
and of the corps artillery, which comprised three batteries
of horse artillery and two batteries of field artillery. This
made up a total of 14 batteries—84 guns. A cavalry division was also contemplated; it was to consist of two
brigades, each including a horse artillery battery.

Although the controversial question of separating the
mounted from the dismounted portion of the Regiment had
been temporarily shelved owing to the inability of the
members of Lord Harris' committee of 1887-88 to come
to an agreement on the subject, the matter was merely in
suspense, and it had been under consideration of the War
Office during the whole of 1890. Discussions carried out
on paper at Headquarters on the separation problem were
moreover wont to become involved with discussions on
another question, that of securing the consent of the
Treasury to augmenting the emoluments of the garrison
artillery. As to the urgent need of rendering the dismounted branch more attractive by increasing the pay, the
Harris committee had spoken with no uncertain voice.

The delay that was taking place in arriving at a solution with regard to the problem had tended to harden
opinion on the subject within the Regiment. It was fully
recognized at the War Office that the majority of artillery
officers who were serving regimentally favoured cleavage,
and that those who had especially identified themselves
with garrison artillery work, and who were quite satisfied

I

to remain permanently in the dismounted branch, were
just as eager for separation as were those serving at the
time in the R.H.A. and in field batteries.   The topic was
no doubt being envisaged mainly from the personal, and
to some extent narrow, point of view.   Officers serving
in the mounted branch wanted to make sure of continuing
to do so.   A considerable minority, who were quite content
to spend their service in the dismounted branch, felt convinced that officers serving in it would benefit by separation.   Only those who preferred the mounted side, but
who feared that they might find themselves permanently
relegated to the other were opposed to divorce, and they
only represented a fraction of the whole body of the commissioned ranks of the Regiment.   That many should have
remembered the extent to which the two branches, assuming them, to be parted, might have to lean on each other
in the event of a great war, would perhaps have been too
much to expect.   Those high military authorities at the
War Office who favoured separation were fully justified in
assuming that they had regimental opinion on their side,
and so, the Treasury having at last assented to proposals
which had been put forward for increases of pay to the
garrison artillery, a special Regimental Order was published on the 28th July, 1891, which paved the way for the
definite parting that was to be carried into effect eight years
later.

The
special
Regimen-
tal Order
of the 28th
July, 1891.
"Certain changes in the organization of the Garrison
Artillery having been decided upon," so ran the preamble
to this order "His Royal Highness the Colonel of the
Regiment, directs that they be carried out, as far as
possible, with effect from the 1st August, 1891.   The
object of these. changes is improvement in the organization
and personnel of the Garrison Artillery, its greater
efficiency in the duties of coast defence, and increased
means of instruction in the higher and more technical
duties connected with the heavy armaments now in use."
The order created a permanent "District Establishment"
in each garrison artillery district.   It substituted the term

"company" for "battery" as designating units of the garrison artillery, and it promised armament pay for officers and promised special pay for certain rank-and-file specialists in the branch. It laid down the establishments of companies at home and abroad (outside of India) on lines calculated to meet local armament requirements, adopting the principle of "double companies" in most cases. It moreover created the appointment of "armament major" —a field officer who was to be accountable for the armament within the area allotted to him.

The garrison artillery was to remain organized in three large groups—Eastern Division, Southern Division and Western Division—although a re-distribution of units within these divisions was to take place. No important change was made as regards depôts, the three main depôts remaining at Dover, Portsmouth and Devonport, with affiliated sub-depôts; the main depôts were however, made responsible for finding drafts for units abroad. The exact establishment of companies, and also the establishment of the special district establishment in each station, were laid down in voluminous appendices. The double companies were allowed 8 officers (1 major, 2 captains and 5 subalterns) and their establishment in non-commissioned officers and gunners was in most cases over 200, 243 being the highest figure. Some of the single companies, i.e., at St. Lucia,[1] Jamaica and Mauritious, on the other hand, had no major and were allowed an establishment of barely 100 non-commissioned-officers and men. The details given as to the district establishments indicated the stations to which the newly created armament majors were to be posted. The order did not actually lay down details as to armament pay and pay of specialists, but it announced that a Royal Warrant on the subject would shortly be issued. The specialists were to include position-finders, depression range-finders, siege-train specialists, machinery gunners and layers.

---

[1] This island had recently became a station for a unit.

CHAPTER
V.

The
special
Regimen-
tal Order
of the 28th
July, 1891.

A very important matter, which affected not merely the
garrison artillery but also the Regiment as a whole, seeing
that it contained the germ of separation, was relegated to
an appendix—Appendix E.   This laid down that young
officers would be posted as heretofore and would be interchangeable as between the field and garrison artillery, but
that they would after three years be considered as definitely posted to whichever branch then bore them on its
rolls and that all their further promotions would be effected
in that branch.   It provided for officers already serving,
being interchangeable between the two branches "on the
merits of their various cases" for 10 years to come, but it
ordained that after that date they would remain for good
in whatever branch they were then in.   It, moreover, included the following provision :—"Promotion to lieut.-
colonel will be by selection, and the officers will be selected
from the two arms[1] according to the nature of the duties
they will have to perform."   The effect of these provisions
will be considered in a later paragraph.

Local
garrison
artillery
unit in
certain
oversea
stations.

Demands for an augmentation in the strength of the
garrison artillery required at certain oversea stations,
notably in the Far East, had been causing the War Office
anxiety for some years before 1891.   One reason why service in the dismounted branch of the Regiment was less
popular than in the mounted branch was admittedly the
amount of foreign service which fell to the lot of the garrison artillery.   The authorities were therefore most unwil-
ling to increase this amount if it could be avoided, and the
financial side of the question had also to be taken into
consideration.   So they fell back upon the plan of utilising
native personnel to some extent in substitution for British.

Three companies of "gun lascars" had been maintained
at Hong Kong and Singapore since the early 'seventies';
but these units had been looked upon as acting in the
capacity of assistants to the regular batteries quartered in

---

[1] The two portions of the Regiment were called "corps" in one
place and "arms" in another.

those stations for the purpose of looking after armament, of acting as guards and so forth, rather than as providing detachments for manning the guns of the defences. The number of companies of these gun lascars had been increased to seven by the year 1889; but the personnel was not adjudged to be wholly satisfactory and, after a project of enlisting Chinese had been rejected, it was decided to fall back upon the fighting races of India to provide not only rank-and-file but also a proportion of officers for these local companies. The plan proved successful, and by the year 1891 a Hong Kong-Singapore battalion of 5 companies and a Ceylon-Mauritius battalion of 4 companies were in being. An African company of Houssas had also been raised for Sierra Leone. But these local formations were not looked upon then, nor were they looked upon until several years later, as actually part of the Royal Artillery. They in this respect stood on a footing analogous to that of the Indian native mountain batteries.

The "double company" system introduced in 1891 had been popular in the garrison artillery, and it had possessed certain undoubted advantages. The larger unit had made a satisfactory command for a field officer. The absence of one or two officers—whether on leave, or on special duty, or on some course or courses—caused much less inconvenience out of a total of eight than it did out of a total of five. With over 200 non-commissioned-officers and men on the books, the finding of the inevitable fatigue parties interfered less with training than when the total borne on the strength was considerably less. The higher establishment was also advantageous from the point of view of institutions—recreation rooms, canteens, and so forth—to companies that were isolated. But the system was not without certain drawbacks. Many stations existed where the available barrack accommodation in out-lying forts and batteries did not lend itself to the housing of so large a body of officers and other ranks as were included in a double company. From the point of view of reliefs also, the time-honoured, smaller company admittedly was preferable.

CHAPTER
V.

Changes in
garrison
artillery
organiza-
tion in
1894.

The matter was settled by a Regimental Order appearing in 1894 which practically reverted to the old plan.

Double companies were by the terms of this order abolished, except at the Cape and in Ceylon. The establishments of the companies told off to the various stations were laid down afresh and, as in the organization devised in 1891, they varied considerably. Range-finding specialists, although continuing to belong to the various District Establishments, were now to be attached to companies. The whole tendency of these newest instructions was indeed to associate companies more closely than had previously been the case with the batteries and works which they would actually man in case of war. The circumstances of the case do not admit of coast-defence artillery units being linked to their armament quite in the sense that horse, and field, and mountain, and even siege, artillery units are linked. But the conditions in this respect were appreciably improved by the issue of the order. Armament majors were abolished, except in a few places where armament existed but where no company was stationed; the other armament majors were indeed required to command companies now that the number of units had been substantially increased. The Eastern Division was now to comprise 26 companies, the Southern Division 36 companies and the Western Division 25 companies.[1]

Augmenta-
tion of the
number of
service
units in
1895.

An increase in the number of service units was carried out in all branches of the Regiment except the mountain artillery in the year 1895, but it was to a large extent effected by the conversion of depôt units into service bat-

---

[1] The distribution had, under the provisions of R.O. 89 of 1889, been 29 batteries to the Eastern Division, 42 to the Southern and 25 to the Western. The figures under the provisions of the Special R.O. of 28th July, 1891 had been respectively 23, 29 and 22. Whatever benefits these successive rapidly recurring re-organizations may have conferred on the garrison artillery as a whole, they necessarily imposed changes of nomenclature upon a number of units. It was found possible however, in most cases for the companies of 1894 to revert to the numbers which had distinguished the batteries of 1889. 30 Southern of 1889, for instance, had become 25 Southern in 1891, but it found itself 30 Southern again in 1894.

teries and companies. The question of depôts had in the case of the field artillery been a bone of contention ever since 1884, when depôt batteries had been re-introduced within three years of their having been abolished. Regimental officers serving in the field artillery were disposed to take what was perhaps the narrower view of the problem involved. They maintained that, if the responsibility of training recruits and of furnishing drafts for the batteries abroad were imposed upon service batteries at home, the training and general efficiency of these latter must suffer to a very appreciable extent. The higher military authorities outside of the Regiment, as well as some of those belonging to the Regiment, held that such depreciation in practical value as the service batteries were likely to suffer from being charged with these duties, was not sufficient to justify maintaining horses and armament for batteries which could not be placed in the field in the event of war. They were strengthened in their view by the knowledge that additional service field batteries were needed, and, their view having prevailed, R.O. 38 of 1895 conveyed the following instructions :—

One of the two depôt batteries, R.H.A. was to be transformed into a service battery, lettered U; there was in future only to be the one depôt battery.

As regards the field artillery, three of its four depôt batteries were to be transformed into service batteries, and four new service batteries were to be raised. These latter were to be numbered 81 to 84; the converted batteries were to be numbered 85, 86 and 87. The remaining depôt battery became a simple depôt without guns or horses, stationed at Woolwich; it was in future only to be charged with receiving and clothing recruits and with their brief elementary training. A decision had also been arrived at to the effect that field batteries were henceforward to have the clothing and equipment for their reservists on charge, and that they were to fit their reservists out in the event of mobilization.

The garrison artillery was increased by six service companies. Three of these were produced by transforming
Augmenta-
tion of the
number of
service
units in
1895.
three of the sub-depôts into service companies; the remaining three were freshly raised. Three of the new companies were told off respectively to Ceylon, Singapore and the Cape, additional garrison artillery being required at those stations in consequence of the armament having been increased; the remaining three were told off to home stations. The order also prescribed that depression range-finder and telephonist specialists were in future, except at one or two specified stations where no companies were quartered, to belong to companies instead of their belonging to the district establishments. Recruits were in future only to be received and clothed and to undergo a brief elementary training at the depôts. Service companies at home were to find the drafts for companies abroad.

The authorities thus, in so far as the depôts were concerned, reverted to the principle which had been adopted for the field artillery in 1882 and had been abandoned two years later in deference to complaints—the principle that service batteries should, apart from the very elementary instruction at the outset, train their own recruits, and that they should moreover be charged with finding the drafts for batteries abroad. Commanders of service units in the garrison artillery had generally rather favoured the plan of training their own recruits (although no more anxious to find drafts than battery commanders in the field artillery), but the conditions are of course very different between the two branches.

The marked interest in the dismounted branch of the Regiment which had of late years been displayed in high places, coupled, as it was, with the introduction of measures improving its organization on well-considered lines, was rendering service in it more popular than had previously been the case.[1] There had indeed been unmistakeable

---

[1] The appointment of Colonel F. T. Lloyd to be D.A.G., R.A., in 1894, an officer who for a number of years had been entirely identified with the garrison artillery, had been significant.

signs of this even before armament pay and specialists extra pay had been granted in 1891.   A gratifying advance had also, as will be seen in part III, been taking place in the development of gunnery efficiency alike in the coast-defence side and the siege-train side of garrison artillery work.   The principle of associating the companies told off to our maritime fortresses as closely as possible with the works which they would man and with the armament they would fight in the event of the fortresses being attacked, was helping to render service in the dismounted branch of the Regiment more interesting than had formerly been the case.   The fact that a large proportion of the young officers now joining it realised that they were to spend their military career in it was likewise exercising a beneficial effect.   It is indeed no exaggeration to say that the garrison artillery had made distinctly greater progress between 1887 and 1895 than had any other portion of the Royal Artillery. Whereas the horse artillery, the field artillery and the mountain artillery had all been efficient services at the be-ginning of that period, the garrison artillery admittedly had not.

But it still laboured under considerable difficulties, at least in so far as its coast-defence companies were con-cerned, owing to the armament of our maritime fortresses, alike at home and abroad, being out of date.   This point is dealt with in Part II.   But, besides the fact of its being discouraging to the personnel, this caused serious manning difficulties for large numbers of virtually or wholly obsolete guns which were of no practical use at all required, or seemed to require, detachments.   The consequence was that C.R.A's at home and abroad, and especially abroad, were pressing for a substantial increase in personnel, seeing that the personnel under their orders was insufficient to man the armament under their charge.   Their appeals gradually won the ear of the War Office, and the result was that provision was made in the Army Estimates of 1897-98 for the greatest expansion of the dismounted

CHAPTER
V.

Decision
to increase
the
garrison
artillery
in 1897-98.

War estab-
lishments
of horse
and field
artillery
at home.

branch of the Regiment which had taken place since the absorption of the Indian Artilleries.

These estimates provided for an increase of 3,641 of all ranks to be made to the existing numbers, although it was foreseen that, in view of recruiting difficulties, the whole of this could not be effected within the one financial year. The number of companies at home was to be increased from 35 to 40, and that of the companies abroad was to be increased from 31 to 37—a total addition of 11 companies. But the figure of 3,641 would naturally represent more than 11 normal companies, and great part of the expansion was, notably in the case of the Mediterranean garrisons, to take the form of virtually reverting to the principle of double companies, although that term was not on this occasion made use of. The numbers at Malta were to be increased by the addition of one company, and by raising the total establishment from 1,248 to 2,007; no new unit was to be added at Gibraltar, but the total was to be increased from 1,134 to 1,547. Additional companies were to be provided for Bermuda, Singapore and Hong Kong; and Sierra Leone and St. Helena were now to have companies permanently quartered in place of their depending upon detachments which were stationed at home in peace time. These expansions had all been carried into effect by the beginning of 1899, in which year a company was sent out from home to Wei-hai-wei—a new garrison artillery station.

When the question of mobilization for war and of war establishments had been seriously taken up in 1886-87, the decision arrived at had been, as was shown in the last chapter, to base calculations upon ensuring the placing of a cavalry division and of two army corps, together with some line of communications troops, in the field. The military authorities had however since that time been coming to the conclusion that, with the number of cavalry regiments and of infantry battalions on the home establishment that were available, it ought to be feasible to mobilize three instead of two army corps, and four cavalry brigades

instead of two.[1] Artillery had been one of the main difficulties; but, in so far as service batteries were concerned,
this had been to some extent got over by the addition of the
one R.H.A. battery and the 7 field batteries to the existing
strength in 1895 which was mentioned in p. 121.   The
intention then was that, instead of corps artillery consisting
of 3 horse artillery batteries and 2 field artillery batteries,
it was to consist of 2 horse artillery batteries and 3 field
batteries.   Four cavalry brigades would require 4 horse
artillery batteries, and three army corps would require 6
horse artillery batteries and 36 field batteries.

Foreign countries were however, augmenting the proportion of field artillery in their armies, the military
authorities at the War Office were becoming very anxious
to follow suit, and they had come to the conclusion that
the corps artillery of an army corps ought to include two
brigade-divisions of field artillery instead of only one.
Nine more field batteries would in fact have to be mobilized
if the field army was to be brought up to its war footing.
To render this practicable an increase in the number of
units and in the total peace establishments was called for.
As an expansion in the peace establishment of the garrison
artillery was being urged at the same time, and as this
question was given the preference, only one additional field
battery was provided for in the estimates for the financial
year 1897-98.   But a very substantial increase was provided for in the estimates for the ensuing year.   It should
be mentioned that an increase of the field artillery was
rendered all the more necessary by the fact that a brigade-
division had been sent out from home to Natal in 1897 in
view of the growing tension between H.M. Government and
the government of the Transvaal; relations between the
parties had been strained ever since the Jameson Raid of

---

[1] Lord Wolseley had succeeded the Duke of Cambridge as Commander-in-Chief at the end of 1895, with restricted powers; but the
Mobilization and Intelligence branches were directly under him and
he devoted especial attention to this question.   Lord Lansdowne had
become Secretary of State at the same time as Lord Wolseley took up
the appointment of C.-in-C.

CHAPTER V.

War establishments of horse and field artillery at home.

1895-96.   Some improvement had, it should be mentioned, been effected at home of late years in respect to concentrating the field batteries, but the majority of them were still quartered in single-battery stations. Only five brigade-divisions (two at Aldershot, two at Woolwich and one at Shorncliffe) were assembled complete in any one place, and only at Colchester, Exeter, Weedon and Athlone were two batteries to be found along-side each other.

Increase of the field artillery in 1898-99.

The calculations on which the strength in artillery for our field army had latterly been based had been the figure of four guns to 1,000 combatants. Following the example of foreign countries, the military authorities were now anxious to reach a five guns to 1,000 combatants standard. A decision had also been arrived at in 1896 to arm one brigade-division at home with field howitzers, and this had been carried into effect in 1897. Working from these bases, the Army Estimates for 1898-99 included amongst its items a substantial increase in the number of field batteries that were to be maintained on the home establishment.

These Estimates provided for the addition of 15 field batteries to the number stationed at home within the succeeding three years. Four of these batteries were actually formed before the end of 1898, and three more had been formed by the summer of 1899 before the outbreak of the South African war. The remaining eight were, together with many others, as will be related in Volume II, created during the progress of that struggle. There had been 80 field batteries at the time of the re-organization of 1889. The 81st to the 87th had, as mentioned on p. 121, been formed in the year 1895. The 88th had been formed in 1897. The 89th to the 95th were in existence before mobilization was ordered for the campaign in South Africa.

Disturbed conditions in the years 1897 and 1898.

Troubles, by which our army had been to some extent affected, had taken place in various parts of the world during the years 1897 and 1898, quite apart from the somewhat threatening situation that was arising in connection with the Boers. Unrest in Crete, which synchronised with the Turko-Greek war, had led in 1897 to the mountain battery which was ordinarily quartered at Newport being sent to that island and remaining there for some months. The most serious troubles which had yet been encountered on the North-West Frontier of India also came to a head during the course of that same year.   A number of distinct campaigns had to be undertaken against different tribes or collections of tribes.   These involved the majority of the mountain batteries in India, British and Native, taking the field, together with certain of the horse artillery and field batteries stationed in the Punjab.   The operations did not however, in most cases last long, and the artillery actually serving in India was able to provide all that was necessary without its having to call for aid from home.   The campaign for the final recovery of the Soudan was undertaken and carried through triumphantly in the year 1898.   One of the newly armed field howitzer batteries was especially sent out from home to take part in the advance to Omdurman; the field battery and the garrison battery already quartered in Egypt provided the rest of the artillery required by the British portions of Sir H. Kitchener's command.[1]

As described in Chapter XIV much attention had of late years been devoted both at home and in India to improving the armament and the training of the garrison artillery companies that were told off as siege companies. A Regimental Order, which appeared in 1898, laid down what was to be the war establishment of such companies at home.   The military authorities were moreover anxious to establish a system by which the four siege companies at home, together with the three siege companies and the four heavy batteries maintained in India, should form a special branch of the Regiment on lines similar to the mountain artillery.   But as will be told in Chapter XIV, no decision had been arrived at before the close of the century.

---

[1] That representatives of the Regiment were in the field in other regions besides those above referred to, is indicated by R.O. 72 of 1897 which promoted two non-commissioned-officers R.A. to the rank of sergeant for gallant conduct at Bida in West Africa.

CHAPTER
V.

The
question
of field
artillery
depôts.

The old question of depôt batteries for the field artillery
was revived in 1897, owing to representations made by
C.R.A's and battery commanders as to the unfortunate
effect which the responsibility for training recruits and for
providing the drafts for service batteries abroad was exercising over service units at home. All the arguments for
and against the existing plan of a single depôt at Woolwich,
which, for practical purposes, merely clothed the recruits,
were produced. The inconvenience had been aggravated
from the point of view of the service batteries by an order
in virtue of which no men were to be considered eligible for
India or the tropics until they were over 20 years of age.
A system which might work fairly well in the case of the
infantry was not, so it was contended, equally applicable
to field artillery, owing to its varied personnel, to the
number of drivers and of specialists—layers, range-takers,
artificers, and so forth—who were indispensible in a battery. But no method of establishing depôt field batteries
could be suggested other than that of converting service
batteries into such batteries, or else of increasing the Army
Estimates.

But a fresh aspect of this depôt question was brought
under examination while the above discussions were still
in progress. Under the existing system, reservists were
on mobilization to be clothed at the service batteries that
they were to join. Their documents, on the other hand,
were under charge of the depôt, and they received their
orders to join up from that unit. This was adjudged—not
altogether unnaturally—to be a clumsy and inconvenient
arrangement. There was much to be said for the clothing of the reservists being carried out at depôts, as was the
practice in the infantry. But, with only one single depôt
at Woolwich to carry out the operation, such a plan would
have had little to commend it. The proposal was however now made that, in place of there only being one
single field artillery depôt at Woolwich, this should be
split up so as to form four or five depôts and that these
should be distributed at convenient centres about the

United Kingdom, a suitable re-appropriation of barrack CHAPTER V.
accommodation being apparently practicable. But nothing
had in fact been settled in September 1899, and the South
African war then intervened.

From the putting in force of the provisions of the Regi-   Progress of the separation question.
mental Order of 25th July, 1891, up to the year 1896,
most difficult problems to solve with regard to individual
officers had troubled the D.A.G., R.A. Appendix E to
R.O. 76 of 1891 had, for instance, contained the following direction:—"Promotion to lieut.-colonel will be by
by selection, and the officers will be selected from the two
arms according to the duties they will have to perform."
This promotion by selection had commenced in December
1891, but it had been discontinued in January 1893, and
one anomalous consequence of its being put in force had
been that certain majors had been passed over for promotion by juniors because there was not a vacancy available
in their proper branch at the moment. Such superses-
sions were to prove common after the Regiment was
actually split up at a later date; but the sufferers had not
become used to such experiences in 1892, and they took
exception to the system. A number of officers (not newly
joined), who wished to serve in the mounted branch and
who could put forward strong claims to do so, also found
themselves in the garrison artillery. The order had distinctly laid down that no transfers from one branch to the
other were to be entertained after ten years and, with
half of that period of ten years already elapsed, many
doubtful cases in 1896 still remained to be settled.

A committee, consisting of Lieutenant-General W.
Stirling as president, with Major-Generals H. le G. Geary,
S. J. Nicholson and J. Alleyne as members, was therefore
appointed to go into each individual case and to make
definite recommendations. This committee reported in
February 1897 and allowed 34 appeals out of a total of
126 sent in. Its report was accepted by the military
authorities at the War Office, although the committee
admitted that a certain amount of hardship was being in-

flicted on individuals by its terms. The report was in fact
to a great extent governed by the principle of *beati possi-
dentes* which meant that officers then serving in the field
artillery were to remain in it unless they wished to transfer
to the dismounted side, while only a very few of the officers
then serving in the garrison artillery who wished for service
in the mounted side could be found room for in the field
artillery. The Secretary of State—Lord Lansdowne—was,
however, most anxious that no injustice should be done to
individuals if it could possibly be avoided, and during the
discussions that ensued it was suggested that the Royal
Artillery should be broken up into a number of distinct
regiments of horse and field artillery, and of garrison
artillery. So a fresh committee was set up under the presidency of Major-General G. H. Marshall, and this drew up
elaborate proposals on the subject. But on further considerations it was decided that the recommendations of the
committee would not prove satisfactory if put in force. So
the plan of a number of regiments was dropped, and it was
decided that the Royal Artillery should be divided into two
distinct "corps", while still remaining the Royal Regiment
of Artillery. The authorities realised that the disappearance of the old name would arouse great opposition, and it
came about therefore that, when the very important Army
Order 96 of June 1899[1] was drafted, the Regiment was
allowed to remain the Regiment—although split in two.

 The preamble to the Royal Warrant quoted in this Army
Order read as follows :—"Whereas we deem it expedient
to re-arrange our Royal Regiment of Artillery, our Will
and Pleasure is that, from the 1st June, 1899, the
mounted and the dismounted branches of our Royal Regiment of Artillery, shall be separated into two corps,
under the general title of the Royal Regiment of Artillery, to be named respectively :

    (a) The Royal Horse Artillery and the Royal Field
         Artillery.

    (b) The Royal Garrison Artillery.

---

[1] The full text of the Order is given in Appendix B.

The names of the officers who have elected, or who have been selected, to serve with either corps shall be published in the Monthly Army List, and they shall then be considered as having been duly gazetted to their respective corps."

CHAPTER
V.

The split-
ting up of
the
Regiment
in 1899.

It was laid down that officers were henceforward to be promoted in their own corps, but that exchanges would be permitted under certain reservations. Those officers serving at the time in the R.G.A., whose names had been noted for transfer to the mounted branch, would be considered for such transfer as opportunities offered. Officers appointed to either corps from the 1st June 1899 onwards would not be eligible for transfer. Officers for appointment to the R.H.A. would be taken from the R.F.A., officers for appointment to the mountain artillery would be taken from the R.G.A. Recruits would be enlisted for either one corps or the other; they would not be available for transfer from one corps to the other without their own consent. The Regiment was thus definitely split in two, and it is a matter for congratulation that, illogical as the arrangement perhaps seemed at the time, the Royal Artillery were allowed to retain their old title and to remain a Regiment. Within a very few months the plan was to be put to the test on the veld of South Africa, and numbers of R.G.A. officers were before long to be found serving in field batteries.

A very important change in respect to the administration of the Regiment was however carried into effect within the War Office before the appearance of this momentous order. The higher military authorities had some months before determined to abolish the post of Deputy Adjutant-General, R.A., and to divide up the duties that had hitherto been carried out in that official's branch between the departments of the Adjutant-General, the Military Secretary and other chiefs in Pall Mall. Lieut.-Colonel Ritchie, who had acted for 26 years as the confidential assistant of successive D.A.G's., R.A., had retired in August 1898, and the then A.A.G. had left

CHAPTER
V.

Abolition
of the ap-
pointment
of D.A.G.,
R.A.
shortly afterwards, the vacancy not being filled up.   This
paved the way for the re-arrangement of duties which was
put in force on the 1st April 1899.   In place of a D.A.G.,
with an A.A.G. and a D.A.A.G. as aids (Lieut.-Colonel
Ritchie had held no actual staff appointment), there was
now to be an A.A.G., R.A. to act as an artillery adviser
in the Adjutant-General's department on all subjects affecting artillery and requiring technical knowledge, and there
was to be an Assistant Military Secretary to act as adviser
to the Military Secretary on questions concerning appointments of artillery officers, their promotions, retirements
and so forth.   Certain matters which had previously been
dealt with in the branch of the D.A.G., R.A. were also
turned over to the Quarter-Master-General's and Director-
General of Ordnance's departments.   Colonel E. O. Hay
took up the appointment of A.A.G. and Colonel J. C.
Dalton that of A.M.S., and upon the latter devolved the
difficult task of dealing with the problems which arose in
connection with certain officers of the Regiment on its
being split up.

The old system had perhaps tended to keep the Royal
Artillery as a service too much apart from the rest of the
army, and it may not have been altogether sound in
principle.   But it worked well upon the whole.   That
substituted for it differed widely from the system which had
been adopted in India a dozen years earlier, on the occasion
when the appointment of D.A.G., R.A. was abolished and
when its functions were to a great extent merged in the
holder of the position of Inspector-General of Artillery.

Changes
in India.
The unification of the military forces in that country,
and the disappearance of the time-honoured Presidential
system in so far as it affected the troops, had been gradually accomplished under Sir F. Roberts' supervision
during the first half of the nineties.   The fighting forces
in India were now organized as four armies, stationed
respectively in the Punjab, in Bengal, in the Madras
Presidency and in the Bombay Presidency.   To each of

these armies had been allotted in 1895 a C.R.A., with the grading of brigadier-general and provided with a D.A.A.G. as staff officer. The Inspector-General of Artillery still occupied to some extent the position of C.R.A. over all, but without the title. The A.A.G's, R.A. in the Madras and Bombay Presidencies had disappeared, but there remained the A.A.G., R.A. on the staff of the Commander-in-Chief in India.

CHAPTER V.

Changes in India.

The senior officers of the Regiment had latterly been receiving decidedly more generous recognition in respect to appointment to army commands at home and in the colonies, than had been the case in years gone by. Their claims, as will be seen from the following details, were upon the whole being adequately met during the period with which this chapter deals. Improvement in this matter had also, it may be mentioned, come about as regards army staff appointments, although officers of the Regiment still scarcely obtained their fair share.[1]

Holders of high appointments at this time.

Lord Roberts had laid down the commandership-in-chief in India in 1893 after an eight years' tenure of the position; he was promoted Field-Marshal early in 1895, and towards the close of that year he succeeded Lord Wolseley as commanding the forces in Ireland. General Sir R. Biddulph acted as Quarter-Master-General for several months in 1893, and he then took up the appointment of Governor and Commander-in-Chief at Gibraltar. Major-General E. F. Chapman followed Lieutenant-General Brackenbury as Director of Military Intelligence in 1891; after holding that position for five years he was appointed to the command of the troops in Scotland.

Lieutenant-General W. H. Goodenough went out to South Africa to command the troops in 1894. Major-General B. L. Forster took over the command at Chatham

---

[1] "No never!" said another distinguished veteran when it was proposed to place one engineer and one artillery officer on the General Staff; "no never! If you place an artilleryman or an engineer on the General Staff of the Army it is the thin end of the wedge; they will never rest until they have driven out everybody else but themselves." See Colonel Jocelyn's *Crimean Period*, p. 42.

CHAPTER
V.

Holders
of high ap-
pointments
at this
time.

in 1892, and Major-General E. Markham became Governor and Commander-in-Chief in Jersey in the same year. Major-General A. H. W. Williams assumed command at Woolwich in 1893, where he was followed in 1895 by Major-General J. F. Maurice. Major-General H. le G. Geary took over the Belfast District in 1895. Major-General Sir H. M. L. Rundle (who had been promoted to that rank for distinguished service in 1896, after holding high appointments in the Egyptian Army) took up command of the South Eastern District in 1898. Major-General M. H. Saward became Governor and Commander-in-Chief in Jersey in 1899. Lieutenant-General Sir E. Markham was appointed Commandant of the R.M. College, Sandhurst, in 1898—a post usually reserved for general officers of cavalry or infantry. Colonel (local Major-General) G. A. French [1] was for a number of years Commandant of the forces in New South Wales.

In India, Lieutenant-General H. Brackenbury took up the post of Military Member of Council in 1891. Major-General C. E. Nairne, who had been Inspector-General of Artillery in India since 1887, took up command of a division in 1892; he was a year later transferred from this position to that of Commander-in-Chief in Bombay; he acted as Commander-in-Chief in India for several months in 1898. Besides certain officers mentioned in the last chapter whose terms of service had not yet expired, Brigadier-Generals E. R. Elles, A. G. Yeatman-Biggs and J. H. Wodehouse were given command of mixed brigades during the period covered by this chapter. Major-General T. Graham commanded the expeditionary force sent against the Manipuris in 1891, Major-General Yeatman-Biggs commanded one of the divisions which took part in the Tirah campaign in 1897-98, Brigadier-General Wodehouse commanded a brigade of the Malakand Field Force in 1897, and Major-General Elles commanded the Mohmand Field Force in 1897-98.

---

[1] The inventor of "French's Sights", so extensively used in the Siege Artillery.—see p. 284.

As regards purely regimental appointments, it should be mentioned that Major-General A. H. Williams succeeded Major-General Markham as D.A.G., R.A., in 1892 and that he was followed by Colonel (temporary Major-General) F. T. Lloyd in 1894, Major-General W. F. N. Hutchinson followed General Lloyd in 1897, but the appointment was, as we have seen, abolished in 1899. Major-General A. H. King took up command of the artillery at Aldershot in 1891, being succeeded at Malta by Major-General O. H. A. Nicolls, who however only held the appointment for a year, when he was followed by Major-General S. J. Nicholson. Major-General G. J. Smart became C.R.A. at Gibraltar in 1892, and he was succeeded by Colonel (temporary Major-General) J. B. Richardson in 1894. Major-General Nicholson was transferred from Malta to Portsmouth in 1895 and was followed by Major-General J. F. Owen. Major-General J. Alleyne succeeded Major-General King at Aldershot in 1893; he was followed by Major-General G. H. Marshall in 1898. Major-General R. M. Stewart became C.R.A. at Portsmouth in 1897, Major-General F. G. Slade at Gibraltar in 1898, and Major-General D. O'Callaghan at Malta in 1899. Colonel H. C. Lewes in 1892 succeeded Major-General Nairne as Inspector-General in India, with rank of major-general; he gave place five years later to Major-General T. B. Tyler. The artillery commands in the Punjab, Bengal and Bombay were made brigadier-generals' appointments in 1896 and Colonels T. B. Tyler, H. Pipon and C. Spragge respectively were selected to fill the posts; Colonel W. F. de H. Curtis succeeded General Tyler in 1897.

Although Sir Collingwood Dickson only passed away in the year 1904, this famous son of a famous father played so prominent a part in connection with the Regiment during the period from 1860 to 1899, and he was looked upon with such admiration within its ranks during the forty years, that it seems appropriate to include a brief biography of him in this chapter. The practice of indi-

cating Crimean and Mutiny veterans by the letters "C"
and "M" before their names in the *Army List* had not,
it may be observed, been adopted by the end of last
century.

Lieutenant-General Sir E. B. Hamley, K.C.B., K.C.M.G.,
was born in 1824, joined the Regiment in 1843, and turned
his attention to literature while still a lieutenant. He went
to the Crimea as adjutant to Lieutenant-Colonel R. Dacres,
was present at the battles of the Alma and Inkerman and
served through the siege of Sebastopol; he was awarded
brevets of major and lieut.-colonel for his services. He
was appointed the first professor of military history at the
newly created Staff College in 1859 and he held that position until 1866, when he became a member of the Council
of Military Education. It was then that he published his
great work *The Operations of War*. In 1870 he was appointed commandant of the Staff College and he remained
at Camberley until he was promoted major-general in 1877.
In the following year he was appointed British commissioner for the settlement of the Turko-Bulgarian frontier,
in 1880 he acted in a similar capacity in respect to the
Turkish frontier in Armenia, and in 1881 he dealt in like
manner with the Turko-Greek boundary in Thessaly and
Epirus. For his services in the near East he was given
the K.C.M.G. As mentioned in the last chapter, he commanded the 2nd Division during the Egyptian Expedition
of 1882; for this he received the thanks of Parliament and
the K.C.B. In 1886 he became M.P. for Birkenhead, and
a year later he was especially retained on the active list
although under regulations due for retirement owing to
non-employment. He died in 1893. He was the author
of several other books besides his famous military volume;
the diversity and brilliance of his literary power can best
be judged by a study of works so various as *Lady
Lee's Widowhood, Our Poor Relations* and *Shakespeare's
Funeral*.

General Sir D. E. Wood, G.C.B., was born in 1812,
joined the Regiment in 1829, and served in the Kaffir

war of 1842 as a 2nd captain. He went out with the
expeditionary force to Turkey in 1854 in command of the
artillery of the 4th Division, was present at Balaklava
and Inkerman and served during the siege of Sebastopol,
for which he received the c.b. and was promoted brevet
colonel. He went out to India in 1857 in command of the
R.H.A., was engaged in the action of Pandora, and, as a
brigadier, commanded the field artillery at the siege and
capture of Lucknow; he was awarded the k.c.b. for his
services. As mentioned in Chapter II he was appointed
commandant at Woolwich in 1869. He died in 1894.

Lieutenant-General Sir C. E. Nairne, k.c.b., was born
in 1836. He joined the Bengal Artillery from Addiscombe
in 1855 and served during the Indian Mutiny. He commanded a horse artillery battery with the Peshawar Valley
Field Force during the second phase of the Afghan War,
and he was in command of the horse artillery in the
Egyptian Campaign of 1882, being present at Kassassin
and Tel-el-Kebir. It was after returning from Egypt that
he especially identified himself with securing progress in
the training of the horse and field artillery, as is related
in Chapter X. He was Commandant of Shoeburyness
from 1885 to 1887, and he then proceeded to India to take
up the appointment of Inspector-General of Artillery.
After 18 months in command of a district in Bengal he
in 1894 became Commander-in-Chief in Bombay and he
then played an important part in promoting the merging
of the three Presidential armies into one. He was advanced to the rank of lieutenant-general in the year 1895
and he was given the k.c.b. in 1897. From March to
November 1898 he acted as Commander-in-Chief in India.
Returning to England at the end of 1898 he died early in
1899 when about to take up the appointment of President
of the Ordnance Committee.

General Sir Collingwood Dickson, V.C., g.c.b., was
born in 1817, son of Major-General Sir Alexander Dickson,
g.c.b., k.c.h., who had commanded the artillery in the
Peninsula. Joining the Regiment from the R.M. Academy

CHAPTER
V.

Some dis-
tinguished
figures
in the
Regiment.
in 1835 Collingwood Dickson was one of the young artillery
officers who served under de Lacy Evans against the
Carlists between 1837 and 1840.   He then went out to
Turkey as an instructor to the Ottoman artillery and he
served there four years; it was in consequence of this
that he joined Lord Raglan's staff as Turkish interpreter
at the outset of the Crimean War, with the rank of
captain and bt. lieut.-colonel.   He was at the Alma, where
he helped to work the two guns which were brought forward
into the heart of the Russian position and which caused
so great an effect.   Returning to regimental duty he took
over command of the right attack of the siege train at the
commencement of the siege of Sebastopol and he was
awarded the **V.C.** for gallant conduct on the 18th October,
1854.   On the day of Inkerman he brought up the 18 prs.
which exerted a decisive influence over the course of the
fight.   He was wounded early in 1854, but on returning
to duty took part in the Khertch expedition, and was afterwards attached to the Turkish contingent till the end of
the war, when he took over charge of Waltham Abbey
as a brevet colonel and c.b.   He was promoted major-
general in 1866 and, as mentioned in an earlier chapter
held the appointment of Inspector-General R.A. from 1870
to 1875, having been given the k.c.b. in 1871.   From 1877
to 1879 he was, as we have seen, military attaché at
Constantinople, having a number of attachés under him
during the progress of the Russo-Turkish war and during
the period of strained relations between the British and
Russian Governments in the early part of 1878.   He was
President of the Ordnance Committee from 1881 to 1885,
was given the g.c.b. in 1884, and was Master-Gunner, St.
James's Park, from the year 1891 to his death in 1904.

The dis-
tribution
of the
Royal
Artillery
at the be-
ginning of
September
1899.
The South African dispute came to a head within five
months of the splitting of the Regiment into two distinct
corps.   The story of the struggle which ensued will be
told in a later volume.   But as the first movement of
troops in connection with this was ordered early in September 1899, it will be appropriate to indicate the actual

distribution of the service units constituting the Royal Artillery on the 1st day of that month. Some figures showing the growth of the Regiment during the period with which this volume deals are also instructive.

Of the 21 R.H.A. batteries, 10 were stationed in the United Kingdom and 11 in India.

Of the 95 R.F.A. batteries then in existence, 49 were in the United Kingdom, 3 were in Natal and 1 was in Egypt. 3 of the batteries at home were armed with field howitzers.

Of the 10 mountain batteries, 1 was in the United Kingdom, 1 was in Natal, and the remaining 8 were in India.[1]

Of the 99 R.G.A. companies, 36 were stationed in the United Kingdom (4 of them siege companies) and 27 were stationed in India (3 of them siege companies and 4 of them fitted out with heavy-battery equipment). The remaining 36 were distributed as follows : 1, St. Helena; 1, Egypt; 2, Hong Kong; 1, Wei-hai-wei; 3, Ceylon; 2, Bermuda; 2, Singapore; 1, Jamaica; 1, St. Lucia; 2, Mauritius; 2, Cape; 1, Halifax; 1, Esquimalt; 7, Gibraltar; 9, Malta. The companies that were stationed abroad outside of India however varied considerably in establishment according to the station they were in; as was indicated on p. 124, a considerable proportion of them were virtually double companies.

CHAPTER V.

The distribution of the Royal Artillery at the beginning of September 1899.

---

[1] The native Indian mountain batteries at this time numbered nine. They were :—

> No. 1. (Kohat) Mountain Battery, Frontier Force.
> No. 2. (Derajat) Mountain Battery, Frontier Force.
> No. 3. (Peshawar) Mountain Battery, Frontier Force.
> No. 4. (Hazara) Mountain Battery, Frontier Force.
> No. 5. (Bombay) Mountain Battery.
> No. 6. (Jacob's) Mountain Battery.
> No. 7. (Gujrat) Mountain Battery.
> No. 8. (Lahore) Mountain Battery.
> No. 9. (Murree) Mountain Battery.

The last three had been raised since the amalgamation of the Indian artilleries with the R.A., the last of all had only been raised in 1898.

CHAPTER
V.

The distribution
of the
Royal
Artillery
at the beginning of
September
1899.

A comparison between these figures (reckoning mountain batteries, for convenience, as garrison artillery units) and the figures of the Regiment just before and just after the amalgamation of the three Indian regiments with it in 1861-62, is shown in the following table :—

Date.	Horse Artillery.	Field Artillery.	Garrison Artillery.
Before amalgamation ...	10	49	73
After amalgamation ...	29	73	88
September 1899 ...	21	95	109

A comparison between the number of officers borne on the strength of the Regiment at the beginning of 1862 after the amalgamation and the number in September 1899 is shown in the following table :—

	Lieut.-Colonels.	1st Captains Majors.	2nd Captains Captains.	Lieutenants and 2nd Lieutenants.
1862 ...	135	281	305	760
1899 ...	98[1]	323[1]	516[1]	864[1]

The great increase in the number of captains between 1862 and 1899 is largely accounted for by the growth in the figures of officers of that rank who were extra-regimentally employed, e.g., the adjutants of Militia and Volunteer Artillery, during the period.

[1] 45 R.F.A. and 53 R.G.A. lieut.-colonels; 145 R.F.A. and 178 R.G.A. majors; 244 R.F.A. and 272 R.G.A. captains; 390 R.F.A. and 474 R.G.A. subalterns.

PART II.

ARMAMENT.

By Sir CHARLES CALLWELL.

An "Armstrong" Gun.

Ordnance, R.B.L., 40 Pr., 35 Cwt.
Scale ⅛

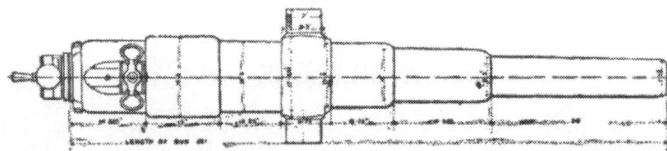

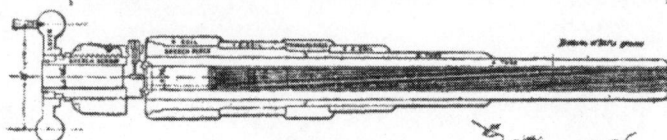

RIFLING UNIFORM RIGHT-HANDED TWIST
OF ⅓ TURN IN 38½ CALIBRES.

SECTION OF RIFLING (FULL SIZE)
38 GROOVES

CHAPTER VI.

1860 TO 1869.

CHAPTER VI.

1859-1860 years of extraordinary importance in the progress of artillery armament.

IN so far as the question of armament is concerned, this volume of *The History of the Royal Artillery* commences at a date of quite exceptional interest. The years 1859-1860 may be said to have synchronised roughly with the greatest step in advance in respect to its weapons taken by the Regiment in the whole course of its existence. For those two years saw our definite adoption of wrought-iron, built-up, rifled, breech-loading ordnance, discharging cylindrical projectiles, in substitution for cast-iron or bronze, smooth-bore, muzzle-loading ordnance, discharging forms of round shot or shell. Singularly little progress had hitherto been made in gun design and gun construction since the days of the Plantagenets and Tudors. Many improvements had been effected in reference to ammunition and to adjuncts since the first appearance of cannon on the battle-field, but very little advance had been made in actual ordnance either in this or in foreign countries.

It is true that cast-iron, muzzle-loading, smooth-bore

CHAPTER
VI.

1859-1860
years of
extra-
ordinary
import-
ance in the
progress of
artillery
armament.
68-prs. and 8-inch guns, converted into rifled ordnance on the Lancaster principle,[1] had been tried before Sebastopol —the first rifled guns ever made use of in war. They had not however proved a success. But it was due to the enterprise and to the inventive genius of Mr. (afterwards Lord) Armstrong that the plan of building up guns on scientific principles out of wrought-iron coils shrunk on to an inner tube, was devised. This was moveover combined with rifling the bore of the piece, as well as with introducing a system of breech-loading which, if far from ideal according to our notions and experiences of to-day, produced none the less a quite serviceable armament for the time being. Thanks to the famous Tyneside civil engineer, the United Kingdom originated and adopted methods of ordnance construction at this juncture which, with certain modifications, came to be followed almost universally abroad, and which in reality form the basis of the methods of ordnance construction which prevail in this country to-day. The 12-pr. R.B.L., and the 7-inch R.B.L. may seem contemptible when contrasted with the 18-pr. Q.F., and the 9·2-inch B.L., which were at the disposal of the Royal Artillery in 1914. But they were weapons of relatively great power as compared with the armament that had been employed by the Regiment during the Crimean War only four years before their introduction.

The Armstrong design, which had first been produced in experimental form with a 3-pr. gun in the year 1854, was definitely accepted for the Royal Artillery in January of 1859. Contracts for the production of large numbers of 12-prs. were thereupon entered into with the newly formed Elswick Ordnance Company, and steps were also at the same time taken to manufacture this equipment in the Royal Arsenal under the guidance of Sir W. Armstrong, who had been appointed Superintendent of the Royal Gun

---

[1] In the Lancaster gun the bore was in the form of a twisted (or spiral) ellipse—that is to say, it was oval in section. The projectile conformed in shape, filling the bore mechanically.

Factory. The result was that before the end of 1860 a
number of field batteries were already fitted out with the
new breech-loading rifled equipment, and that this country
for the moment took the lead in furnishing its mobile
artillery with a modern weapon. Besides the manufacture
of the 12-pr. equipment, that of 6-prs., 20-prs., 40-prs.,
and 7-inch guns after the same design was taken in hand,
although the heavier natures, it is true, were in the first
instance intended mainly for the sea service. Batteries
fitted out with the 12-pr. R.B.L.[1] Armstrong gun were
employed in action in China in 1860, where they gave
satisfaction, and the 6-pr. R.B.L. Armstrong gun was used
in the field against the Maoris in New Zealand in the year
1863.

Seeing that these Armstrong guns were the first rifled,
breech-loading pieces to be introduced into our service, and
that a large proportion of our horse and field batteries were
equipped with them during a period extending over a
number of years, a brief description of their general design
will not be out of place.[2] In all breech-loading firearms,
be they muskets or be they cannon, the first problem that
presents itself is how to close the breech. Under the
Armstrong system the breech was closed by means of a
"vent-piece" (so called because the vent passed through it),
which was a block of wrought-iron that fitted into a slot or
opening in the top of the breech end of the gun. It was
dropped in and lifted out from above, and was pressed
home against the chamber of the gun by means of a
"breech-screw". This breech-screw fitted into threads cut
in the breech end of the gun, it was worked backwards or
forwards by a lever, and it was bored hollow so as to allow
of the charge being passed through it from the rear into
the chamber of the gun after the vent-piece had been
lifted out. The joint was rendered gas-tight by copper

---

[1] The Armstrong guns were at first distinguished as "B.L.R." guns.
This nomenclature was afterwards changed to "R.B.L."

[2] See the diagram facing p. 143, and the photograph facing p. 43.

CHAPTER
VI.

The
Armstrong
R.B.L.
guns.

rings, one affixed to the face of the vent-piece and the other
screwed into the bore of the gun.   The rifling of the gun
was polygroove; the projectile was coated with lead, which
coating made it slightly larger than the bore of the gun;
and to allow for this the bore at the breech end was made
slightly larger in diameter than elsewhere.   On shock of
discharge the force of explosion drove the projectile along
the bore, compressing its soft coating into the grooves of
rifling and by this means imparting to it the required
rotatory motion.

Whereas the vent-piece in the case of the 12-pr. only
weighed 15 lbs., and was therefore easily lifted out and
dropped in by a single man, the vent-piece of the 40-pr.
weighed 59 lbs., and that of the 7-inch weighed $1\frac{1}{4}$ cwt.
Experience speedily proved that the arrangement as regards
a removable vent-piece did not work satisfactorily in the
case of ordnance of above the 20-pr. type; only relatively
small charges could safely be used with the 7-inch R.B.L.
A wedge, side-closing device was within a year or two
adopted for 40-prs. R.B.L. and also for a 64-pr. R.B.L.
which was designed and introduced for the sea service in
1864. $2\frac{1}{2}$ millions sterling were expended on breech-loading ordnance and its equipage for the two services in the
four years 1859-1862.

Rifled
small-arms
introduced
at an
earlier
date.

The advantages arising from rifling firearms had, it
should be understood, been realised in England and on the
Continent for many years before the introduction of the
Armstrong guns into our service.   Those advantages had
indeed received practical recognition in the case of small-
arms in this country so early as the year 1851, when a
rifled muzzle-loading musket, the Minié, was introduced
to some extent; this was superseded in 1855 by the Enfield
muzzle-loading rifle, which weapon was largely used towards the close of the Crimean War and in the Mutiny.
In so far as the breech-loading principle is concerned, this
had received recognition as adapted to small arms so far
back as the year 1841 in Prussia, for it was in that year
that that country adopted the famous "needle-gun" which

thanks to the rapidity of its fire played so important a part in the campaigns of 1864 and 1866 in Denmark and Bohemia. But it is noteworthy, as perhaps to some extent accounting for the fact that the breech-loading principle was not generally adopted sooner for small arms nor yet for ordnance, that the Prussian needle-gun fell far short, in respect to accuracy and range, of our Enfield rifle, as also of muzzle-loading rifles that were in use in most Continental armies during the sixties. The backward state of metallurgy and of mechanism prior to about the year 1860 can perhaps be accepted as a valid excuse for the delay in introducing the principle of rifling for ordnance in this and other countries. Rifled guns of a sort had been produced on the Continent so far back as the seventeenth century : but, owing to lack of suitable materials and of proper machinery, nothing really serviceable had ever been turned out.

In tracing the progress made respectively in regard to small arms and to ordnance immediately subsequent to 1860, it is worth noting that the United Kingdom and also most foreign countries hastened to adopt breech-loading rifles for military purposes after the Prussian victories in 1866, as they had produced such rapid and destructive fire in action. But, as will be seen later, the United Kingdom in that very year 1866, virtually decided to abandon the breech-loading system in favour of the muzzle-loading system for guns. And one important factor in bringing about this seemingly reactionary decision was that it was found after exhaustive experiments that the Armstrong R.B.L. 12-pr. was less rapid in firing than was a specially designed Armstrong muzzle-loading gun of the same calibre.

Thus doubts arose somewhat early after the introduction of the Armstrong gun into the British service as to the relative merits of the breech-loading as compared to the muzzle-loading system, while there still lingered differences of opinion as to the superiority of rifled over smooth-bore ordnance for all purposes. In evidence before a Select

CHAPTER VI.

Rifled small-arms introduced at an earlier date.

Many smooth-bore guns still in the service during the 1860-1869 period.

CHAPTER
VI.

Many
smooth-
bore guns
still in the
service
during the
1860-1869
period.

Committee of the House of Commons in 1862 Colonel
Charles Bingham, D.A.G., R.A., stated that while pre-
ferring the new Armstrong guns for field artillery generally,
he considered the old smooth-bores preferable for horse
artillery attached to cavalry where the range was seldom
more than 200 or 300 yards, and simplicity and rapidity
were all important.   Colonel W. B. Gardner, Chief Instructor of the School of Gunnery, went further and stated
that he would like to see a great proportion of smooth-bore
guns retained in the service for field artillery generally,
supporting his opinion by the experience of the civil war
in America, and maintaining it under cross-examination
even at the disadvantage of having two descriptions of
artillery with the field army, and taking into consideration
the increase in the range of rifled small-arms.   In spite
of such individual expressions of opinion[1] there can be
little doubt that the time-honoured smooth-bore guns and
howitzers and mortars that were in use by the Regiment for
coast defence in the year 1860, would have speedily given
place to rifled pieces, but for the vast cost which such re-
armament would necessarily have involved.   While Armstrong guns were turned out in large numbers for arming
the R.H.A. and our field batteries, it took years before the
smooth-bores, with their spherical shot, their grape, and

---

[1] Sir A. Noble (to whom reference will be again made later) used to
tell a story which deserves to be repeated here.   He was trying to convince an officer of the Regiment of high rank and great distinction, who
was holding a prominent position in connection with problems of
armament, that a certain rifled gun was more accurate than a corresponding smooth-bore gun.   So he
produced a diagram (as shown) displaying the relative
sizes of the "25% rectangles" produced by the fire of
the two pieces at a given range—"R." representing
the shooting of the rifled gun and "S.B." that of its
rival.
  "That only proves that I have been right in what I
have always maintained" rejoined the eminent gunner.
"Our S.B. is the finest gun in the world.   With your
new-fangled gun firing at one, one only has to keep
outside of the space R. and one won't be touched.
But with the S.B. gun firing at one *One is'nt safe anywhere!*"   Sir
A Noble always frankly acknowledged that this aspect of the question
had not before occured to him.

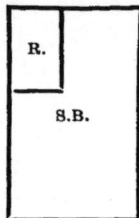

their carcasses, ceased to find place in the armament of the numerous British fortresses existing within the confines of the United Kingdom and in foreign parts.   During the whole of the succeeding decade, and indeed for several years later, an immense number of different types and calibres of smooth-bore ordnance, with their various forms of carriage and mounting and their divers antiquated paraphernalia, remained officially recognised.

A Royal Commission, already referred to on p. 95, had assembled in 1859 to report upon the question of defences for dockyards and naval stations at home, and this reported in February, 1860.   Its recommendations were in the main accepted by the Government, and a Bill was introduced and passed towards the end of the session in Parliament authorising the necessary expenditure.   The consequence was that, not only were the existing coast batteries defending the approaches to Portsmouth, Plymouth, the Thames, etc., modernised and added to, but the elaborate system of land forts defending Portsmouth and Plymouth was decided upon and these costly works were shortly afterwards commenced.   In the plans then adopted, the certain eventual supersession of smooth-bores by rifled ordnance was fortunately provided for.   The policy decided upon had moreover the effect of attracting attention to the need of progress in ordnance of a heavier nature than what was required for service in the field.   As has already been mentioned in Chapter I, the acceptance of the Royal Commission's Report, gave rise to an immediate increase in the strength of the garrison artillery at home.

The armament of British horse and field batteries was, as we have seen, in a transition state in the year 1860,[1] The situation at the end of that year may however be summed up as follows :—all horse artillery batteries serving on the home establishment were still armed with four smooth-bore 9-prs. and two 24-pr. smooth-bore howitzers;

Marginal notes: Chapter VI. Many smooth-bore guns still in the service during the 1860-1869 period. Development of fixed defences in the United Kingdom after 1860. Armament of horse and field artillery during this period.[1]

---

[1] Appendix C shows the number of horse and field batteries armed with each nature of gun in use on five dates between 1860 and 1899.

Chapter
VI.

Armament
of horse
and field
artillery
during this
period.

for this equipment one of six 9-pr. R.B.L. Armstrong guns
was substituted in the year 1862.[1]   The majority of the
field batteries on the home establishment were in 1860 still
armed with four smooth-bore 9-prs. and two 24-pr. smooth-
bore howitzers, like the horse artillery; but this equipment
was rapidly being exchanged for one of six 12-pr. R.B.L.
Armstrong guns,[2] In so far as position artillery was concerned the 20-pr. and the 40-pr. R.B.L. Armstrong guns
had not yet been introduced into the land service, except
experimentally; so that in that year, and immediately subsequently, the Army still had to depend for its position
artillery upon the smooth bore types—18-pr., 24-pr., and
32-pr. guns; 8-inch howitzers; 8-inch and 10-inch mortars.

The rifled gun possessed, it should be mentioned, one
merit as compared with the smooth-bore gun—a very important merit from the point of view of horse and field
artillery.   This was that, weight for weight of the projectile fired, the rifled gun was much lighter than the smooth-
bore one.   That this was so is shown clearly in the
following comparative table :—

Nature of gun.		Bore of gun in inches.	Weight of gun in cwt.
6-pr.	S.B.	3·66	6
	R.B.L.	2·5	3
9-pr.	S.B.	4·2	13
	R.B.L.	3	6
12-pr.	S.B.	4·62	18
	R.B.L.	3	8

Batteries armed with the 9-pr. S.B. required gun-teams
of eight horses, whereas batteries armed with the 9-pr.

---

[1] This 9-pr. was of the same calibre as the 12-pr. but was shorter,
and it fired a shorter projectile, with a smaller charge.

[2] The replacing of smooth-bores by rifled ordnance was a much
slower process in India. In January 1867, for instance, 14 R.H.A.
batteries in that country were still armed with the 6-pr. S.B., and 39
field batteries were still armed with the 9-pr. S.B.

R.B.L. and the 12-pr. R.B.L. only required gun-teams of six horses.[1]

The acceptance of the Armstrong gun as that best suited to our requirements did not prevent a continuation of the experiments with various forms of rifling, which had been in progress in this country ever since the Crimean War. Amongst the various systems that came into notice in the course of these investigations, was the French plan, which consisted in a limited number of shallow grooves in the bore of the gun, and of rows of studs let into the side of the projectile corresponding to the grooves. This plan differed essentially from the Armstrong design, in that it could be employed with muzzle loading pieces. In this French plan, as in use about 1860, the studs were made of zinc; but the Ordnance Select Committee found after experiments that gun-metal studs were preferable to zinc studs. Such satisfactory results were obtained from using this system of studded projectiles with rifled muzzle-loading guns of experimental type, that, almost before our horse and field artillery had been fully equipped with the 9-pr. and the 12-pr. Armstrong guns, and before any serious attempt had been made to replace the smooth-bore guns in our fortresses by Armstrong breech-loading pieces, the adoption of the system of built-up, wrought-iron, muzzle-loading guns for all types of artillery heavier than the 40-pr. was finding favour. Force was given to this movement by the fact that the 7-inch R.B.L. Armstrong gun did not prove altogether a success, and by the further fact that, already early in the sixty decade, it was foreseen that guns of even larger bore than the 7-inch were becoming a necessity. The Armstrong breech-action was also found by experience to be cumbrous and slow, as well as somewhat insecure.[2] The consequence was that a special committee

CHAPTER
VI.

The
muzzle-
loading
versus the
breech-
loading
principle.

---

[1] Appendix D gives the main particulars of each nature of gun and howitzer with which horse and field batteries were armed between 1860 and 1899.

[2] Ordnance Committee Minutes of the time are full of complaints from battery commanders, who apparently kept "Armstrong Diaries" for the express purpose of recording defects.

CHAPTER
VI.

The
muzzle-
loading
versus the
breech-
loading
principle.

was appointed on the 1st of June 1863, with instructions
to examine and report upon different descriptions of guns
and ammunition which had been proposed respectively by
Sir W. Armstrong and Mr. (afterwards Sir J.) Whitworth.[1]

This committee carried out prolonged and exhaustive
competitive experiments as between Whitworth muzzle-
loading 12-prs. and 70-prs., Armstrong R.B.L. 12-prs.
and 70-prs., and specially designed muzzle-loading 12-prs.
and 70-prs. produced for the purpose by Elswick.   The
Whitworth guns had hexagonal bores and mechanically
fitting projectiles, while the specially designed Elswick
guns were rifled on the French system with studded projectiles.   The committee did not report until the 3rd of
August 1865, and they then declared :—"That the breech-
loading gun is far inferior as regards simplicity of construction to either of the M.L. guns and cannot be compared
to them in this important respect in efficiency for active
service . . . .   That both Sir W. Armstrong's and Mr.
Whitworth's muzzle-loading systems, including gun and
ammunition, are on the whole far superior to Sir W.
Armstrong's breech-loading system for the service of
artillery in the field . . . .   That the many-grooved
system of rifling with its lead-coated projectiles and complicated breech-loading arrangements, entailing the use of
tin cups and lubricators,[2] is far inferior for the general
purpose of war to both the M.L. systems, and has the
disadvantage of being more expensive both in original cost
and ammunition.   That M.L. guns can be loaded and
worked with perfect ease and abundant rapidity."   These
remarks referred alike to field guns and to heavier natures.
Although the report of this committee exercised no immediate influence in the direction of bringing about a fresh
re-armament of the horse and field artillery, it did help to
establish the principle that ordnance of a heavier nature

---

[1] Sir J. Whitworth was a great scientist and inventor, the result of
whose labours in connection with gun design and gun construction
rivalled what was accomplished by Sir W. Armstrong.

[2] The tin cups were only used in the case of the 64-pr. R.B.L. and
the 7-inch R.B.L.

must henceforward be of a muzzle loading type, with few grooves for rifling purposes in the bore of the piece, and with rotation given to the projectile by means of studs. The plan actually adopted after experiments, and which came to be known as the Woolwich system of rifling, was that of having only three grooves—a wide departure from the polygroove design which was a feature of the Armstrong guns.[1]

A fresh committee, with Sir R. Dacres as president, was set up in 1866 to investigate the subject yet further, especially in connection with the field gun. This committee in due course reported that "the balance of advantages is in favour of M.L. field guns", and it recommended their adoption. By many, unacquainted with the actual facts, the reversion from the breech-loading to the muzzle-loading system, which these committees brought about, has been regarded as a retrograde step on the part of the Royal Artillery. But the step was taken as a result of trials which had been most exhaustive, in which the muzzle-loaders had held their own on most counts—range, accuracy, rapidity of fire—and in which they had won on the important counts of simplicity and of cost.

Reference was made above to the financial obstacles to the provision of an armament more powerful than the smooth-bore ordnance that was employed for coast defence purposes in 1860. It has to be remembered in this connection that the period just about that year synchronized with a departure of vast importance in the construction of ships of war. The first sea-going, armoured, iron ship to

CHAPTER
VI.

The
muzzle-
loading
versus the
breech-
loading
principle.

Conse-
quences
of the in-
troduction
of armour
for ships.

---

[1] The "new-fangled" ideas that had gained approval in the Regiment with regard to rifled guns, and so forth, were not universally popular in its ranks, and were looked upon with profound suspicion amongst some of its senior members. One very distinguished veteran, who had performed good and gallant service in the Kaffir and Crimean Wars, and who had played a prominent role in the Mutiny, used to grumble:—"First of all they insisted on having a lot of grooves in the bore of the gun. Now they are only going to have three grooves in the bore of the gun. Please goodness, they will next have no grooves at all, and we shall get back to the good old smooth-bores which did all that was necessary to beat the Russians and to smash the Mutiny."

CHAPTER
VI.

Conse-
quences
of the in-
troduction
of armour
for ships.

The intro-
duction of
heavy
R.M.L.
guns.

be designed—*La Gloire*—was launched in France in 1859,
and this significant event was followed in December 1860
by the launching in the Thames of the first British ironclad—*H.M.S. Warrior.*   A number of wooden warships
intended for the Royal Navy were moreover provided with
armour between the years 1860 and 1865.   The introduction of armour for fighting ships created automatically the
demand for a great increase in power of ordnance for sea
service.   The need was met by the introduction of a 64-pr.
R.M.L. gun of 64 cwt. in 1864, and of a 7-inch R.M.L.
gun of $6\frac{1}{2}$ tons, an 8-inch R.M.L. gun of 9 tons, and a
9 inch R.M.L. gun of 12 tons in 1865.   Within a year or
two, some of the earlier marks of these different types
were allotted to the Royal Artillery.[1]   The 10 inch R.M.L.
gun of 18 tons was introduced for the Royal Navy in the
year 1868, and later marks of this type were to play an
important part in the armament of our coast defences in
the years to come; but up to the year 1870 very few had
been devoted to land service.

The Armstrong R.B.L. guns, it should be mentioned,
were built up on the principle of having a large number of
comparatively thin coils.   In 1867, however, a plan devised
by Mr. R. S. Fraser of the Royal Gun Factory, was introduced of depending instead upon a very few heavy coils.
This appreciably reduced the cost of manufacture, and all
the heavier R.M.L. guns of calibres already introduced,
as also yet heavier R.M.L. ordnance to be introduced a few
years later, were built up after this Fraser model.   Thus,
while the 7-inch R.B.L. gun (a 110 pr.) had six coils, the
10-inch R.M.L. (a 400-pr.) only had the one coil, besides
an outer tube strengthening the chase.   Some guns of
larger calibre than those above mentioned were experimented with between 1865 and 1869, but only a very few
such were actually turned out, and none had been adopted
by the end of 1869.

---

[1] In all later marks of these guns steel was used in place of wrought-
iron for the inner tube.

The wants of the Navy have always in this country, very properly, been the first consideration while coast defence has taken second place, so that the introduction of these various heavy muzzle-loading rifled types affected the land service only very gradually. This was partly because the guns were required for warships, but still more because the necessary funds for a re-armament of coast fortresses at a rapid rate were not at the disposal of the War Office. The question of converting some of the old cast-iron smooth-bore guns that were available in large numbers into rifled ordnance had, in the meantime, received attention, and in the year 1863 Captain (afterwards Major Sir William) Palliser[1] proposed a plan of lining cast-iron guns with wrought-iron tubes. A number of guns, so converted, were experimented with during the ensuing five years. Conversion on a large scale was finally decided upon in 1868, with the result that by the year 1870 many of the more important batteries in British coast fortresses were, in default of built-up R.M.L. guns of more powerful type, armed with these improvised rifled pieces. S.B. 32-prs. were converted into rifled 64 prs. and 8-inch S.B. were also converted into rifled 64-prs; S.B. 68-prs. (10-inch) were converted into 80-prs.; the rifling selected was in each case of the "Woolwich" pattern intended for studded projectiles. Many hundreds of old smooth-bore pieces that had become practically useless as they stood were by this means transformed into reasonably serviceable fortress and coast defence guns. They were however necessarily on the light side for the purposes which they were intended to fulfil, the 80-pr. (the heaviest) falling considerably short of the built-up R.M.L. 7-inch gun, which fired a 115 pound shell, and still shorter of the R.M.L. 8-inch, which fired a 180 pound shell.

Reverting to the lighter types of ordnance which came into use in this 1860-69 period—guns intended for work in the field and mounted on travelling carriages—some

Chapter VI.

The converted smooth-bores.

Mountain guns of this period.

---

[1] A Cavalry officer of inventive genius who had started his service in the Rifle Brigade.

CHAPTER
VI.

Mountain
guns of
this period.

reference must in the first place be made to mountain
artillery.   In the year 1860, and during the following four
or five years, a mountain battery was supposed to be armed
with four smooth-bore 3-prs. and two smooth-bore $4\frac{2}{5}$-inch
howitzers, and this actually formed the armament of the
native Indian mountain batteries which took part in the
Ambela campaign.   The 6-pr. R.B.L. Armstrong gun had
originally been designed as a portable gun; but its weight
(3 cwt.) was found excessive for the purpose; it was in fact
never used as a typical mountain gun, but was employed
instead as a light field gun for Colonial service, notably in
New Zealand, and, carried on elephants, in Bhootan.   In
view of Ambela experiences, some bronze S.B. 3-prs. were
in 1865 hastily bored out to 3-inch calibre and rifled to take
part in the second phase of the Bhootan campaign.   Others
of these bronze guns were turned down so as to reduce their
weight, and were similarly bored out and rifled.   So converted pieces were supplied to one of the batteries taking
part in the Abyssinian Expedition and were used on the
Red River Expedition of 1870.   Some steel, rifled, muzzle-
loading 7-prs. were however constructed in 1866, and
twelve of them were used as mountain artillery during the
Abyssinian Expedition of 1868.   An improved pattern of
this particular piece moreover became the approved pattern
of mountain gun for India shortly afterwards, and it
remained so for several years.

Proposals
to revert
to muzzle-
loaders in
the field
artillery.

The Dacres Committee had, as we have seen, pronounced itself uncompromisingly in favour of the muzzle-
loading as opposed to the breech-loading system of ordnance for field and horse artillery.   Owing however to the
very heavy outlay which a re-armament would involve,
and to the fact that the question came to a head just at
the very time when the substitution of the Armstrong guns
for the old smooth-bores had been completed at home, no
steps were taken for the moment towards carrying out this
fresh change.   Experiments were nevertheless set on foot
in 1869, and a 9-pr. R.M.L., constructed of bronze, was
definitely approved in that year as the field gun for India,

where many of the horse and field batteries were still CHAPTER
VI. equipped with smooth-bores. There was also some question of introducing this bronze piece for service at home, but the project never materialized. The adoption of bronze for India was largely the outcome of a desire that our great Asiatic dependency should be placed in a position to produce its own material, the casting of a bronze gun being naturally a much simpler undertaking than the building up of a wrought-iron gun. Actual issue of the bronze equipment did not begin before 1870.

Proposals to revert to muzzle-loaders in the field artillery.

Great changes were of necessity carried out during this 1860-1869 period in regard to ammunition, seeing that elongated projectiles took the place of spherical ones. The projectiles introduced with the Armstrong breech-loading guns were segment shell, common shell and case shot. The segment variety were thin, cast-iron shell, inside of which were placed a number of rows of cast-iron segments round a cavity which enclosed the bursting charge. On explosion, the burst had all-round effect; and these projectiles in fact proved effective in the Maori wars, where attacks on stockades played an important part in the proceedings, for they burst as they passed through the stockading and the segments then dealt havoc amongst the defenders lining the inside. A shrapnel shell was however devised in the year 1865 for the various patterns of R.B.L. guns by Colonel E. M. Boxer, R.A., Superintendent of the Royal Laboratory.[1]

Progress in respect to gun ammunition.

---

[1] This distinguished inventor and officer of the Regiment had, while still a captain and after serving in a subordinate position in the Royal Arsenal, been made Superintendent of the Royal Laboratory during the Crimean War. His achievements there have been referred to by Colonel Jocelyn in his History of the Regiment during that period. He was given a fresh term of five years as Superintendent of the Royal Laboratory at the end of 1859, having by that time arrived at the rank of lieutenant-colonel.

At the end of 1864, now a full colonel, he was granted a yet further term of five years in his position at the head of this portion of the Royal Arsenal, and he remained in charge of it till the year 1869. In him inventive genius was combined with boundless energy and with a most effectual driving force. During his prolonged term of control all manner of new devices in connection with artillery ammunition—many, if not most, of them of his own design—were turned

CHAPTER
VI.

Progress
in respect
to gun
ammu-
nition.

But another very troublesome problem had also to be
solved in connection with projectiles during this period, as
a consequence of the introduction of armour for ships of
war.   Some form of armour-piercing shot or shell was
rendered a necessity by this development.   As had been
the case in the matter of converting old, cast-iron, smooth-
bore guns into rifled ordnance, Major Palliser came to the
assistance of the Ordnance Select Committee in their
difficulties.   He advocated the plan of casting the projectile
head downwards, with the head in an iron mould, a process
which chilled, and in doing so, hardened the head. Palliser
shot and shell consequently came to be a cardinal feature
in the ammunition approved for the various natures of
R.M.L. ordnance of 7-inch calibre and upwards, which
were being introduced into the sea and the land service.

No small progress was likewise made in respect to fuzes
during this period.   Most important perhaps were two new
patterns of wooden time fuze intended respectively for
R.B.L. and for R.M.L. ordnance—modifications of the
wooden time fuze devised by Captain Boxer in 1854 for
spherical shrapnel which had proved so useful in the Crimea
and during the Indian Mutiny.   The earlier types of this
wooden time fuze had been set in action by the flame which
surrounded the projectile on discharge from a smooth-bore
gun.   But, as there was no windage in an Armstrong gun
and therefore no flame surrounding the projectile, Colonel
Boxer invented a special detonator to be inserted in the
head of the fuze, which set the fuze in action on discharge ;
the device did not however give complete satisfaction, and
the detonating composition was moreover found to deterior-

out, and were by practical experience in the hands of the Royal Navy
and the Royal Artillery found to be highly satisfactory.
    In the closing years of his career in the Royal Arsenal his relations
with the War Office became somewhat strained.   A difference of
opinion arose as to how far Boxer was entitled to financial recognition
for some inventions of his which had been adopted for the services.
The official view put forward was that these inventions had been
arrived at in the course of duty—the same point has arisen in connection with other officers holding positions in the manufacturing and
similar departments.

ate in the climate of India.   The other new type of wooden
time fuze was intended for R.M.L. guns; it was set in
action by the flame on discharge, and it came to be the
generally recognized pattern of time fuze used in the land
service in years to come after the reversion to muzzle-
loading guns took place.   More trustworthy forms of percussion fuze than had been available before the introduction
of rifled ordnance were also adopted during this 1860-1869
period, during which the Royal Laboratory was kept very
busy.

Some reference is necessary here to the question of
the forms of propellant in use.   This question had offered
little difficulty in the days of smooth-bore ordnance.
Ordinary black gunpowder of finest grain—actual powder,
in fact—served the purpose quite satisfactorily.   The
spherical projectile was so light, relatively to the calibre of
the piece, and (owing to there being no rifling) there was
so little resistance to the motion of the projectile in the
bore on the explosion of the charge, that a very rapid
burning propellant, such as black powder was, did all that
was required.   But on the introduction of rifling, and of
elongated projectiles of relatively greater weight for a given
calibre, a somewhat slower rate of burning became desirable.   The difficulty was met by manufacturing the black
powder in the form of fine gravel rather than in the form of
powder, the size of the grains of gravel being increased
as guns grew larger and as the charges grew correspond-
ingly heavier till they came to be pellets and pebbles.[1]
The problem of producing a really slow-burning propellant
had however hardly become urgent by the end of the year
1869.   The actual ingredients of the powder used, as also

---

[1] In the case of "L.G.", the powder used in the R.B.L. guns and
in the R.M.L. guns introduced into the land service between 1864 and
1869, the grain would pass through a sieve of $\frac{1}{4}$ inch mesh but was
retained by one of $\frac{1}{16}$ inch mesh.   Powders of larger grain, "R.L.G."
and "Pebble", had been introduced into the sea service by the end of
1869.   The R.L.G. powder would pass through a sieve of 4 meshes to
the inch, but it was retained by one of 8 meshes to the inch.   Pebble
powder would pass through a sieve of $\frac{5}{8}$ inch meshes, but was retained
by one of $\frac{1}{2}$ inch meshes.

their respective proportions (75 p.c. saltpetre, 10 p.c. sulphur and 15 p.c. charcoal), remained in the meantime the same as had been accepted in this country since the middle of the eighteenth century.

The remarkable advances made in respect to gun design and to gun construction subsequent to the year 1860 necessarily demanded corresponding advances in respect to the design and construction of gun-carriages and of the mountings for the heavier types of ordnance. Wood constituted the principal material used in the putting together of field carriages in the year 1860, and this lasted during the subsequent decade. Manufacturers were however before the year 1869 recognizing that wrought-iron was preferable to wood as material for the trail and the axletree of a travelling gun-carriage, and the one designed to carry the bronze 9-pr. R.M.L. gun which was approved for India, was constructed almost entirely of iron.[1] Wood remained the main material out of which mountings for fortress and coast defence guns of below 6 tons in weight were fashioned, although some wrought-iron carriages were especially introduced as mountings for medium guns to be used in climates where wood was liable to rapid decay. For the heavier natures of R.M.L. guns that were being introduced from 1865 onwards, on the other hand—the 7-inch, the 8-inch and the 9-inch—both the carriage and the slide were constructed mainly of wrought-iron. It should be added that in the case of the mountings for these heavier classes of ordnance, the principle of the hydraulic buffer for recoil-checking purposes was beginning to be applied in place of older and cruder devices—a reform which constituted a great step in advance.

Hale's war rockets still formed a part of Royal Artillery equipment at this time, and practice was occasionally carried out with them. There were two kinds in the ser-

---

[1] The carriages of the 12-pr. R.B.L. and the 20-pr. R.B.L. had a traversing arrangement capable of giving 3° deflection to the gun on either side; it did not however work altogether satisfactorily, and no device for traversing formed part of the various field gun carriages approved between 1869 and 1880.

vice :—the 9-pr., intended for work in the field, and the
24-pr., which formed part of the siege equipment.

Reference has been made in the course of this chapter
to the Ordnance Select Committee. This body was composed in 1860, and during the immediately succeeding
years, almost entirely of officers of the Regiment, chosen
on the grounds of their technical attainments. The President of the Committee in 1860 was Colonel J. St. George,
and its Secretary was Lieut.-Colonel J. H. Lefroy.[1] The
Vice-president of the Committee was an officer of the Royal
Navy, and one of the members for a short time was
Captain A. Noble.[2] Colonel Lefroy succeeded to the

---

[1] *Major-General Sir J. H. Lefroy*, K.C.M.G., C.B., F.R.S., was born
in 1817 and joined the Regiment in 1834. Together with Lieutenant
(afterwards Major-General F. M.) Eardley-Wilmot, he was largely
concerned in the creation of the R.A. Institution, and he was its first
Secretary. A pioneer of magnetic research under Sabine, he, after
joining the Toronto observatory in 1842 where he served for eleven
years, carried out vast surveying operations about Hudson's Bay, resuming the position of Secretary of the R.A. Institution in 1853. He
shortly afterwards produced his *Handbook for Field Service*, which
went through several editions, and which served to some extent as the
model on which *Wolseley's Pocket Book*, appearing in 1869, was based.
He became the Duke of Newcastle's confidential adviser on artillery
matters in 1854, and in 1856 he was invited to prepare a detailed
scheme of military education for the authorities. In 1858 he prepared
a paper urging the establishment of a School of Gunnery, and his
suggestions were shortly afterwards adopted. In 1859 he was a
member of the Royal Commission on the Defence of the United
Kingdom, after which he became, first Secretary and then President,
of the Ordnance Select Committee. In 1868 he was appointed
Director-General of Ordnance, and he then created the "Advanced
Class". He retired as a major-general in 1870, and in 1871 was
appointed Governor and C.-in-C., Bermuda. He was Governor of
Tasmania from 1880 to 1882. He died in 1890.

[2] *Sir Andrew Noble, Bart.*, G.C.B., F.R.S., was born in 1832 and
joined the Regiment in 1849. He was promoted Captain in 1855,
became Secretary of the R.A. Institution in the year 1857, and acted
as Secretary of the Select Committee on Rifled Cannon set up in the
year 1858. He joined the Ordnance Select Committee in 1860, and
he was then being brought much into contact with Sir W. Armstrong
then Superintendent of the Royal Gun Factory, who prevailed upon
him to retire from the army and to join the Elswick establishment.
This however by no means closed his connection with the Regiment,
although that connection necessarily became indirect instead of direct.
At Elswick he was at the outset placed in charge of its ordnance
department; but his inventive genius and his rare business capacity
caused him gradually to become the leading spirit in this great industrial concern and to succeed to the chairmanship. He was given

M

CHAPTER VI.

Responsibility for progress.

Presidency in 1865 ; but the Committee was abolished two years later—only to be revived in the year 1881 (as will be mentioned in the ensuing chapter) under the title of the "Ordnance Committee."

One of the duties of the President of the Ordnance Select Committee in 1860—and a very important one—was that of acting as adviser to the Secretary of State for War on artillery and armaments. He was relieved from this responsibility in the following year owing to the creation of the appointment of Director of Ordnance, Major-General A. Tulloh, R.A. being the first to fill the post; the Director of Ordnance became the adviser of the Secretary of State on these questions for some years to come.[1] Tulloh was succeeded in 1866 by Major-General St. George, transferred from the Ordnance Select Committee. St. George in his turn was succeeded by Brig.-General Lefroy in 1869, and that officer was given the title of "Director General of Ordnance and head of the Arsenal." "The arrangement was strongly objected to by the heads of departments in the Arsenal, who argued that it was not desirable to diminish their individual responsibility, and the subject came before Mr. Cardwell within a few days of his entering into office. He suspended his decision

---

the K.C.B. in 1893 and a baronetcy in 1902. He died in 1915. His presence in the great manufacturing establishment on the Tyne was of immense advantage to the military authorities responsible for effecting progress in the design and production of artillery armament in this country.

---

[1] It has to be remembered that during the sixties—and earlier— the War Office and the Horse Guards were for all practical purposes distinct; they communicated with each other by formal letter, as different Departments of State do. The Director of Ordnance, the Ordnance Factories, and the Experimental Detachment at Shoeburyness were, except in the matter of discipline (and even in that to some extent) under the Secretary of State for War. The Inspector-General of Artillery (Major-General Bloomfield in 1860) was under the Horse Guards. This dual system was put an end to by the War Office Act of 1870, after Cardwell had been S. of S. for a year and a half.

pending the enquiry of Lord Northbrook's committee.[1]
Their report, largely influenced by the weighty opinion of
Lord Dalhousie, was adverse to the appointment of a head
of the Arsenal."[2]

CHAPTER VI.

Responsibility for progress.

The School of Gunnery had been established at Shoeburyness by a General Order dated the 1st April 1859, and
shortly afterwards the experimental work to be carried out
there was placed under the superintendence of the Commandant (Colonel J. W. Mitchell).   The instructional work
of the School will be dealt with in Part III—Training, but
it must be remembered here that the Commandant at this
time, and for several years to come, acted in a two-fold
capacity and was responsible for experiments as well as for
instruction.   For a year or two he only had a small staff
of non-commissioned-officers and men to help him.   But
an "Assistant Superintendent of Experiments" and a
"Second Assistant Superintendent of Experiments" (who
had nothing to do with training) were appointed in the year
1862, and an increase to the staff of non-commissioned-
officers and gunners maintained for experimental purposes
making the total 19 was sanctioned at the same time.   It
came to be known as the "Experimental Detachment".
Great developments took place at Shoeburyness during this
1860-1869 period in respect to ranges and appliances of
various kinds connected with the work of testing the
different patterns of ordnance, fuzes and so forth under
consideration of the military authorities.   A considerable
extension of War Department lands had been secured in
1860 by the purchase of a farm, and various questions as to
foreshore and rights of way had been satisfactorily settled.
But the gradually increasing extreme ranges which the guns
brought under trial were able to obtain, was already by the
year 1869 creating serious difficulties.   It was pointing to
the urgent need, if experimental labours and responsibilities

---

[1] This committee had been appointed by Mr. Cardwell to enquire
into the arrangements in force for the conduct of business in Army
Departments.

[2] From Sir R. Biddulph's *Lord Cardwell at the War Office.*

CHAPTER
VI.

Responsi-
bility for
progress.

The
Ordnance
Factories
during this
period.

were to be carried out with efficiency and with a due regard
to the safety of the public, of securing rights over additional stretches of the foreshore and sands which serve as
ranges for the very progressive institution on the Essex
side of the mouth of the Thames.

And if great developments took place during this period
in respect to the experimental side of the School of
Gunnery, even greater developments were taking place in
the Royal Arsenal at Woolwich. This consisted of the
three main branches—each under its own Superintendent—
the Royal Gun Factory, the Royal Carriage Department
and the Royal Laboratory. The two latter were under
charge of officers of the Royal Artillery of acknowledged
standing; but the former had, as already mentioned, been
placed under the control of Sir W. Armstrong in the year
1859, and it was in this that the most far-reaching expansion took place during the 1860-1869 period.

The acceptance in the year 1860 of the principle that
the Royal Gun Factory was to play an important part in
producing guns of the Armstrong pattern, was in itself
sufficient to necessitate the setting up of much entirely new
plant for dealing with wrought iron. Steam hammers of
the Nasmyth type had to be erected, fresh furnaces had to
be constructed, and machinery on the most generous scale
had to be introduced. Even before the programme in connection with the turning out of the Armstrong guns had
been completed, the demand was already arising for the
construction on a large scale of the heavy types of R.M.L.
gun—the 8-inch, the 9-inch and the 10-inch. Sir W.
Armstrong resigned his position as Superintendent in the
year 1863, and he was succeeded by Colonel (afterwards
Major-General, Sir F. A.) Campbell, R.A., on whom devolved the responsibility for grappling with the problem of
how to produce this heavy R.M.L. class of ordnance. The
R.G.F. was now being called upon to turn out the huge
wrought-iron coils which played so conspicuous a role in
the construction of the muzzle-loading ordnance constituting the main armament of our warships in the immediate

future, and which was to constitute the main armament of our coast fortresses for a good many years to come. Notable developments in connection with proof-butts at Woolwich and with the accommodation connected with these took place *pari-passu* with the expansion of the actual factories.

If the Royal Laboratory did not during these years experience quite the same need for expansion in respect to its plant and to its buildings as did the Royal Gun Factory, it none the less underwent amplification under its energetic Superintendent, Colonel Boxer. Shells, fuzes, friction-tubes, and so forth, of entirely new patterns were manufactured during these years in a variety and in quantities such as had scarcely been known in the Royal Laboratory even during the busiest days of the Crimean War.

The other main branch of the Royal Arsenal, the Royal Carriage Department likewise expanded very considerably during this 1860-1869 period. Mainly occupied in the early days with the production of travelling carriages for the Armstrong guns, it was called upon at a later date to turn out the mountings for the heavy types of R.M.L. gun introduced subsequently to the year 1865. Colonel H. Clark R.A., who served two terms as Superintendent, was in charge of the R.C.D. during practically the whole of this period. The growth of the Royal Arsenal, as a whole, it should be added, necessarily carried with it a large increase in the number of the civilian personnel employed within its walls.

As was the normal practice at this time the Superintendents of the Small Arms Factory at Enfield and of the Gunpowder Factory at Waltham Abbey were both senior officers of the Regiment. This arrangement continued for the whole of the period under consideration, and for many years to come.

CHAPTER VII.

1870 to 1883.

CHAPTER
VII.

Main
features
of this
period.

THIS period may be said to synchronise roughly with the brief epoch during which the armament in the hands of the Royal Artillery consisted almost entirely of rifled muzzle-loading ordnance; the R.B.L. type of gun was however, it is true, only superseded gradually in so far as it had been adopted. Our coast batteries had already during the latter part of the preceding period been very largely armed with rifled muzzle-loading pieces converted from smooth-bores, and a fair number of the built-up R.M.L. guns had also been mounted in them before 1870. By that year smooth-bores had for practical purposes disappeared (except in India), and the principle that the R.M.L. type of ordnance was to be the type to be used in future both in the land service and in the sea service was fully accepted, alike for naval and for military purposes, by H.M. Government. R.M.L. ordnance still continued to play an important part in our artillery armament for several years subsequent to 1883; but this was owing to the great cost involved in replacing it by the improved breech-loading guns of the day, and not because (except perhaps in the case of mountain guns and howitzers) muzzle-loading pieces were not admitted by that time on all hands to have become virtually obsolete.

But for the great prominence which the R.M.L. guns enjoyed during the 1870-1883 period, and for the high favour in which they stood in the Royal Artillery during all the earlier years of that period, those fourteen years were, in so far as artillery armament in, this country and in British Possessions was concerned, chiefly noteworthy for the far-reaching progress made during their course in respect to propellants. The notable advances made with regard to this moreover exercised a dominating influence during the last three or four years of this period over theories concerning the principles of gun-design. The period was however also signalised by the introduction of rifled howitzers into the land service, by the change from wood to wrought-iron as the material out of which travelling gun-carriages came to be mainly constructed, and by the increased use of steel in the manfacture of the newest types of ordnance being taken over by the Regiment.

Important influence as some of the lessons taught by the Franco - German War of 1870 - 71 unquestionably exerted over the British Army in general and over the Royal Artillery in particular, those lessons did not in fact to any very appreciable extent affect questions of detail in respect to the armament upon which in the immediately succeeding years the Regiment depended. Such influence as the experiences of that great campaign exerted in this country were exerted in respect to various aspects of organization, to problems connected with the recruiting of military personnel and the length of service of non-commissioned-officers and men, and—at least in theory—to the training of troops and the tactics to be employed by them in the field. The highly meritorious achievements of the German field artillery on the battlefield were recognized by our experts to have been due to bold, skilful and appropriate

CHAPTER VII.

Main features of this period.

Little learnt from the Franco-German War as regards artillery material.

CHAPTER
VII.

Little
learnt
from the
Franco-
German
War as
regards
artillery
material.

handling of batteries and their component parts on the part of the personnel, rather than to any especial efficiency that could fairly be claimed for the material.   Alike in the case of the German and the French horse and field artillery equipments, the material was upon the whole inferior to that with which our corresponding units were fitted out at the time.   The mitrailleuse, of which the French had entertained somewhat extravagant hopes at the outset of the struggle, had proved a grievous disappointment when brought into action in face of the enemy.   As regards siege equipment, that in the hands of the German gunners when attacking Strasbourg and certain other enemy strongholds had performed its task quite adequately; but what it had accomplished had been attributable to its having been pitted against fastnesses that were out of date, rather than to the ordnance and ammunition actually employed having ranked as high class.   Of neither belligerent had the coast defence armament been on a single occasion put to the test.

But the interest in defence questions which the dramatic events of 1870-71 on French soil excited, not merely in service circles in this country but also amongst men of affairs and the general public, did undoubtedly, from one point of view exert a considerable influence over the question of the weapons to be in the hands of the Royal Artillery during the immediately succeeding years.   It accelerated the re-armament of our horse and field artillery, in the sense that the funds required were furnished a good deal more rapidly than, it is reasonable to suppose they would have been furnished had no Franco-German War, with its startlingly decisive conclusion, provided those responsible with a compelling object lesson.

The
reversion
to muzzle-
loading
guns for
field
artillery.

The position of the Regiment as regards the equipment of its horse and field batteries at home in the year 1870 was that all of them were fitted out with the Armstrong R.B.L. guns, but that Sir R. Dacres' Committee had pronounced itself in favour of a reversion to muzzle-loading guns.   The majority of the horse and field batteries in

India were also by this time armed with the R.B.L. guns, but some units in that country still depended upon smooth-bore equipments,[1] and it had recently been decided to intro-duce a bronze 9-pr. R.M.L. gun. A fresh committee to examine into the whole matter was however set up in the summer of 1870, and this, after carrying out exhaustive trials with muzzle-loading and breech-loading field guns (one of them a Prussian 9-pr. breech-loader of Krupp's) reported at the end of November strongly in favour of re-verting to the muzzle-loading system. In a minute for-warding the report to higher authority the Director of Artillery declared that the great majority of officers of the Royal Artillery were convinced that no system of breech-loading was necessary for the field—an opinion in which his views entirely coincided.

The result was that the 9-pr. R.M.L. wrought-iron[2] gun was definitely adopted in the following year as the gun for horse artillery and light field batteries, in sub-stitution for the 9-pr. R.B.L. and the 12-pr. R.B.L.[3] The replacement of the Armstrong equipments at home was consequently taken in hand at once—i.e., approxi-mately ten years after they had first been introduced.[4] Experiments were moreover initiated about the same time in order to secure a pattern of R.M.L. gun for field artil-lery to fire a projectile heavier than 9 lbs., and the first 16-pr. battery appeared at the manœuvres of 1871; this pattern of gun was in due course adopted for a proportion

---

[1] An examination of the Regimental Lists, prepared monthly by the R.A. Institution, for the forty years from 1860 to 1899 conveys the impression that every successive armament adopted for horse and field batteries had become obsolete before the whole of the batteries con-cerned had been equipped with it.

[2] Like all guns of the R.M.L. type it had a steel inner tube.

[3] The decision to revert to muzzle-loaders appeared to be fully justified when the news leaked out that during the 1870-71 campaign over 200 Krupp breech-loading field guns had failed owing to their crude mechanism.

[4] The 9-pr. R.M.L. guns were at first of two patterns, a light gun of 6 cwt for the horse artillery and a heavier type of 8 cwt for field batteries; but the latter soon disappeared, the lighter gun being found quite efficient.

Chapter
VII.

The
reversion
to muzzle-
loading
guns for
field
artillery.

of the field batteries at home.   The idea of light field
batteries was moreover abandoned about the year 1874,
and the 16-pr. was thenceforward supposed to be the sole
armament of field batteries on the home establishment:
but some remained armed with the 9-pr. for several years
subsequent to 1874.   It should be mentioned that even the
9-pr. was adjudged to be too heavy a piece for service in
road-less territory and in countries where only the lighter
types of draught-horse were procurable.   The consequence
was that a special "Kaffraria pattern" field carriage was
designed for use with the 7-pr. R.M.L. (the mountain gun);
and this equipment was that mainly used by the Royal
Artillery in the successive South African campaigns which
took place between 1875 and 1880[1]

CARRIAGE.FIELD R M L .16-P? MARK II.

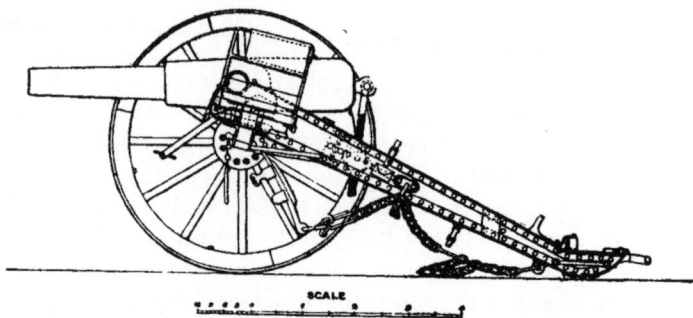

SCALE

The bronze 9-pr. R.M.L. had not in the meantime been
giving entire satisfaction in India.   The 14th Brigade
(Field Artillery) had by the year 1872 been re-armed with
it; but, as a consequence of unfavourable reports received
from batteries concerning it, the responsible authorities
decided to adopt the home pattern wrought-iron 9-pr. in
its place.   The substitution of the R.B.L. pattern guns
for the smooth-bores in batteries on the Indian establish-

---

[1] The weight behind the team was only 25 cwt, as compared with
the 35 cwt of the 9-pr.

ment had however been proceeding very slowly—in the year
1871 there still remained 13 horse artillery and 27 field
batteries equipped with the obsolete ordnance—and the dis-
favour into which the R.B.L. guns had fallen at home
checked the process of replacing the smooth bores in India
with the only rifled guns that were at the time available.
The decision to arm all field batteries on the home establishment with the 16-pr. subsequently to 1874, on the other
hand served to facilitate the replacement of the smooth-
bores in India, because large numbers of 9-prs. of the home
pattern were released. These were in due course sent to
supersede, first the smooth bores, and afterwards the
R.B.L. guns; some Indian field batteries however remained armed with the 12-pr. R.B.L. so late as the year
1881.

Steps in the direction of substituting muzzle-loading for
breech-loading ordnance in the case of position and siege
artillery, were taken at about the same time as the decision

CHAPTER
VII.

The
reversion
to muzzle-
loading
guns for
field
artillery.

CARRIAGE, SIEGE, R.M L. 40 PR TOP, OVERBANK.

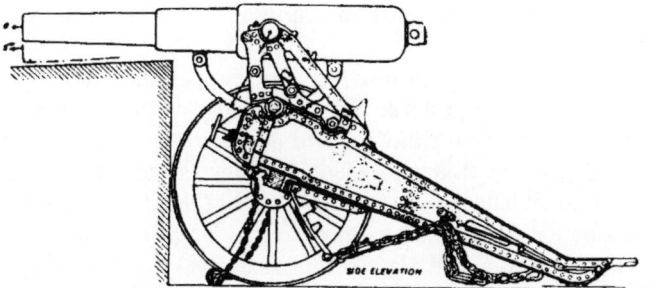

SIDE ELEVATION

was arrived at in respect to changing the armament of the
horse and field artillery on the home establishment. The
manufacture of R.M.L. 40-prs., intended to replace the
R.B.L. 40-prs., was undertaken in 1871, and this step was
followed by approval being in 1874 given to a pattern of

25-pr. R.M.L. which was to replace the 20-pr. R.B.L.
The discarded R.B.L. guns of position however proved useful for many years to come as reasonably serviceable items
in the "Moveable Armament" of fortresses, both at home
and abroad.

Coast
defence
armament
in 1870.

As regards the armament of coast defence batteries, the
position at home and abroad in the year 1870 was, expressing the situation in general terms, that a certain number
of the new wrought-iron, built-up R.M.L. guns, of calibres
from 7-inch to 9-inch, were already mounted in some of the
more important works, but that the bulk of the ordnance in
use (apart from some old smooth-bores and a few 7-inch
R.B.L. guns) was composed of the "converted" 64-prs.
and 80 prs. R.M.L.—smooth-bore ordnance which had been
transformed into rifled ordnance by the Palliser process.
In so far as mountings were concerned, these were for the
most part designed for the gun to fire through an embrasure
or else through a gun-port.   The wrought-iron R.M.L.
guns which were in process of being introduced to supersede older patterns, were, furthermore, for the most part
being emplaced in casemate batteries, of which Garrison
Point Fort at Sheerness—still so conspicuous a feature at
the mouth of the Medway as viewed from vessels on their
way to and from the Port of London—may be cited as a
typical example.

Improve-
ments in
the pro-
pellants.

The question of improving the propellant used with
rifled ordnance in general, and especially with the heavier
natures, was at this time beginning to receive very serious
consideration in this and also in other countries, and in
the course of the exhaustive researches that were taking
place during a succession of years in England (the then)
Captain A. Noble and Mr. (afterwards Sir. F.) Abel played
a particularly prominent part.   The result of their labours,
as time went on, was to produce much slower-burning forms
of gunpowder than those which had found favour in 1870
and earlier.   The production of these new types of powder
characterised by gradual combustion exercised a far-reaching influence over what came to be regarded as the correct

forms of built-up gun construction. Slower burning propellant demanded an increased length in the bore of the
piece, otherwise some of the powder was discharged from
the bore before the whole was fully consumed. Relatively
to the weight of the charge used, slow-burning powder
also decreased the strain on the gun.

The consequence was that the guns which came to be
introduced into the service subsequently to about the year
1876 were all considerably longer, relatively to their calibre,
than had been those approved before that time. Experiments carried out in connection with improved forms of
pellant moreover indicated that the strain on the bore of
the gun was decreased if the gun was "chambered", i.e., if
the bore was given a slightly larger diameter at the breech
end, where the cartridge rests, than along the remainder
of its length, thus allowing an "air space" which caused
pressure to rise more gradually. Owing to the strain at the
breech end of the piece being reduced, it was furthermore
found possible to decrease the bulk of the coils which had
latterly been employed along the greater part of the length
of the gun. The discoveries made in respect to the propellant, coupled with additional experience gained in relation
to ballistics in general, may in fact be said to have brought
about a revolution in the accepted principles of gun construction as they were understood in this country. And
it so happened that this revolution took place within ten
years of that remarkable reversion from the breech-loading
to the muzzle-loading system, which the military authorities had finally decided upon (in connection at least with
all the lighter patterns of ordnance) about the year 1870.

But a very important modification which had taken
place in projectiles intended for muzzle-loading ordnance
already in the service some time before this, as also in
those intended for guns and howitzers about to be introduced into the service, must here be touched upon. This
was the adoption of the gas check. Windage, such as of
necessity existed within the bore of the gun under the
approved R.M.L. system, with its "Woolwich" plan of a

limited number of rifling grooves and its studded projectiles, was found by experience to cause very serious erosion
in the bore—especially so in the case of heavier natures of
ordnance with which large charges were employed.
Various forms of gas-check for attachment to the base of
the projectile—some of them rigidly fixed to it, others capable of rotating independently of it—were tried as antidotes
to this scoring of the bore. The result of exhaustive trials
carried out with different patterns of gas-check and with
different natures of gun, ultimately led to the gas-checks
being always rigidly fixed, and to their in fact to all intents
and purposes forming part of the projectile.

It was moreover discovered that the rigidly fixed gas-
check sufficed by itself to give rotation to the projectile on
discharge, so that studs could be dispensed with altogether
The employment of the gas-check was furthermore found
somewhat to increase the range of the gun for any given
elevation, inasmuch as its presence led to the whole effect
of the combustion of the charge being expended on propel-
ling the projectile instead of some being wasted owing to
windage.[1]   The acceptance of the principle of the gas-
check very soon led to the adoption of a plan of polygroove
rifling with shallow grooves, in substitution for the "Woolwich" plan of a few and deeper grooves.   Although steps
were early taken to supply gas-checks for R.M.L. projectiles already on charge, the full results of their adoption
only began to take effect in connection with new patterns
of ordnance towards the close of the 1870-1883 period.
We must therefore revert to the progress made subsequently to 1870 in respect to producing ordnance more
powerful than the 9-inch R.M.L. gun.   Reference has also
to be made to the introduction of rifled howitzers.

---

[1] It is recorded that one of the ironclads engaged in the bombardment of Alexandria in 1882 had only just received its complement of
projectiles with the gas-check fitted, but had not received copies of the
modified range tables. Its practice at the Egyptian batteries in consequence was mortifyingly ineffective.

The 10-inch R.M.L. gun, which had been approved for the Royal Navy in the year 1868, was approved at the same time for the land service whenever it should become

CHAPTER
VII.

Developments
in the
heaviest
guns.

CARRIAGE GARRISON R M. L 10 INCH. CASEMATE OR DWARF

SLIDE. R, M.L. 10 INCH CASEMATE.

REAR

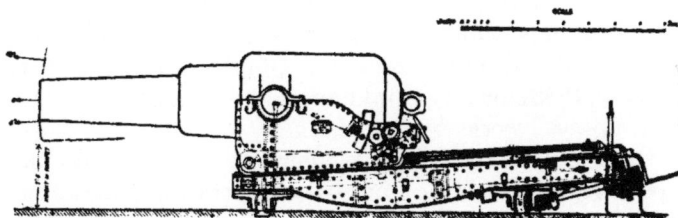

ELEVATION

available. The consequence was that some of these guns were introduced into our coast fortresses soon after 1870, and that for a number of years they became an important feature in our coast defence system. A few 12-inch R.M.L. guns of 35 tons—they were nicknamed "Woolwich Infants"—were constructed experimentally in 1871[1] but were found inaccurate when tested on the ranges; so a longer 12-inch gun weighing 38 tons was constructed. But after prolonged trials the experts decided to give the 38-ton guns a calibre of 12·5 inches, and large numbers of these ponderous pieces were approved for the armament of battleships; and as soon as naval requirements had been met they began also to be issued to the land service. These 12·5 inch R.M.L. guns may indeed almost be looked upon as the heaviest R.M.L. pieces with which the Regiment has had to deal; so few 80-ton or 100-ton R.M.L. guns were ever mounted on land that they almost partook of the

---

[1] Only two of these guns were actually issued—both to the Royal Navy. They were mounted in H.M.S. "Thunderer" as a pair in one of her turrets; One of them had a tragic history, for it was the gun which burst during practice with disastrous results in the year 1879, owing to its having inadvertently been double-loaded.

CHAPTER
VII.

Develop-
ments
in the
heaviest
guns.

nature of freak armament. Originally intended to have a
14·5-inch calibre, the 80-ton gun ended in being a 16-inch
gun ; the only two of these employed ashore were mounted
in a turret at what was then the end of the Admiralty Pier
at Dover. Then, at the time when relations with Russia
became strained in 1878, four 17·72-inch muzzle-loading
guns of 100-ton weight each, were purchased from Elswick;
two of them were mounted at Gibraltar and two at Malta.[1]
The more important coast batteries at home and abroad
had been mainly armed with the 10-inch R.M.L. gun by
the year 1883, but a sprinkling of 38-ton guns was also
found in these works by that date.

Reference has been made above to the fact that the
heavier types of R.M.L. guns—those from the 7-inch type
upwards—were for the most part mounted in casemates
previously to 1870. Those introduced subsequently to that
date were likewise very generally placed in casemates.
This was mainly due to the casemates being already in
existence and only requiring some modification to adapt
them for the big muzzle-loading guns. Where moreover
such ordnance happened to be mounted in open batteries
the guns generally fired through embrasures. The consequence was that the field of fire of the individual gun was
of necessity seriously restricted and that in many maritime
places of arms a considerably larger number of guns were
required than would have been necessary had the guns been
mounted *en barbette*. It was an extravagent plan from the
point of view of the number of guns required, and also from
the point of view of gun-detachments. One consequence
was that during this 1870-1883 period (and also, it may be
added, during the succeeding 1884-1889 period) the artillery personnel allowed to our maritime fortresses at home
and abroad was never nearly sufficient to man the whole of

---

[1] As showing the consequences of the developments taking place
with regard to slow-burning propellants, it may be mentioned that,
whereas the 10-inch R.M.L. gun of 1869 was one of 14½ calibres, the
17·72 R.M.L. of 1877 was one of 20 calibres.

those guns mounted in them. Smoke was apt to interfere with the service of the guns when in casemates. Casemates moreover almost inevitably offered well-defined targets to hostile warships, and they thus sacrified the one undoubted advantage which shore artillery ought to enjoy over ship's artillery, seeing that a ship must inevitably offer a good mark to the shore battery, whereas a shore battery need not necessarily offer a good mark to the ship.

Realising the vital importance of high-angle fire for siege purposes, our artillery experts had begun to take up the question of adopting some form of rifled howitzer to meet the case as early as the year 1867. But it was not until 1872 that an 8-inch R.M.L. howitzer of 46 cwt. was definitely approved for the land service; a number of these howitzers were turned out during the next two years. A lighter piece, one of 6·3-inch calibre, was proposed about the same time, but none of them were actually introduced until the year 1878; it was in that year decided to allow two of these howitzers to each heavy battery in India.[1] The early 8-inch howitzers adopted for the service were dumpy ordnance of comparatively speaking limited range, having a bore of only six calibres in length; a greatly improved pattern, with a bore of twelve calibres, was therefore introduced in 1880. A 6·6-inch howitzer was moreover also introduced about that same time, and this gradually superseded the 6·3-inch type. It may be mentioned here that in 1878 a "Heavy Siege Train Unit" was composed of eight 64-pr. guns and fourteen 8-inch howitzers. A "Light Siege Train Unit" was at that time composed of ten 40-pr. guns, ten 25-pr. guns and ten 6·3-inch howitzers; 6·6-inch howitzers were substituted for the 6·3-inch as soon as they had become available in sufficient numbers.

Chapter VII.

Developments in the heaviest guns.

Rifled howitzers.

---

[1] The Peshawar Heavy Battery took part in the first phase of the Afghan War, armed with four 40-prs. R.B.L. This armament was changed in 1879, and the battery took part in the second phase of the war with two 40-prs. R.M.L. and two 6·3-inch howitzers.

A very important advance in armament for mountain artillery was made in the year 1879 by the introduction of the jointed 2·5-inch R.M.L. gun of 400 lbs. This piece was noteworthy, not merely owing to its being constructed in two parts that screwed together, but also owing to its being the first of the longer types of ordnance to be introduced into the land service. (It was a piece of $26\frac{1}{2}$ calibres, as compared to the 9-pr. R.M.L. of 17 calibres). Generally spoken of as the "screw gun", it was a weapon very superior to the 7-pr. of 200 lbs. with which the mountain batteries in India were equipped at the time. Relatively to its calibre it was a much more powerful gun than were either the 9-pr. or the 16-pr. on which the horse and field artillery at home depended. A battery equipped with the 2·5-inch took part in the later phase of the Afghan War and was also present at Tel-el-Kebir in 1882. These screw guns were largely used during the various campaigns on the North-West Frontier of India of the closing two decades of the nineteenth century, and a battery fitted out with them (still firing "smoke" powder) fought in Natal in the year 1899.

CARRIAGE MOUNTAIN R. M. L. 2 5 INCH MARK II.
STEEL (WITHOUT LIMBER)

SIDE ELEVATION

Reverting now to the subject of horse and field artillery armament, it has to be noted that artillery experts in this country had by the year 1878 come to realize that both the 9-pr. and the 16-pr. R.M.L. guns, were out of date as

compared to the armament which certain foreign countries
were adopting, or had already adopted.　So experiments
were set on foot with 13-pr. designs, some of the first of
which were completed as breech-loaders.　The responsible
authorities however remained convinced that the muzzle-
loading plan was the most practical and satisfactory, and
in due course a pattern was adopted which admittedly
represented a great advance on the 9-pr. and the 16-pr.
This gun was one of 28 calibres; it was chambered;
although Mark I had a wrought-iron jacket, Mark II was
fashioned wholly out of steel.　It proved an accurate piece,
possessing much longer range that its predecessors, and it
began to be issued to both horse and field batteries at home
in the year 1880.　Re-armament was however only carried
out by slow degrees, so that when the equivalent of an
army corps was mobilized to undertake the Egyptian Campaign of 1882, although both R.H.A. batteries sent out
from home had the new gun, the field artillery despatched
from the United Kingdom was armed partly with the 13-pr.
and partly with the 16-pr.[1]　The 13-pr., although giving
satisfaction in most respects, caused trouble in battle owing
to its violent recoil, the 16-pr., as was only to be expected,
threw a severe strain on the gun-teams in the sands border-
ing the Wady Tumailat.　Moreover, before re-armament
with the 13-pr. had at a later date been nearly completed
at home, the gun was already superseded by a new breech-
loading 12-pr.

This 12-pr. B.L. (which was not adopted until subsequent to the 1870-1883 period, with which this chapter
is concerned) was not however the first of the novel type
of breech-loading ordnance to be introduced into the Service.　A number of 6-inch breech-loading guns of quite a
new pattern were purchased from Elswick for the Royal
Navy in the year 1880.　None of these pieces, nor of the
later "Marks" of the 6-inch B.L., had, it is true, been

---

[1] The one field battery furnished to Sir G. Wolseley's force by India
was a 9-pr. R.M.L. one.

CHAPTER
VII.

The
Elswick
6-in. B.L.
guns, and
the effect
of their
intro-
duction.

mounted ashore by the end of 1883; but owing to the influence which their introduction exerted in connection with gun design, as accepted by the freshly set up Ordnance Committee and by our artillery experts in the mass, some reference to them appears to be called for in this chapter.

The reduction of pressure in the bore of the gun—so important a feature in connection with the slow-burning propellants—naturally tended to simplify the problem of producing a satisfactory breech-mechanism. The original Armstrong design—the R.B.L. design—with its removable breech-piece screwed home from the rear—had proved unsatisfactory because the design was not strong enough to stand the shock of the quick-burning powders which it was the practice during the early sixties to employ for the charge. The plan of the interrupted screw combined with the De Bange obturator, borrowed from France by Elswick and adapted to these 6-inch pieces, also connoted a very great step in advance as compared with the abandoned "Armstrong" system of closing the breech. Thanks to employing appropriate propellant, to chambering, and to a length of bore of 25 calibres, these 6-inch guns attained a muzzle-velocity of close on 2,000 f.s., whereas in the comparatively recently designed 80-ton and 100-ton R.M.L. the muzzle-velocity fell short of 1,600 f.s. In respect to range and accuracy they were ahead of the 38-ton R.M.L. gun, and were well ahead of the 10-inch gun—the two natures of much heavier ordnance which constituted the most effective armament of British coast batteries at the time. The obvious convenience and the proved trustworthiness of the breech mechanism employed in these Elswick 6-inch guns, had much to say to the belated decision to revert to the breech-loading system for almost all natures of ordnance. In so far as this decision affected the Regiment, it found early expression in the prolonged experiments that took place during the years 1882 and 1883 with samples of a breech-loading 12-pr. constructed wholly of steel, experiments which led to the eventual adoption of one of them for both horse and field artillery.

To turn from the subject of guns and howitzers to that
of ammunition, some further details must be given of the
results of the experiments with propellants. The progress
made in this matter has been already touched upon in this
chapter. One result of the labours of the explosive experts
was the definite adoption into the land service of a large
number of new patterns of gunpowder to meet the requirements of different types of ordnance already introduced
and about to be introduced. The ingredients of the various
patterns of propellant, as also the relative proportion of the
different ingredients, remained as before,[1] but by the year
1883 the number of different powders on charge of units
of the Regiment amounted to twelve. They varied between
the finest grain powder (such as was suitable for small
arms and was used for bursting charges in shrapnel and
common shell), and what was called "Prism Powder".
This latter took the form of hexagonal prisms, 2 inches in
height and about $2\frac{1}{2}$ inches in diameter, with axial per-
foration; it was only used for the largest natures of R.M.L.
gun, the prisms being built up in layers within the
cartridge.

The projectiles intended for mobile guns used in the
field at this time were shrapnel shell, common shell and
case shot. This held good for the R.H.A., for the field
artillery, for the siege artillery and for position artillery.
But the 2·5-inch jointed gun was allowed in addition a
supply of special star shells. R.M.L. howitzers also were
allowed a proportion of spherical star shell. Besides a
quota of ordinary common shell, the 7-pr. mountain gun
was supplied with a special "double" common shell for use
against villages and *sangars*. The proportions of shrapnel
shell to common shell per gun in the case of the three
natures of ordnance with which the field artillery was armed

---

[1] This is only correct in the case of the land service. For "Prism
Brown Powder" had been adopted for the heavy B.L. guns which by
the year 1883 were already being mounted in H.M. Ships. In this
compound the proportion of sulphur was less than in black powders,
while a special component in it took the place of carbon.

in 1882 were : 9-pr. R.M.L. 112 shrapnel to 32 common;
16-pr. R.M.L. 76 shrapnel to 24 common; 13-pr. R.M.L.
112 shrapnel to 30 common.

The projectiles in use with heavy R.M.L. guns mounted
in coast defence works were Palliser shot, Palliser shell
(this contained a bursting charge, whereas Palliser shot
did not), common shell and case shot. The projectiles for
all the later natures of R.M.L. gun introduced during this
period, viz. : the 2·5-inch, the 13-pr., the 16-inch and the
17·72-inch, as also the projectiles for the 6·3-inch, the
6·6-inch and the later 8-inch howitzer were studless;
rotation was given them by what for all practical purposes
corresponded to a fixed gas check. Although projectiles
were still for the most part constructed out of cast iron,
a move in the direction of steel had been made in the case
of the shrapnel for the 2·5-inch gun, which was of cast
steel.

Great progress was made within this period in fuze
design. A wooden time fuze furnished with a trustworthy
detonator, for instance, was introduced for use with projectiles fitted with the gas-check. A metal "Time and
Concussion Fuze", proved in the field in Afghanistan, was
adopted for service after that campaign. Certain improved
forms of percussion fuze also became items of equipment.

Numbers of new patterns of gun carriage and mounting
had necessarily to be adopted between 1870 and 1883, as
fresh natures of ordnance were introduced into the land
service. A noteworthy development in respect to travelling
gun carriages moreover began to take place towards the
close of this period in that the superiority of steel over
wrought-iron for construction purposes received practical
recognition. In illustration of this it may be mentioned
that the gun-carriages for the 2·5-inch and the 13-pr.
R.M.L. were constructed wholly of steel. One consequence
of the increase in the charges used in the later patterns
of R.M.L. gun, consequent upon developments in respect
to slower burning powder, was that the recoil of the gun
increased more or less proportionately. The charge for

the 13-pr., for instance, was slightly greater than that for
the 16-pr.—a heavier gun with a heavier carriage. The
13-pr. carriage was not provided with recoil-checking
appliances such as were introduced in the different patterns
of carriage to be employed with the 12-pr. B.L. gun; its
recoil was excessive and, as was found in the Egyptian
campaign, imposed a great strain on the gun detachment
in case of prolonged or of rapid fire.

Much had at the outset of this period been hoped for
from the "Moncrieff" disappearing form of mounting for
coast defence armament, with its ingenious form of counter-
weight. The design did not however prove wholly satisfactory when put practically to the test even with comparatively light forms of ordnance (64-pr. R.M.L., 7-inch
R.B.L. and 9-inch R.M.L.), for which it was actually
adopted. It was not tried as a mounting for the 10-inch
R.M.L. In respect to the more normal forms of mountings
for heavy guns, it should be mentioned that various improvements were effected in the system of hydraulic buffers
for checking recoil, as adapted to the mounting of guns of
the 10-inch R.M.L. and 38-ton type. The improved hydraulic buffers indeed rendered their service as rapid as
could reasonably be hoped for with ponderous, muzzle-
loading ordnance.

Some headway was made during the seventies in the
matter of designing and adopting range-finding instruments
for the service of batteries in the field, as also for use in
connection with coast defence operations. The Watkin
Range-Finder, introduced in 1881, came to be a recognized
item in the equipment of the horse and field artillery on
the home establishment. The Weldon Range-Finder had
already been introduced for service in the field in India
and it had been found useful in Afghanistan. The more
elaborate Nolan Range-Finder was taken into use for coast
defence batteries; this instrument was also adopted for
employment with siege artillery units and in position batteries. Telescopes were approved for use with horse and
field batteries in 1883.

War rockets had for many years, down to 1870, been regarded as part of the material in charge of the Royal Artillery. They were moreover actually made use of by the Regiment during the Ashanti Campaign of 1874, and also in the course of the Zulu War. But batteries ceased to carry out practice with them in peace time during the period under review, and all idea of employing them—except possibly in small wars—was definitely abandoned before its conclusion. It was nevertheless enacted that stores of war rockets were to be maintained in charge of the Ordnance Department in certain specified stations oversea, so that some should be available on the spot to meet the case of possible hostilities with savages in forest country and jungle-clad regions.[1]

Responsi-
bility for
the
supply of
artillery
material.

The great reforms effected by Mr. Cardwell in connection with terms of service for the rank-and-file, with the creation of an adequate reserve, and with placing officers of the R.A. and the R.E. on a proper footing as regards promotion have been referred to in Part I of this Volume. But the famous War Minister also carried out reforms of far-reaching importance within the War Office itself. Under the terms of the War Office Act of 1870, which was largely based on the recommendations of Lord Northbrook's Committee already mentioned on p. 163, the actual central army administration was divided between three great officials. These were the General Commanding-in-Chief, the Surveyor-General of the Ordnance and the Financial Secretary. It is with the Surveyor-General of the Ordnance that we are here concerned.

The post of Controller-in-Chief (a military Under-Secretary of State) had been created in 1868 and had been conferred on Major-General Sir H. Storks, under whom were placed the Commissariat, Barrack, Military Stores

---

[1] For many years to come the work of the Horse and Field Artillery Branch of the School of Gunnery included "Colonial Courses" for aspirants to posts in various colonial constabulary corps; and the syllabus of these courses included practice with rockets as well as with the earliest patterns of 7-pr. R.M.L. guns.

and Clothing Departments. By the War Office Act these duties were transferred to the Surveyor-General of Ordnance, who also assumed responsibility for the supply of artillery material, which, as already mentioned in Chapter II, was placed under a Director of Artillery and Stores (Brig.-General J. M. Adye) who replaced General Lefroy, the Director-General of Ordnance. General Adye was replaced by Colonel F. A. Campbell in 1875, but he returned to the War Office as Surveyor-General of the Ordnance in 1880, and he held that position until he went out to Egypt for the 1882 campaign as Chief of the Staff. Sir H. Storks was for some time, while Surveyor-General, a Member of Parliament, and before Adye's appointment to that position it had been for some years occupied by politicians.

The abolition of the Ordnance Select Committee in the year 1867 was recorded in the last chapter. The Committee had at that date been composed almost wholly of officers of the Royal Artillery. It was reconstituted on the 1st of April, 1881, bearing the title of "Ordnance Committee", under the presidency of General Sir Collingwood Dickson, ꟾꟾꟾ. By an agreement come to between the War Office and the Admiralty the constitution of the Committee was expanded in its new guise in a direction of great importance. The arrangement arrived at was that, while (as had been the case in 1867) the President was to be an officer of the Royal Artillery and the Vice-President was to be a naval officer, two officers of the Royal Navy were in future to be Members of the Committee. The membership was in addition to these to consist of three R.A. officers (one of them especially representing Indian requirements), of one officer of the Royal Engineers, and of two civilian Members. The Secretary was to be chosen from the Royal Artillery; but there was also to be an Assistant Secretary who would be selected from the Royal Navy. The Experimental Staff at Shoeburyness was yet further expanded during this 1870-1883 period.

The progress that was being made during the years under consideration in the design of armament and in the pre-

Side notes:

CHAPTER VII.

Responsibility for the supply of artillery material.

The Ordnance Committee.

The Manufacturing Deparation of explosives, led of necessity to expansion taking place in almost all the different branches of the manufacturing departments of the army.   The growth in the dimensions and the weight of the heavier natures of ordnance— the adoption of the 38-ton and the 80-ton guns, for instance—could only be rendered practicable by setting up much new plant within the Royal Arsenal.   The increasing use of steel in gun construction subsequent to about the year 1875 tended to direct the energies of the Royal Gun Factory into new channels, and it led to the installation of much fresh machinery.   Developments in the Royal Carriage Department were on scarcely less important a scale, seeing that mountings had to be turned out for far heavier ordnance than only a very few years before.   The abandonment of wood as the material for travelling gun carriages, also called for the adoption of new methods and demanded the provision of new plant.   The Royal Laboratory, like the rest of the Royal Arsenal, underwent some amplification.

But it was at Waltham Abbey perhaps that the most important changes of all took place between 1870 and 1883, changes which, as in the case of the Royal Arsenal, were carried out under the superintendence and on the responsibility of officers of the Regiment.   The fashioning of an explosive substance in the form of "Prism Powder" involved far more elaborate mechanical processes than did the manufacture of the fine-grain powders which had served all purposes quite adequately a few years earlier.   The introduction of propellants characterized by slow combustion automatically carried with it a need for new buildings and for the introduction of machinery of novel design. The Royal Small Arms Factory likewise felt the effect of the progress taking place in respect to the design of firearms.   For during the period that is under consideration in this chapter the infantry were re-armed with Martini-Henry rifles and the cavalry and artillery were re-armed with Martini-Henry carbines, all of which were produced either at Enfield or else in its Birmingham branch.

CHAPTER VIII.

1884 to 1899.

Main features of this period—Recognition that the breech-loading was the best system—The 12-pr. B.L.—Heavy ordnance for the field—Howitzers—Siege Train—Coast defence armament—High-angle batteries—Q.F. guns for harbour defence—Wire-construction—Cordite—Shells and fuzes—Carriages and mountings—Systems of draught—Range-finders; the D.R.F. and P.F.—Responsibility for the supply of artillery material—The Ordnance Committee—Shoeburyness—Personnel at the head of the Ordnance Factories—The Inspection Branch—Responsibility for the Manufacturing Departments taken over by the Director-General of Ordnance.

CHAPTER
VIII.

Main
features
of this
period.

THE closing years of the nineteenth century synchronised with a period of yet further progress in connection with most forms of artillery armament. Ranking first perhaps in importance amongst the numerous novelties that came to be introduced into the Service during these years was the adoption of cordite as a propellant—one which, besides the absence of smoke on discharge, possessed properties that influenced gun design. Then there was the introduction of quick-firing guns; this, it is true, affected the Royal Navy far more generally than it did the Royal Artillery up to the commencement of the present century; but certain of the lighter natures of this class of ordnance had taken their place in the land service before 1899. Another noteworthy feature of this particular period was the appearance of the howitzer as part armament of our field artillery—a distinct step in advance, a step which, as it happened. was only taken very shortly before the outbreak of the South African War. The superiority of steel hoops over

CHAPTER
VIII.

Main
features
of this
period.
wrought-iron coils for use in gun construction had already
been recognised in the Royal Gun Factory before the year
1884; but the adoption of steel wire in place of the steel
hoops a few years later connoted a yet further advance.
Then again, the efficiency of our coast defence artillery
was much increased during this period consequent on the
introduction first of the Depression Range-Finder, and later
of the Position-Finder (the inventions of Major H. S. S.
Watkin). Both siege artillery and field howitzers acquired
increased destructive effect in 1898 by the introduction of
a high-explosive for charging projectiles in the shape of
lyddite.

Recogni-
tion
that the
breech-
loading
was
the best
system.
Practically all artillery experts in this country were at
one by the commencement of this 1884-1899 period in
recognising that, for all types of ordnance other possibly
than howitzers and mountain guns, the muzzle-loading system was in reality totally obsolete, and that a complete re-
armament of our horse and field artillery, as also of our
coast defence artillery, was already overdue. As the
recently adopted 13-pr. R.M.L. gun was by no means one
to be set down as ineffective at that date, the need of re-
armament was in reality perhaps greater in the case of our
coast batteries than it was in the case of the field artillery.
Still the military authorities—quite rightly no doubt—
looked upon the batteries which formed part of the mobile
army as of primary concern. So a B.L. 12-pr. was already
(as has been mentioned in the last chapter) undergoing
trials in 1884, and it had indeed virtually been adopted.

The greatly increased length of the bore of the gun of
any given calibre consequent on the introduction of propellants of gradual combustion, as compared with the
length previously regarded as appropriate, had much to do
with the substitution of the breech-loading system for the
muzzle-loading system—certainly so in the case of ordnance
of a heavy type. For this greater length of bore created
serious difficulty with regard to the rammer and sponge in
the case of a muzzle-loading gun. But great improvements
in connection with breech-loading devices had also pro-

foundly altered the relative merits of the breech-loader and the muzzle-loader, as compared to the situation existing in the years 1866 and 1871. In those years committees had pronounced themselves uncompromisingly in favour of the muzzle-loading system, and they had brought about what was undoubtedly in many quarters looked upon as a retrograde step. Still, the position in the year 1884 was that, although guns of the new B.L. pattern had been mounted in large numbers in H.M. Ships, none such had as yet come under charge of units of the Regiment.

The 12-pr. B.L. was however approved for issue both to the R.H.A. and to the field artillery in the year 1885, and during the succeeding four or five years it gradually replaced the 9-pr. R.M.L., the 13-pr. R.M.L. and the 16-pr. R.M.L.[1] The new guns were received with pæans of praise, and the writer of the Prize Essay of 1888 affirmed that with them "and Scott's Revolving Telescopic Sight which leaves nothing to be desired" it became "almost impossible to miss the mark after a couple of trial shots". Sir F. Roberts (who, when the suggestion was put forward in 1883, had discouraged the idea of a field gun lighter than a 12-pr. for India, maintaining that there was no justification for adopting a less powerful gun that was considered suitable for field artillery in Europe) held the opinion that for work beyond the frontier field guns were no use. His view was that for such operations pack artillery alone possessed the requisite mobility, while for destructive effect heavy guns or howitzers were needed. He moreover pronounced the new piece, after it had been issued, to be too heavy for horse artillery in India.[2] The situation as regards the R.H.A. gun in that country was shortly afterwards brought to a head by the experiences encountered during the course of the great cavalry man-

---

[1] The 12-pr. B.L. was sighted up to 5,000 yards, as compared with the 9-pr. R.M.L. up to 3,500 yards, the 16-pr. R.M.L. up to 4,000 yards, and the 13-pr. R.M.L. up to 4,800 yards. It was provided with a telescopic sight in addition to the usual tangent scale and foresight.

[2] He pressed for a high velocity 10-pr. to secure which he was ready to sacrifice uniformity of calibre.

œuvres conducted by Sir G. Luck at Muridki and between Aligarh and Meerut, when the gun-carriage was found to be much too complicated, the axle-traversing device in particular giving great trouble owing to the dust causing the metal surfaces to "seize".[1]

——— CARRIAGE, FIELD, B.L. 12 PR. 6 CWT. ———

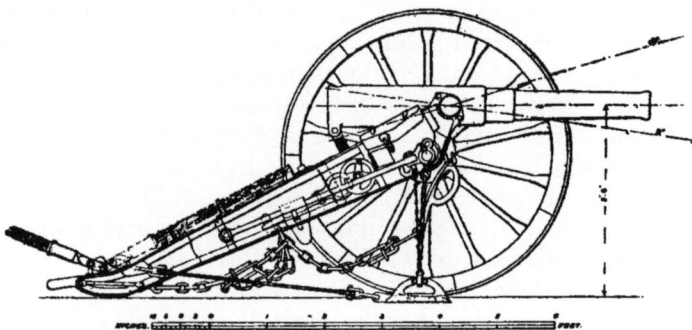

The equipment was also found too heavy and too complicated for horse artillery at home, where it was held moreover that a field gun ought to fire a projectile heavier than 12 lbs. The consequence was that a Committee was assembled in 1892 under chairmanship of General Sir R. Biddulph to consider the question, very shortly after cordite had been adopted. Cordite, materially altering ballistic properties as it did, provided an opportunity for adding to the weight of the shell, without such increase demanding any very important alteration in the actual gun. The Committee recommended that the existing 12-prs. should be converted into 15-prs. A somewhat lighter pattern of 12-pr. (weighing 6 cwt. instead of 7 cwt.), furnished with a lighter and less complicated carriage than the old one, was at the same time introduced for horse artillery.[2] These

---

[1] The guns of the Chestnut Troop which had just been armed with the new guns were out of action from this cause after two days of the manœuvres.

[2] Although they were known officially as the 12-pr. B.L. and the 15-pr. B.L. the two guns were in reality respectively a 12½-pr. and a 14-pr.

two patterns of gun, it may be mentioned, constituted the
armament of the horse and field artillery (apart from the
field howitzer batteries) when the forces were mobilised
for the South African War in the year 1899.[1]

In respect to the heavier natures of mobile artillery,
the British military authorities remained satisfied for
nearly the whole of the 1884-1899 period with the various
patterns of R.M.L. ordnance that were already in the
service. Sir F. Roberts, on the other hand, when C. in C.
in India, pressed for guns of heavier type than what was
suitable for field artillery, as part equipment for that
country. His experiences in Afghanistan had convinced
him that armament of the nature of the 40-prs. and the
6·3-inch howitzers which had taken part in that campaign,
was indispensable for dealing with the mud-walled forts
and the mud villages found so largely in the east. A 30-pr.
B.L. gun of 20 cwt. and a 4-inch B.L. (jointed) howitzer
were therefore especially introduced for employment in
India—the former as the armament for heavy batteries
in place of the 40-pr. One result of the less progressive

[1] Two field batteries stationed at Hilsea (12th and 80th) took over
a special experimental equipment in 1894-95—the military authorities
had conceived the idea that a very light form of field artillery might
prove of service for campaigning purposes in South Africa. The gun
was the 2·5-inch R.M.L. "screw" gun, mounted on its usual carriage,
but with a special limber added. The gun was drawn by a pair of
cobs abreast, with pole and breast harness, and driver mounted. The
ammunition was carried in trench carts, with special lids, drawn by a
pair of cobs like the gun. Officers, Nos. 1, trumpeters, etc., were
mounted on cobs. A sub-section comprised gun and carriage, two
ammunition carts and a kit-cart; there were also two store carts per
battery. The two batteries carried out practice at Okehampton in
1895, where it was found that the gun was very prone to capsize when
traversing rough country or when firing from unlevel ground; but it
could always be turned right side up again, without damage sustained.

As the detachment had to walk, the battery did not possess the
speed mobility of a normal field battery on ordinary ground. Nor
did it possess the mobility of a pack battery armed with the same gun
in difficult mountainous terrain. Short trots were indulged in when
coming into action, the detachments doubling behind, but for practical
purposes the pace was the pace of a pack battery. (On march in the
United Kingdom the gunners went by train if the distance exceeded
20 miles). The 2·5-inch gun of course fell far short of the 12-pr. B.L.
or the 15-pr. B.L. in respect to power. The idea of introducing batteries of this type into the service was abandoned in 1896.

CHAPTER
VIII.

Heavy
ordnance
for the
field.
attitude adopted in regard to this matter at home was that, when urgent demands for mobile heavy guns reached the War Office from South Africa shortly after the outbreak of hostilities in that quarter in 1899, improvisation had hastily to be resorted to.

That so little advance in respect to heavy artillery for the field was made in England during these fifteen years was however very largely due to a growing recognition in the Regiment of the value of howitzers.   In respect to this form of ordnance very important developments were taking place.

Howitzers.   A brief reference has already been made to the adoption of the field howitzer. This made its first appearance in 1896[1] although trials had taken place some years earlier. The pattern adopted was a 5-inch breech-loading piece, which fired a 50 lbs. projectile—a piece which was signalised by its having a comparatively short length of bore and by its possessing but a limited range.   Other natures of B.L. howitzer which were introduced between the years 1884 and 1899 were :—(a) a 5·4-inch of 13-cwt., which was designed exclusively for use in India, where the military authorities insisted upon having a 60 lb. shell; (b) a 6-inch of 25 cwt. which was likewise intended exclusively for India; (c) a 6-inch of 30 cwt.   The authorities in India had moreover for some years been desirous of introducing some form of portable howitzer for employment in the hill campaigns which had so often to be undertaken on the north-west frontier, their great difficulty being that a mule load must not exceed a total of about 200 lbs.   To meet their requirements, a 4-inch, jointed, R.M.L. howitzer of 600 lbs. was designed, and this was in due course introduced for service with mountain batteries.

**Siege
Train.**   It should be mentioned that, during the greater part of this 1884-1899 period, the authorised organization for

---

[1] Sir John Headlam in Chapter XI explains how the abandonment of common shell for field batteries helped to bring about the introduction of field howitzer batteries into our service.

a siege train should one be mobilised, remained as follows.
There were to be three different units—"Heavy", "Medium" and "Light", and their composition was laid down
in Regulations as :—

Heavy Unit.	Four 40-prs. R.M.L., two 6·6-inch R.M.L. howitzers, and ten 8-inch R.M.L. howitzers.
Medium Unit.	Six 40-prs. R.M.L. and ten 6·6-inch R.M.L. howitzers.
Light Unit.	Eight 25-prs. R.M.L. and eight 6·3-inch R.M.L. howitzers.

But on the introduction of the 6-inch B.L. howitzer of
30 cwt., this came for practical purposes to be looked upon
as the sole armament of a siege train. Guns dropped out
altogether—at least in principle. An 8-inch B.L. howitzer
was, moreover, in the experimental stage in the year 1899;
but it had not yet at that date been definitely introduced
into the service.

In the meantime the re-armament of our coast defences
made but slow progress. Although ordnance of the new
B.L. type had been introduced into all ships building for
the Royal Navy between the years 1880 and 1890, and had
also to some extent been substituted for the R.M.L. guns
in ships already in the service, coast batteries, alike at
home and abroad, remained until about the year 1899
armed solely with the virtually obsolete muzzle-loading
guns. A Committee appointed to enquire into the fortification and armament of our military and home commercial
ports in 1887 had come to the conclusion that deficiencies
existed in each of them which rendered our position
dangerously insecure. Their criticism was directed partially at the design and the situation of the batteries, but
was largely, if not mainly, directed at the obsolete char-

CHAPTER
VIII.

Coast
defence
armament.

acter of the armament.[1] The question was thereupon taken in hand by the Secretary of State for War (the Hon. E. Stanhope) and his military advisers, and it was decided to allot considerable sums within the ensuing three years to the re-armament of coast defences in general.

A number of different "Marks" of the 6-inch B.L., of the 9-inch B.L. and of the 10-inch B.L. were in use by that time in the sea service, and the guns of these natures which were now mounted in our coast batteries were mostly of the latest patterns approved by the Ordnance Committee. The original 6-inch B.L. guns purchased from Elswick (as related in the last chapter), were pieces of 81 cwt., built up after the old plan of a steel inner-tube with wrought iron coils shrunk on to it. But the guns of this calibre introduced into the land service were of improved pattern; they weighed 5 tons and were constructed of steel hoops shrunk over a steel inner-tube, and by the year 1899 a considerable number of them had been mounted in the various maritime fortresses. Some 8-inch B.L. guns, especially purchased from Elswick, were mounted at Hong Kong. But, as regards the heavier natures of B.L. ordnance, that which was most freely introduced for coast defence during this period was the 9·2-inch constructed wholly of steel and weighing 23 tons. A few 10-inch B.L., of 32 tons, had also been mounted before 1899, but the 6-inch and the 9·2-inch were considered to be those most suitable for this class of battery. They were in many cases combined, two of each, in a single work.

Still, even so late as the year 1899, the armament of British maritime strongholds (leaving that intended purely for anti-torpedo-boat defence out of consideration) consisted largely, if not indeed mainly, of old 10-inch and 12·5-inch R.M.L. guns—ordnance completely outranged

---

[1] Speaking in the House of Commons in March 1888, Lt.-General Sir E. B. Hamley, R.A., referred to "the ridiculous spectacle of defensive works which are not defensible, armed with obsolete and dismounted artillery."

by that mounted in the modern warships maintained by this country and by most foreign naval Powers. These R.M.L. guns, housed in casemates, were to be found in very large numbers both in the more important fortresses such as Plymouth and Malta, and in the numerous coaling stations maintained oversea. Such armament, obsolete except where it was being employed to defend a channel, absorbed, gun for gun, as many officers and men for its service, as did the modern effective B.L. ordnance. The military authorities were however by that date coming to realise that maintaining this antiquated armament at all— and particularly when the armament was (as was usually the case) emplaced in works of antiquated construction— was unwarrantable and was terribly wasteful in personnel.[1]

High-angle batteries, armed with guns which were in reality the equivalent of howitzers (although not originally designed as such) became a feature in the defences of certain of our maritime places of arms subsequent to the year 1893. These batteries were fitted out either with the old 9-inch R.M.L., or else with the old 9-inch R.M.L. converted into a 10-inch, the guns being mounted on specially designed high-angle carriages. They were intended to meet the case of hostile warships lying far out to sea off a dockyard and bombarding its establishments at extreme range. Even if they provided against a contingency which might not be very likely to occur, these batteries did enjoy one advantage in that they could be planted down, completely concealed, behind cover.[2]

The Royal Artillery had no quick-firing guns until subsequent to the year 1888. Light Q.F. ordnance for dealing with torpedo craft—3-pr. and 6-pr. Nordenfelt and Hotchkiss guns, firing from fixed pivots, with "elastic-frame mountings"—had been introduced into the Royal Navy

---

[1] In practice the establishment was not kept up.

[2] See p. 319. The advantage was not however so great as might, at first sight, be supposed, for cordite could not be used with these H.A. muzzle-loading guns and the smoke on discharge would indicate the position of the battery to an enemy.

CHAPTER
VIII.

Q.F. guns
for
harbour
defence.

even before 1883; and by that year most of the newer
battle-ships and cruisers flying the White Ensign were provided with a quota of them.   The 4·7-inch Q.F., produced
by Elswick in the year 1887, was moreover at once accepted
for the sea service, and its introduction was followed up a
year or two later by the adoption of the 6-inch Q.F.   Ten
of these latter powerful pieces were allocated as auxiliary
armament to each of the eight "Royal Sovereign" battle-
ships, laid down as a principal item of construction under
the memorable Lord George Hamilton naval programme
of the year 1889.   The land service on the other hand—
necessarily so owing to the lack of funds for the purpose—
lagged far behind the sister service in this respect.

CARRIAGE, GARRISON, Q.F. 12 P^R MARK I
SCALE - ABOUT ⅛

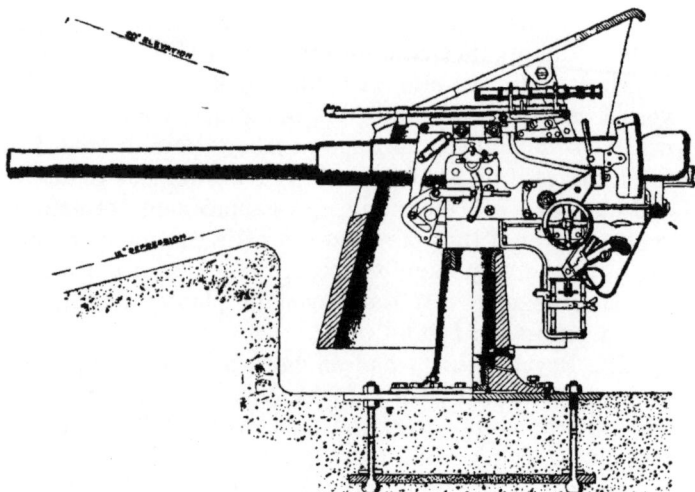

In the Stanhope programme adopted in the year 1888,
the provision of light Q.F. guns and the construction of
appropriate emplacements for them however played an
important part.   It was estimated that the cost of the

steps about to be taken to improve harbour defence would come to £799,000, spread over three years.[1] The result was that, by the year 1892, large numbers of 6-pr. Q.F. and of 12-pr. Q.F. had been mounted at the entrances of the most important defended havens at home and abroad. As the importance of this class of armament became still better appreciated, practically all our defended ports were protected by an adequate number of these light pieces by the year 1899. Moreover the merits of a type of Q.F. gun heavier than the 12-pr. for dealing with enemy destroyers, were fully appreciated by that date; some 4·7-inch Q.F. guns had therefore been mounted about the entrances of harbours of first class naval importance.[2]

With a view to still further increasing the circumferential strength of guns, besides obtaining other advantages, a method of manufacture called "wire construction" was introduced about this time. It was simply a development of the principle of making the exterior part of a gun take a due share of the strain, and it is impossible to accord absolute priority of invention to any one individual, but Mr. J. A. Longridge, c.e., was the first patentee, and to him belongs the credit of consistently following up and strongly advocating the system from the very first.[3]

The advantages of the wire system of construction may be stated briefly as follows :—

CHAPTER VIII.

Q.F. guns for harbour defence.

Wire construction.

---

[1] A portion of this sum was allocated to the development of submarine mining and to installations for the Brennan torpedo.

[2] Although the merits of quick-firing armament for horse and field artillery were generally realised if a suitable carriage could be designed, the difficulty of completely overcoming recoil on a travelling carriage had not been met by the year 1899.

[3] See his "Treaties on the Application of Wire to the construction of Ordnance " (1884), and "Further investigations regarding Wire Gun Construction " (1887).

(1) Absolute soundness of the material . . . . whereas no possible testing or care in manufacture could ensure this result in forged steel hoops.

(2) Possibility of regulating the tension of the successive layers with the utmost nicety.

(3) Greater tensile strength of steel in the form of wire or riband[1] than in hoops.

ORDNANCE, B. L. 12-PR. 6 CWT.

— SCALE ⅟₁₀. —

— DEVELOPMENT OF GROOVE —

SECTION OF GROOVE
FULL SIZE
Nº OF GROOVES 18

RIFLING A UNIFORMLY INCREASING TWIST FROM I TURN IN
105 CALIBRES AT BREECH END OF RIFLING 10 I TURN IN 28 CALS AT 15
FROM THE MUZZLE THE REMAINING 15 BEING UNIFORM AT I TURN IN 28 CALS.

On the other hand the wire provided no longitudinal strength, and in the long guns then coming in this required special measures. But by the end of the period most of the later marks of guns (except siege and light Q.F.) were constructed on this principle, viz. :—

B.L. 12 pr. of 6 cwt., 6″ VII, 9·2″ VIII—X, 12″ VIII—IX. Q.F. 4″, 4·7″ IV, 6″ II.

Cordite   Improvements in ammunition advanced *pari passu* with improvements in gun construction. The progress made in ammunition indeed helped to some extent in shaping the progress made with regard to ordnance. Brief reference has already been made to the adoption of cordite as a

---

[1] The actual form used was a riband, rectangular in Section, ·25″ × ·66″.

propellant. A compound composed of 58 p.c. of nitro-
glycerine, 37 p.c. of gun-cotton, and 5 p.c. of mineral
jelly, cordite was approved for general purposes in the year
1891. It differed totally as regards ingredients from the
gun-powder which had hitherto in various forms been the
accepted propellant for use alike with small arms and with
cannon. Virtually smokeless owing to its products being
all gaseous, cordite does not foul the bore of the gun or
howitzer, it permits of a relatively smaller charge being
used to ensure a given pressure on the projectile than
where gun-powder is employed, and, thanks to its more
controllable combustion, the strain upon the bore of the
piece can be better distributed than was the case with older
forms of propellant. That its introduction permitted of the
12-pr. B.L. field artillery gun being converted into a 15-pr.,
has already been mentioned. It became, as soon as was
practicable, the approved propellant for all B.L. and Q.F.
ordnance in the land service.[1] The older forms of propellant however continued to be in use with the heavy
R.M.L. guns which still remained mounted in so many
of our coast defence works, as also with the R.M.L. howitzers and with the mountain guns that were in use.

The projectiles for the B.L. guns and howitzers which Shells and
came into the hands of the Royal Artillery during this fuzes.
period, were distinguished from the projectiles employed
with R.M.L. ordnance in that rotation was given by means
of driving bands, instead of its being imparted by means of
gas-checks or (as held good with the older natures of
R.M.L. ordnance) by means of studs. Another step in
advance was that steel came to be brought largely into use
as the material for the body of projectiles, in substitution
for cast iron. Then again, bursting charges for common
shell had always up to the year 1898 consisted of gun-

---

[1] Cordite is manufactured in the form of sticks of different
diameters. Just as in the case of the different forms of gun-powder
the rate of burning is varied by the size of the grain, or pebble, or
cube, or prism, so in the case of cordite the rate of burning is varied
by the diameter of the stick. Some of the sticks are made tubular.

powder. But in that year a high explosive in the shape of lyddite was introduced for this purpose. This was adopted for the bursting charges of common shell for all natures of B.L. guns and howitzers of over 4·7-inch calibre.[1]

It has also to be noted in connection with projectiles that for some years past there had been a tendency to reduce the proportion of common shell as compared to that of shrapnel in the equipment of horse and field batteries. Although the employment of steel enabled the body of common shell to be thinner, and the bursting charge proportionately greater, experiments satisfied the authorities that common shell fired from light guns had little effect. This form of projectile consequently ceased to be included in R.H.A. and R.F.A. equipment.[2]

Marked improvement was effected in the design of fuzes. Metal time fuzes gradually superseded the old Boxer pattern and modified Boxer patterns of wooden fuzes. Those in store were used up at practice. Improved forms of percussion fuze were also adopted. The introduction of lyddite rendered imperative in itself, it should be observed, the devising of a percussion fuze which could be relied upon under no circumstances to act prematurely on shock of discharge.[3]

Wrought-iron was already before 1884 beginning to give place to steel as the main material out of which gun-carriages and gun-mountings of all kinds were being constructed, and between 1884 and 1899 this material practically ceased to be employed. The elaborate mountings that were coming into use for the heavy B.L. ordnance

---

[1] Powder filled shell were thenceforward called "common" while shell filled with high explosive was called "high explosive common" at first, but later on came to be called simply "H.E."

[2] Sir John Headlam deals with this point in greater detail in Chapter XI.

[3] The risk of a powder-filled shell bursting in the bore could be faced because it usually only damaged the bore, whereas the detonation of a H.E. shell would shatter the gun and be disastrous to the detachment.

employed by the Royal Navy and in coast defence works were of steel. It was the material out of which the pivots, the cradles, etc., connected with the light Q.F. guns employed for harbour protection were manufactured. The new patterns of field and siege travelling carriages likewise were constructed almost entirely out of steel.

The increase of power in the various new types of ordnance being brought into use during this 1885-1899 period automatically carried with it an increase in the recoil of the actual gun when fired. It rendered improved recoil-checking devices imperative. The problem presented to designers was necessarily easier of solution in the case of ordnance on fixed mountings, than it was in the case of travelling carriages, seeing that weight was not a matter of vital importance when a fixed mounting was in question. But in the case of a travelling carriage, and particularly in that of a gun-carriage for horse or field artillery, weight was a governing factor. Buffers, springs and similar devices could be multiplied in the fixed mounting, but not in the travelling carriage. The recoil of the 13-pr. R.M.L. (the recoil, that is to say, of the gun and carriage on discharge of the piece) had, as mentioned in Chapter VII, proved excessive. Particular attention was therefore paid to this very important point when the carriages for the various experimental 12-pr. B.L. guns were being constructed; but wholly satisfactory results had not been arrived at when a design was definitely approved and introduced.

In the early 12-pr. gun-carriage the plan adopted for controlling the recoil was that of a form of break which acted on the flange of the wheel and by which the wheel was jammed. Shoe brakes were employed in addition; but, even with the help of these latter, the recoil was found to be excessive by batteries at gun practice. When it was decided to employ a lighter 12-pr. for the R.H.A., and to convert the existing 12-pr. into a 15-pr. for the field artillery, the carriages were modified to some extent. But it

Chapter VIII.

Carriages and mountings.

was not till a year or two later that the plan of an "axle spade", coupled with tyre brakes, was hit upon. Although this arrangement had been applied to the carriages of all field and horse artillery batteries stationed at home by the year 1899, the design had not come into use in India, so that the field batteries included in the Indian Contingent which arrived in Natal at the time of the outbreak of the South African War, were not equipped with it.[1]

In the case of the 5-inch field howitzer the recoil problem was partially met by the howitzer recoiling in a cradle provided with an hydraulic buffer and spring, while the recoil of the carriage was checked by shoe brakes. The recoil of the carriage was not however sufficiently controlled by this. In the case of siege guns and howitzers the intention was that recoil should be checked by a tension, hydraulic recoil-buffer, one end fixed to the carriage and the other end to the platform; but this plan did not meet the case of such guns or howitzers when used in the field without platforms. The travelling carriage for the 6-inch B.L. howitzer of 30 cwt marked a distinct advance; it was so contrived as to be capable of employment with or without the wheels when bringing the piece into action. Without its wheels, the carriage resting on a platform, the design admitted of the howitzer being given extreme degrees of elevation.

When the 6-inch B.L., the 9·2-inch B.L. and the 10-inch B.L. guns were first introduced into our coast defence works, their mountings were almost entirely of the disappearing, hydro-pneumatic type. These "H.P. mountings" gave satisfaction in what may be called the mechanical and technical sense as soon as the R.G.A. personnel

[1] In certain "Marks" of gun carriage for the 12-pr. B.L. of 7 cwt., and the 15-pr. B.L. there was a top carriage, with a buffer absorbing some of the recoil of the gun and moreover admitting of a traverse of 4 degrees, independently of the trail (see p. 190). The old R.B.L. horse and field gun-carriages had been fitted out with a traversing device, but the plan had been dropped for the sake of simplicity when the carriages for the 9-pr. R.M.L. the 16-pr. R.M.L. and the 13-pr. R.M.L. were designed.

grew used to them.   They did undoubtedly in spite of their
many complications, prove serviceable during the stress of
actual gun practice.   But R.G.A. officers concerned in

CARRIAGE, SEIGE, TOP, B.L. 6-INCH. 25 CWT, HOWITZER, MARK I.

SCALE ⅒

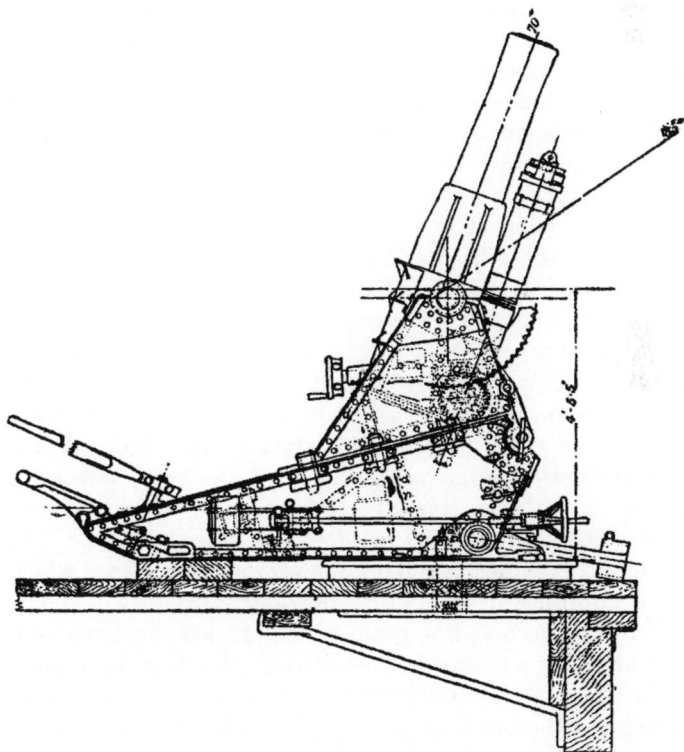

coast defence began towards the end of the 1884-1899
period to perceive that, besides the objections to it due to
its complexity, this H.P. disappearing system of gun-

mounting necessarily checked the rapidity of fire of the
gun as compared with that of a gun on a non-disappearing
mounting. The truth is that the efficiency of our coast
defence artillery often suffered during the last thirty
years of the nineteenth century owing to tactical requirements being insufficiently kept in mind as compared with
the attractions afforded by mechanical ingenuity. The
H.P. mountings might delude the gunnery-expert pure and
simple; but the disappearing principle, however suitable
when applied to artillery intended to fight an enemy on
land where protection was of cardinal importance, was
fundamentally unsound when applied to ordnance ashore
intended to oppose the guns of a hostile warship. The
fire of the ship would not, in all reasonable likelihood, be
sufficiently accurate to justify that retardation in the rate
of discharge which the vanishings of the gun into its pit,
and its return to the firing position, rendered inevitable.

The question of pole versus shaft draught had been a
subject of debate in the Regiment for years. The Bengal
and Madras Artilleries had, as already mentioned in
Chapter I depended upon pole-draught in their horse and
field batteries, whereas the Bombay Artillery, like the
Royal Artillery, employed shafts. Subsequently to the
amalgamation all batteries were fitted out with shafts.[1]
But, as the years passed, and when it was observed that
practically all foreign artilleries used the pole, advocates
of the shafts grew fewer and fewer and it was at last
decided in the year 1889 to adopt the other method. The
system actually decided upon was very similar to that which
had been in use in the Bengal horse artillery.

During the first few years of this period the horse and
field artillery continued to rely upon the Watkin Range-
finder, in so far as they depended upon any means of range-
finding at all other than the gun itself; but the Mekometer

---

[1] It had only been by the casting vote of the chairman (who belonged to the Royal Artillery) of the Committee which settled the
matter in 1859 prior to the amalgamation, that shaft draft was decided
upon for the amalgamated regiment.

supplanted it in 1895 owing to ranges being taken more
rapidly with it and because it was not so conspicuous as
the Watkin range-finder when being used. Great progress was in the meantime made in this respect in our
coast artillery. The efficiency of coast batteries was, in
the first place, vastly increased by the introduction, early
in the eighties, of the Depression Range-Finder, even if
the device was from its nature but ill adapted for employment in the low-lying works found in many maritime places
of arms. The appearance of the Depression Range-Finder
was followed within a very few years by the introduction
into the service of the Position-finder coupled with electrical communications. By the year 1899 all our first class
maritime fortresses were furnished with P.F. installations
in connection with most of the B.L. guns, as also of the
high-angle batteries included in their seaward defences.[1]
The D.R.F. and the P.F. were both the product of Major
H. S. S. Watkin's inventive brain.[2]

The system that had been introduced by Mr. Cardwell,
under which a Surveyor-General of the Ordnance dealt
with supply in general, as head of one of the three great
departments into which the War Office was divided, was
retained until the end of the year 1887. The post was then
abolished by Mr. Stanhope, the Secretary of State for War,
the department was broken up, and its various branches
and sub-divisions were transferred either to the Commander-in-Chief's department or to the Finance Depart-

---

[1] Use of the P.F. practically neutralised difficulties caused by
smoke, but cordite was introduced about the same time as the P.F.
In later days the P.F. instrument depending on angle of depression
was called the D.P.F., as distinguished from the H.P.F.—the horizontal position-finder used for low sites.

[2] Colonel H. S. S. Watkin c.b., had joined the Regiment in 1864;
he became full colonel in 1895 and died in 1905. Besides his range-
finder used in the field, and the D.R.F. and P.F., he invented various
devices of the clinometer type. He held the post of Inspector of
Range-Finding for some years, and in his particular line he had no
rival. The effect of his inventions on the training of the Royal Artillery is dealt with in Chapter XVI.

CHAPTER
VIII.

Responsi-
bility for
the supply
of artillery
material.
ment. The Commander-in-Chief under this new dispensa-
tion became generally responsible for the housing, the
clothing, the food and the armament of the soldier, as well
as for his discipline and training.   In so far as artillery
material was concerned, previously under the Director of
Artillery and Stores, this vitally important branch of the
Surveyor-General's department was transferred to the
charge of the Commander-in-Chief.   Without appreciably
altering his duties and responsibilities, its Director became
head of one of the five main departments on the military
side of the War Office.   His title was at the same time
altered to that of Director of Artillery, Major-General Sir
H. J. Alderson continuing to hold the appointment.

A noteworthy change as regards responsibility for the
Government Manufacturing Departments was however carried out at the same time. A committee had been appointed
by Mr. Campbell-Bannerman as S. of S. for War in 1886
to enquire into their organization and administration.
The main recommendation of this body had been that a
Superintendent of Ordnance Factories should be created
who would be under the Director of Artillery and Stores,
and that an Inspector-General of Warlike Stores should
be appointed who would be under the Surveyor-General of
Ordnance.   The principle of separating manufacture from
inspection, to which the committee had attached great importance, was adopted in 1887 by Mr. Stanhope (who had
succeeded Mr. Campbell-Bannerman), but the plan arrived
at did not follow the actual recommendations of the committee, the post of Surveyor-General of the Ordnance
having indeed been abolished.   Inspection of warlike
stores, whether produced by Government factories or furnished by contractors had hitherto been carried out by the
Assistant-Superintendents of the five great Government
factories—The Royal Gun Factory, the Royal Carriage
Department, the Royal Laboratory, Waltham Abbey and
Enfield—each of whom had under him a Captain In-

spector.[1] Contractors were wont to complain of a system CHAPTER VIII. under which the Government institutions enjoyed the advantage of to some extent inspecting their own produce as Responsibility for well as the produce tendered from outside.   Under the plan the supply introduced in 1887 the Government factories were placed of artillery under the Financial Secretary to the War Office, while in-material. spectional responsibilities remained under the Director of Artillery and Stores. The appointment of Director-General of Ordnance Factories was at the same time created.

Sir Henry Alderson was succeeded in 1891 by Major-General R. Hay, whose title was in 1895, at the time of Lord Wolseley's assumption of the position of Commander-in-Chief, changed to Inspector-General of Ordnance; the position was at the same time under the provisions of an Order in Council raised (together with that of the Adjutant-General, the Quarter-Master-General and the Inspector-General of Fortifications) to that of being virtually a colleague of the Commander-in-Chief.   The title was changed afresh in 1899, the more appropriate one of Director-General of Ordnance being chosen when the appointment was taken over by Lieut.-General Sir H. Brackenbury.

Although the constitution of the Ordnance Committee The remained practically the same during this period as had Ordnance Com- been laid down in respect to its personnel at the time when mittee. it was resuscitated in the year 1881,[2] the principle of "Associate Members", definitely appointed as such, was introduced.   These Associate Members were only called upon to attend meetings of the Committee when questions directly affecting their own branch of the Regiment were to come up for discussion. They were drawn from officers of experience holding actual commands, and who were therefore in close practical touch with units and in a posi-

---

[1] In the case of the Royal Gun Factory, the Captain Inspector was also "Proof Officer" and carried out all firing tests for the proof of guns, as well as all experimental firing for other departments of the Arsenal and for the Ordnance Committee. He also carried out the firing experiments of powder for Waltham Abbey.

[2] President, Vice-President, 2 members R.N., 3 members R.A., 1 member R.E. and 2 civilian members, with a secretary and an assistant secretary.

CHAPTER
VIII.

The
Ordnance
Com-
mittee. tion to gauge the views concerning matters of armament and equipment held by officers serving with the troops. The normal arrangement followed was for two senior officers to represent the R.H.A. and the field artillery, for one such officer to represent coast defence artillery, for another to represent siege artillery, and for yet another to represent mountain artillery. Besides these representatives of the Royal Artillery, the list of Associate Members included delegates from the Royal Engineers, as well also as certain civilian specialists. These assistants of the Ordnance Committee drew allowances for days when they were employed with it, but did not receive special pay in addition to their ordinary emoluments.

Lieut.-General Sir M. A. S. Biddulph succeeded Sir C. Dickson as President in the year 1886, and at the end of his five years term he was replaced by Major-General Sir H. S. Alderson from the War Office. Alderson was succeeded in the year 1896 by Lt.-Genl. Sir H. Brackenbury, who had recently given up the appointment of Military Member of Council in India. On Brackenbury becoming Director-General of Ordnance at Headquarters early in 1899, Lieut.-General H. le G. Geary became President.

The experimental side of Shoeburyness enjoyed some further expansion in respect to the staff and personnel of the Experimental Detachment, as also in respect to the lands, the plant and the buildings under charge of the detachment, during this period. The Commandant of the School of Gunnery continued to duplicate responsibility for instruction with that of general supervision over experiments; but during all the latter years he had to aid him a First, a Second and a Third Assistant Superintendent of Experiments. Although minor contretemps had occurred on one or two occasions, causing slight injuries to individuals, the personnel of the Experimental Detachment had happily, since it had been created, enjoyed almost complete immunity from really serious accidents in connection with its labours, up till the 26th February 1885. But on that day a terrible disaster occurred at Shoeburyness.

Trials were being carried out in connection with a
sensitive percussion fuze of delayed action. It was a base
fuze, the invention of Colonel F. Lyon, Superintendent of
the Royal Laboratory, and it was about to be tried with a
6-inch common shell. The fuze had been screwed into
the shell, and a lead washer was being tapped into a
recess in the shell to protect the fuze, a number of officers
and rank-and-file standing around, when the shell ex-
ploded. Gunner Allen, who was carrying out the work,
was killed on the spot. Colonel W. M. Fox-Strangways
(Commandant of the School of Gunnery), Colonel Lyon,
Captain F. M. Goold-Adams (Assistant Superintendent of
Experiments), and Sergeant-Major Daykin all received
such grave injuries that they succumbed. Others were
more or less seriously, although not fatally damaged.
Many unfortunate accidents in connection with guns and
ammunition, in which members of the Regiment have lost
their lives, have occurred in peace time and on active
service since the year 1860. But it stands to the credit
of the personnel of the Experimental Detachment, considering the nature of its duties, that this disaster at Shoeburyness in 1885 has been the only really serious mis-
adventure in which its personnel has been involved.

The first to hold the appointment of Director of Ordnance Factories was Major-General E. Maitland, R.A.
His responsibilities covered not only the Royal Arsenal,
but also the Royal Small Arms Factory at Enfield with its
branch at Birmingham, the Royal Gunpowder Factory at
Waltham Abbey, and the Royal Clothing Department in
Pimlico. Up till that year the Royal Gun Factory and the
Royal Carriage Department within the Royal Arsenal had
for long past always (except for the brief period when
Sir W. Armstrong was in charge of the R.G.F.) been under
charge of officers of the Regiment. But an officer of the
Royal Engineers now became head of the Royal Carriage
Department, and in the following year an officer of the
Royal Navy became Superintendent of the Royal Gun
Factory; these arrangements moreover held good up to

P

1899.   General Maitland was succeeded in the year 1889
by a civilian, Mr. (afterwards Sir W.) Anderson, who was
to fill the position of Director up to the year 1899.

As a consequence of the Manufacturing Departments
ceasing to be under the military side of the War Office,
and of their having been placed under the Financial Secretary, it became necessary to establish an Inspection Branch[1]
under the Director of Artillery, and this was set on foot
early in 1888. Its staff were given gradings—Chief Inspector, Assistant-Inspector, and so on— and were in the
first instance found entirely from officers of the Regiment.
At the outset there was only one Chief Inspector—Colonel
W. H. King-Harman, who dealt with small arms. As a
result of experience, however, the authorities found it
necessary to create the appointment of Chief Inspector at
the Royal Arsenal in 1893, and Major (afterwards Major-
General Sir C. F.) Hadden was chosen to fill the position.
The Royal Gun Factory, the Royal Carriage Department
and the Royal Laboratory had each been allotted their
quota of inspectors when the branch was formed, and this
arrangement remained in force; but the Chief Inspector
was in a position to co-ordinate the work besides super-
vising its execution, and was most successful in doing so.
The staff dealt both with the output of the Government
factories and also with the war material that was furnished
by contractors. One of the responsibilities which the
inspectors took over was that of carrying out the proof of
guns at the Woolwich butts, a responsibility which before
the creation of the Inspection Branch had, as we have
seen, rested with the Captain Inspector of the R.G.F. and
his assistants.

The Inspection Branch was thenceforward to provide
employment for a considerable number of officers of the
Regiment who possessed scientific qualifications. The

---

[1] The Inspection Branch cost the country a good deal of money.
Each of the Government factories was obliged to examine its own
manufactures before submitting them to the Branch. The work in consequence was in reality done twice over, which caused expense and
which moreover gave rise to delay.

personnel was mainly furnished from the ranks of those
who had passed the "Advanced Class", or "Senior Class,
Artillery College", as it was called in later years.

The plan introduced in 1887, under which the Manufacturing Departments had been placed under the Financial
Secretary of the War Office while the Inspection Branch
was placed under the Director of Artillery, had not worked
satisfactorily, although the principle of a special Inspection
Branch was acknowledged to be sound.   Friction had
occurred, and that this was the case had become apparent
to Sir H. Brackenbury while he was holding the appointment of President of the Ordnance Committee.   He had
made it a condition of his accepting the appointment of
Director-General of Ordnance in the early part of 1899 that
the Manufacturing Departments should come under his
charge.   This change was carried into effect within a few
months and the result was a marked improvement in the
working of the machinery.

Chapter
VIII.

Responsi-
bility for
the Manu-
facturing
Depart-
ments
taken over
by the
Director-
General of
Ordnance.

PART III.—TRAINING.

A.   HORSE & FIELD ARTILLERY.

PART III.

TRAINING.

By Sir JOHN HEADLAM.

A.   Horse & Field Artillery.

B.   Mountain, Heavy, & Siege Artillery.

C.   Coast Artillery.

CHAPTER IX.

THE FRANCO-GERMAN WAR.

The Troops and Batteries in the 60's—India—The Training Manuals—
The first Manœuvres—The Mobility of field batteries—The new
Training Manuals—The first Practice Camp—Prince Kraft's Letters.

IN 1860—the first year of the period chronicled in this
volume—the Royal Artillery received the famous "Armstrong" rifled guns. They marked the opening of a new
era, but there is little indication that the effect of their
introduction—or that of rifled muskets—on the employment of artillery in the field was at all realised at the
time, either by the Regiment, or by the Army at large.
To understand aright the developments in artillery training which eventually resulted, it is necessary to appreciate
this fact, and also to take cognizance of the state of the
troops and batteries when they first received the new
armament.[1]

CHAPTER
IX.

The
Troops &
Batteries
in the 60's.

In the Horse Artillery rapidity of fire and movement
was still the great desideratum, and with a permanent
organization, regularly maintained, and a picked *personnel*,
this quality had been developed to the highest possible
pitch of perfection. Magnificently dressed and horsed, the
troops were the admiration of all—a *corps d'élite* in the
fullest sense of the term.

Very different was the case of the Field Batteries.

---

[1] For an account of the state of the Regiment in the 50's see *The
History of the Royal Artillery (Crimean Period)*: by Colonel Julian
R. J. Jocelyn.

General
IX.

The
Troops &
Batteries
in the 60's.

Their permanence as mounted troops still in jeopardy;[1] horsed with flat-sided, hairy-heeled, underbred brutes— coarse without being powerful[2]—and condemned to a uniform that was at once incongruous and unserviceable, it is little wonder that they could not compare in appearance or general estimation with the Horse Artillery. Above all, they were not "mobile" as the term is now understood.   In spite of the incident[3] in the Peninsula when the absence of the gunners, labouring breathless behind, nearly resulted in the capture of Wellington; and of the similar episode at the Alma when "Staff Officers and Divisional Artillery Commanders had to throw themselves from their horses to serve the guns until the arrival of their panting detachments", the "Order of March", with the gunners tramping solemnly beside their guns, was still insisted on when acting with other troops.   There is some ground for thinking that this tradition, unknown in any other country, was fostered by jealousy on the part of the horse artillery, many of the officers of which prided themselves on having served only in "The Horse" or "The Foot", and affected to look down on field artillerymen as those who "rode cart horses and called their trousers overalls!"

While in outward appearance, and even in efficiency by the standard of days that had passed, the difference between the troops and batteries was thus great, there was little to choose between them as regards their practical training in the use of their new weapons.   It was not their fault, for the first essential—ground—was denied them. For drill and manœuvre the great majority had only the miserable drill-fields provided at country quarters, or the crowded commons of Woolwich and Plumstead.   For prac-

---

[1] The Regimental Order of 1st April, 1859, stated that field batteries were liable to be changed back to garrison at any time.

[2] There were some favoured batteries which were exceptions.

[3] See *The Mobility of Field Artillery* by Captain H. L. Hime— "Proceedings," Vol. VIII, and *The History of the Royal Artillery (Crimean period)*, by Colonel Julian R. J. Jocelyn, pages 24-5.

tice the only land ranges—so-called—were the Plumstead
Marshes and the sands at Shoeburyness. Elsewhere batteries retired to the nearest seaside resort for a pleasant
picnic, and got rid of their allowance of shot and shell at
a barrel moored off the beach! But of blank ammunition
there was no lack, and the drills were enlivened by a lavish
expenditure, in which rapidity in getting off the first round
was the only thing that mattered. Smart subalterns carried a cartridge or two in their wallets, and it was not uncommon for the gun to be fired while the rammer was still
in the bore—to the consternation of the spectators. So
serious was the tale of accidents that field batteries were
forbidden to practice the favourite manœuvre of "retiring
by alternate half-batteries in action", and were obliged to
use the "prolong" instead.[1]

In the days of short ranges and close-order tactics
elaborate evolutions, exactly executed, had been essential
to that conformity with the movements of the other arms
required of the artillery,[2] and the field-days on Woolwich
Common demanded a continuance of such complicated
manœuvres. The drill of those days was indeed a fine art.[3]
Not only were the movements of the guns intricate to a
degree, but every gun was closely accompanied throughout
by its wagon, which had to "cover off" after every change
of position of the gun however slight, and no movement
might be made without an express order from the No. 1.

---

[1] The prolong was a short rope attachment from the trail eye to
the limber hook, which was used to allow of the gun being withdrawn
without limbering up.

[2] The first order given to "I" Troop at Inkerman, when the
Russians came upon them through the mist, was "Change Front, Right
Back!"—one of the most complicated of the battery evolutions.
(Changes and Chances of a Soldier's Life by Major-General Sir E. S.
May).

[3] Up to 1873 batteries galloped past at close interval, detachments
front. On one occasion Sir W. Bell, who had been adjutant to Sir
Augustus Frazer, commanding the R.H.A. at Waterloo, came down
while in front of his troop during this performance. Wonderful to
relate he come out alive, but the swinging drag-shoe of a gun had
snicked off his ear as clean as if cut with a razor. The No. 1 picked
it up and returned it to its owner.

CHAPTER
IX.

The
Troops &
Batteries
in the 60's.
The words of command were thus long and involved, and those of their superiors had to be repeated—at the top of their voices—by each rank in the hierarchy, from battery commander to No. 1, before the giving by each of his own executive order.

Another legacy from the days when the round shot were apt to knock the equipment about was the importance attached to rapidity in the execution of such operations as changing shafts and wheels, mounting and dismounting guns, and especially to "removing disabled field artillery", for which elaborate drills were laid down covering every conceivable casualty.[1] These were for many years a prominent feature of all artillery competitions, very much on the lines of the Naval field gun events which are now such a popular feature of the Royal Tournament.

What has been said above as regards the conditions of the Horse and Field Artillery at Home applies, broadly speaking, to the troops and batteries of the Indian Artilleries. The troops rivalled those of the Royal Horse Artillery in magnificence of appearance, in pride of bearing, in rapidity of manœuvre, and perhaps outstripped them in fearless horsemanship.[2] For many years to come it was to be an article of faith in the artillery in India that, in this respect at any rate, they could teach those at home a lesson. The field batteries suffered under very similar disadvantages to those in England, in spite of their many brilliant exploits in the Mutiny. Like them they were only temporary formations, and like them they were apt to find their interests sacrificed to those of the more orna-

---

[1] The following were provided for :—
   A gun without a wagon carriage disabled.
   „   with   „   „   „
   „   axletree arm broken.
   A gun and wagon; the gun limber disabled.
   „   „   „ ; the wagon limber disabled.
   „   „   „ ; the wagon body disabled.

[2] A senior officer, who was serving at Woolwich when Indian batteries made their first appearance there, remarked to the writer :—
"They certainly made the R.H.A. *move*, and coddle their fat horses less !"

mental branch. But both troops and batteries enjoyed some marked advantages over those of the "Old Artillery".

There had never been a Master-General of the Ordnance in India, and so there was not the same tradition of a service apart. The artillery lived alongside the other arms in cantonments, and, as late as the end of the century, such an astute observer as Lord Rawlinson, when commenting upon the watertight compartments which still prevailed at home, noted that "things were better in India."

Then both troops and batteries had men and horses,[1] and good ones too, in plenty. While those at home were mere skeletons until they reached the top of the roster for foreign service, and even then were far short of war establishment, every unit in India could march out of cantonments any day practically at war strength, with unlimited ground at their disposal for drill or practice—the "maidan" stretching away to the horizon and all India beyond!

It was in matters of equipment that India lagged behind. Whether it was due to parsimony on the part of the India Office, or to procrastination on the part of the War Office, certain it is that new guns took an unconscionable time getting out to India. Many batteries were still armed with smooth-bores after the first rifled guns had served their turn and been replaced at Home; and the methods of the smooth-bore era prevailed long after the guns themselves had disappeared. Right up to the end of the century the filling of the shell, and the making up of the cartridges for practice—abolished at home in 1877—were regular parts of the year's programme. Batteries arriving in India were horrified at finding themselves served out with guns which they had long looked upon as obsolete, and set to work at such prehistoric tasks, and in consequence all ranks were apt to lose interest in gunnery matters. It is to this

---

[1] In the early days bullock draught had been the ordinary thing for field batteries. Then came the expensive stud system in Bengal and Arabs and Persians in Madras and Bombay. The importation of Australians, commenced under the Company, gradually superseded all other sources for artillery purposes.

cause that is greatly due the tradition, long cherished at home, that gunners in India, however well they might ride, certainly could not shoot!

If, as we have seen, the opportunities for practical training were small, except in India, the theoretical instruction contained in the Manuals was equally meagre. In the days when the Napoleonic wars had been fresh in men's memories it had been different. As late as 1831 the "Field Artillery Exercises" had contained a chapter which dealt very practically with the action of the arm in war, illustrated by diagrams showing the actual distribution of the guns in typical battles. It enjoined, moreover, that these principles were to be kept in view, and conformed to, in all drills and exercises, so that on active service there might be no hesitation in their execution. But the long years of peace and neglect which followed had their inevitable effect. Those sumptuous volumes, the "Manual of Artillery Exercises" of 1860, and the "Manual of Field Artillery Exercises" of 1861, which were the first fruits of the transfer of the care of the Royal Artillery from the Master-General of the Ordnance to the Commander-in-Chief, were devoted almost exclusively to "drill" pure and simple. "Battery Manœuvre" accounted for sixty complicated evolutions, "Brigade Manœuvre" for another forty. From judging distance to pitching camp nothing could be done without an exact drill—so fighting was crowded out.

And in spite of the establishment of Camps of Instruction during the Crimean War, the vast majority of the troops and batteries were hidden away in country quarters, or herded together at Woolwich—"the world forgetting by the world forgot". The "Field Exercises and Evolutions of Infantry", which was at that time the authority for the combined work of the different arms—even for that of horse artillery and cavalry—dismissed the whole subject of the action of artillery on the battlefield in the following short passage, which is worth quoting in full, since it was repeated in the Artillery Manual without comment :—

"POSITION OF THE BATTERY OF ARTILLERY WHEN MOVING
WITH A BRIGADE. [1]

"The usual position of a battery of Artillery, when
in line is on the right, with an interval of $22\frac{1}{2}$ yards,
$28\frac{1}{2}$ yards or $34\frac{1}{2}$ yards, according to the number of
horses in the guns, whether four, six or eight.

"When the battalions are in contiguous quarter-
distance columns, the battery will be on a flank, as
ordered, at a distance equal to the depth of the strong-
est column in rear of the alignment, unless they are
formed for inspection or review, in which case they
will be dressed with the leaders' heads on the alignment. In echelon the battery will be on a flank.

"When squares are formed in echelon, and the
battery is brought into action, the muzzles of the guns
should be in line with the rear base of the rear square.

"N.B. A battery *on all occasions* to keep its full
interval when possible.

"It is the duty of the Commander of the Artillery to
keep his battery so well in hand that he may never
interfere with deployments or other movements of the
brigade; and the Brigadier should impress on the
officers commanding regiments, that they should at
all times give way to the guns when the latter have
occasion to advance or retire through a line, by
smartly wheeling back a section or company.

"Should skirmishers be in front of the battery, and
be obliged to retire, they should only retire to the
guns, and remain with them as long as they continue
in action, retiring with them.

"Should the battery be detached from the brigade,
two companies at least should accompany it as an escort.

"These remarks apply equally to Horse Artillery
when working with Cavalry." [2]

---

[1] No mention of divisional artillery is to be found in the Manuals
until the issue of the "Field Exercises" of 1874.

[2] The Cavalry Regulations of 1876 were the first even to mention
horse artillery, and it was not until 1885 that they contained a chapter
on " the employment of horse artillery with a division of cavalry
acting independently."

To an army trained on such lines, the collapse in 1870
of the French army—which, since its victories over the
Austrians in 1859, had been regarded as the pattern for
imitation—came as a rude shock.   There was a general
stirring of the military world, and proposals for new
systems of tactics, punctuated by grumblings at "the useless manœuvres taught", poured in upon the War Office.
The Commandant at Woolwich asked for permission to
encamp on Dartford Heath, and finally three divisions
were brought together under the Duke of Cambridge for
the great "Aldershot Encampment and Autumn Manœuvres" of 1871.   It was the first assemblage of a mixed
force of any size[1] in England for training, and it aroused
extraordinary interest, for public opinion had been greatly
stirred by Sir George Chesney's brilliant brochure "The
Battle of Dorking", which had appeared in "Blackwood"
a few months before.[2]   From the Royal Artillery the
Manœuvres struck off the fetters of immobility, not only
in the narrow sense of restrictions to the pace of field batteries already described, but in the wider significance of
close conformity to the movements of the other arms.

---

[1] In 1853 a Camp of Instruction had been formed at Chobham, but
the artillery only consisted of one troop and three field batteries.

[2] His vivid picture of a battery in action in those days may well
find a place in Regimental History: it is quoted here by kind permission of Messrs. William Blackwood & Son.

"We could see the gunners working away like fury, ramming,
loading, and running up with cartridges, the officer in command
riding slowly up and down just behind his guns, and peering out
with his field glasses into the mist . . . .   Two of the guns ceased
firing for a time; they had got injured in some way, and up rode
an Artillery General.   I think I see him now, a very handsome
man, with straight features and a dark moustache, his breast
covered with medals.   He appeared in a great rage at the guns
stopping fire.   'Who commands this Battery', he cried.   'I do,
'Sir Henry', said an officer, riding forward.   The group is before
me at this minute, standing out clear against the background of
smoke, Sir Henry erect on his splendid charger, his flashing eyes,
his left arm pointing towards the enemy to enforce something he
was going to say, the young officer reining in his horse just beside
him and saluting with his right hand raised to his busby.   This for
a moment, then a dull thud and both horses and riders are prostrate
on the ground ".

The Inspector-General, Sir Collingwood Dickson, was appointed "Major-General Royal Artillery" for the manœuvres, and to his staff was attached the Brigade-Major of the School of Gunnery, Captain W. S. M. Wolfe. On his return to Shoeburyness he gave a lecture on his experiences which has fortunately been preserved in the "Proceedings", and the story he told is so important that it must be given in his own words :—

"For years a constant agitation had been kept up by artillery officers as to the greater development of their arm, but unsuccessfully, and up to this summer was to be seen the senseless practice of what was called 'Artillery Conforming to Infantry'. No one knew what was meant by this process, and the result was that field artillery with accurate and long shooting rifled guns was 'sentenced' (and I use the word 'sentenced' advisedly as it meant complete destruction) to march side by side—i.e. the Leaders' heads in line with the front ranks of the lines of Infantry; halt when they halted; and move when they moved.

"This pernicious system[1] had become so fixed that no ordinary authority had the power of changing it; but, at the outset of the Campaign, the 'Cry of Lamentation' from Captains[2] of batteries and others 'went up', and, on the recommendation of Sir Collingwood Dickson, H.R.H. was pleased to cause the following order to be promulgated to the Commanders of Corps, Divisions, and Brigades :—

MEMORANDUM RELATIVE TO THE EMPLOYMENT OF
HORSE AND FIELD ARTILLERY.

"General Officers commanding Divisions or detached Brigades should indicate to the Officers Commanding

---

[1] The system took long to eradicate. Major-General E. O. Hay relates how, on asking for orders for the artillery at Kassassin in 1882, all that he could extract was that they should "conform to the infantry".

[2] It was not till a few months later that the importance of battery command was recognized by the promotion of all 1st Captains to the rank of Major, as recorded in Chapter III.

Artillery under their orders the general object of the movements about to be executed, and these officers should give directions to the Captains of Batteries as to the best mode of co-operating with and supporting them.

"Officers Commanding Batteries should be permitted (under the direction of their own commanding officers) to use their own judgment in selecting the best positions to enable them to operate with advantage either in covering an attack or retreat, conforming of course as much as the nature of the ground will permit with the movements of the Corps to which they are attached.

"Any special directions received by the Officer Commanding Artillery from the General or other Officer in command of troops, relative to any change in the disposition of the batteries during the movements, will, of course, be promptly carried out.

"No battery ought to be exposed to the risks of Infantry Fire unless under unavoidable circumstances which occasionally occur in action."

Such a bomb-shell was naturally not received kindly in all quarters, but for the artillery it was a Magna Carta. The Duke noted in his Report that :—

"A marked improvement in manœuvre took place after I had directed an order to be given that the Officers of artillery were to take up their own positions in accordance with the general course of the movement, without adhering too formally to actual alignment or contact with the Brigade of Cavalry or Infantry to which they were attached. The object of this order seemed to be well understood and fully appreciated by batteries generally, and a marked improvement in the taking-up of ground was the result."

Such improvement would, however, have been impossible if the field batteries had not, at last, been given the power of movement for which they had long been striving.

As early as December 1870, Lieut.-Colonel C. C. Chesney, R.E., had pointed out that the distinguishing feature of the Prussian Field Artillery was its mobility, due to the fact that the guns had axle-tree seats, and so could carry a sufficient number of men for their service; and he caught the popular ear with the remark that "to lecture to field artillery officers on tactics so long as they did not possess the means of moving with their gun detachments beyond a walk, though interesting and improving to their minds, was likely to be practically as futile as teaching a bear to dance with its hind legs tied together!" The Press took the matter up, and the provision of axle-tree seats for the new R.M.L. guns then under construction was approved.[1] Their appearance at the Manœuvres of 1871 marked the opening for the field artillery of a greatly extended tactical *rôle*, and thus affords a striking example of the intimate relationship which, in the artillery at any rate, must always prevail between tactical and technical considerations.

There were more manœuvres in 1872 and 1873 which introduced the artillery to Salisbury Plain and Dartmoor. They marked a real advance in field training, and soon showed the necessity of authoritative guidance in the tactics of the three arms. The want of anything of the sort had naturally been severely felt,[2] and had led to the production of various unofficial, or demi-official guides, mostly compiled from foreign sources. An interesting example of these is a collection of papers on "The Move-

CHAPTER IX.

The Mobility of field batteries.

The New Training Manuals.

[1] Up to the adoption of the Armstrong guns horses had not been provided even for the Nos. 1. But even with them, only three numbers were available until the wagon came up, and so, during the Fenian Raids in Canada in 1868, axletree seats were improvised for the 12-pr. R.B.L. guns so as to allow of field batteries carrying sufficient gunners when required to move rapidly to threatened spots.

[2] In evidence before the Warde Committee of 1870-1 on the Education of Artillery officers, Captain T. B. Strange had pointed out that "the special tactics of artillery in the field are scarcely taught at all. That there is no text book in the English language is a proof that the subject is not appreciated in the British Army". The same was true of the other most important subject for an artilleryman—gunnery. The first syllabus for admission to the Advanced Class included a qualifying examination in French—the reason being that gunnery had to be studied in that language.

ment, Tactics, Action and combination of Artillery with
the other Arms, compiled at Headquarters in India for
the use of Officers at the Camp of Exercise at Delhi in
1871." [1]   This included extracts from the works of
Jomini, de Ternay, Okouneff, Taubert, von Moltke and an
anonymous German critic on the war of 1866, with, of
English writers, Owen, Burgoyne, Hamley, Ketchen and
Hime—the latter's Prize Essay of the year.   It is thus a
valuable compendium of the best opinions of the day on
artillery tactics.

By 1874, however, the experience gained at the successive manœuvres had crystallized, and there appeared a
new edition of the "Field Exercises and Evolutions of
Infantry" which at last gave the long looked for official
guidance.   This confirmed the liberty of action given to
the artillery by the Duke's order of 1871, and acknowledged
for the first time the existence of "Divisional Artillery".
Heretofore the artillery attached to a Brigade had been
the only combination recognised in the text books.

The Manual of Field Artillery Exercises which followed
in 1875 repeated and developed these instructions :   no
longer tied to the apron-strings of the other arms, but with
its duty to them definitely defined, the artillery was free to
develop on its own lines.

It was not only in the domain of tactics that the events
of the Franco-German War were causing some searchings
of heart to those responsible for the efficiency of the horse
and field artillery.   A Regimental Order of 1874 shows that,
as regards shooting as well as manœuvring, interest had
been aroused :—

"Frequent instances having of late occurred when the
annual practice of Field Batteries has been carried out
in so short a time as to render it quite impossible for
the non-commissioned-officers and men to obtain the

---

[1] The copy in the writer's possession was given by Colonel M. A.
Biddulph, D.A.G., R.A., in India, to Major-General Sir H. Tombs,
V.C., K.C.B., commanding the 3rd Division; and by him to his staff
officer, Capt. M. H. Saward, R.A.   It has thus had a descent through
the hands of three Colonels Commandant.

full benefit of the practical instruction in that most
important item of an Artilleryman's duty, which the grant of practice ammunition was intended to afford, H.R.H. the Field-Marshal Commanding - in - Chief deems it necessary to call the very serious attention of Commanding Officers thereto &c. &c.'',

Such fulminations could, however, have little practical effect until a change had been made in the conditions under which batteries practised.   The credit for this is due to a Committee under Major-General F. Eardley-Wilmot, F.R.S., who had become impressed with the difficulty of drawing definite conclusions from trials on the ranges at Shoeburyness, which bore no resemblance to anything likely to be met with on service.   They accordingly prepared a programme of experiments for the solution of various problems connected with field artillery under service conditions as regards ground :   the Director of Artillery, in conjunction with the Deputy Adjutant-General, submitted the proposal to the Secretary of State :   the latter approved :   and on the 23rd of June, 1875, two members of the Committee set out on their historic quest—"starting from Exeter in company with the Senior Officer of Artillery of the station."   After first viewing the eastern slopes of Dartmoor, which were rejected on account of difficulty of access, they decided on Okehampton "in view of the camping ground in the park within a quarter of a mile of the station, the good water supply, and the moor forming part of the Duchy and being in every way suitable as a practice range."   On the 26th they took the C.R.A. Western District over the ground ; on the 28th they secured the agreement of the Control Department at Plymouth ; and on the 30th they submitted their report.   By the 17th of July all questions connected with the use of the land had been settled, and on the 2nd of August "the Camp was formed" under the command of Lt.-Colonel Tod Browne, C.B., R.H.A., with E/E from Exeter (9-prs.) and C/25 from

Devonport (16-prs.)—each with 1000 rounds to expend.[1]
The whole business from the submission of the scheme to
the actual presence of the troops on the ground had scarcely
taken six weeks—surely a record.

In their Report at the conclusion of the practice, after
dealing with various tactical and technical matters of great
importance, the Committee recorded their general conclusion as follows :—

> "In equipment the Royal Artillery may fairly claim
> to be equal to that of any nation.   But, judging from
> their knowledge of the requirements and the experi-
> ments at Okehampton, it is evident to the Committee
> that there is very great room for improvement in
> systematic shooting . . . . the Committee cannot too
> strongly urge the importance of making the annual
> practice of batteries more a trial of skill in accuracy
> of shooting than it is at present—by introducing some
> system of field artillery gun practice such as exists in
> Germany and Austria . . . . the great drawback now is
> the use of sea ranges over which the annual practice
> of batteries is to a great extent carried on, and which
> give an unreality to the fire and use of field artillery
> which diminishes the interest in the practice."

The movement for the adoption of "the foreign system
of campaign practice"—as it was then generally termed—
was started.

The liberation of the Royal Artillery from the leading
strings of "conformity" with the other arms in manœuvre,
the endowment of the field batteries with mobility, and
the acquirement of land ranges where troops and batteries
could practice under something approaching service conditions, were the immediate effects of the Franco-German
War.   But its full results did not make themselves felt
until the publication in 1887 of Prince Kraft's famous
"Letters on Artillery."   Their writer had commanded the

---

[1] The head of one of the shrapnel fired on this historic occasion is
in the possession of Major-General E. O. Hay, C.B., who was a
subaltern in C/25 at the time.

artillery of the Prussian Guard Corps throughout the wars against Austria and France, and could thus speak with unrivalled authority.   And the story he had to tell of the rise to fame of the German Artillery was one of absorbing interest to any gunner. Translated by Major N. L. Walford with a literary skill which preserved all the charm of the original, the letters came as a revelation to the great mass of officers when they appeared in the pages of the "Proceedings", and they are still probably the most readable account of the work of artillery in war.   It may be doubted whether any of the invaluable services rendered to the Regiment by the Institution can compare in far-reaching effect with their publication.

A handsomely bound copy of the translation was presented to Prince Kraft, with a letter in which the Duke of Cambridge, as Colonel of the Regiment, expressed the admiration felt for his work by the officers of the Royal Artillery and their appreciation of its utility for the instruction of all ranks.   The volume bore the following inscription :—

"PRESENTED TO

HIS HIGHNESS PRINCE KRAFT ZU HOHENLOHE-INGELFINGEN
KÖNIGL. PREUSS. GENERAL D. INF. U. GENERAL ADJUTANT
S.M. DES DEUTSCHEN KAISERS, KÖNIGS V. PREUSSEN

BY THE

OFFICERS OF HER MAJESTY'S ROYAL REGIMENT OF ARTILLERY
IN GRATEFUL RECOGNITION OF HIS KINDNESS IN ALLOWING

HIS INVALUABLE

LETTERS ON ARTILLERY

TO BE TRANSLATED FOR THEIR BENEFIT."

CHAPTER X.

THE PERIOD OF PROGRESS.

The Practice Camps—Batteries on the March—India—"Field Artillery Drill"—The School of Gunnery—Fire Discipline—The Era of Controversy—The Rival Schools.

As recorded in the last chapter, the first Practice Camp was held at Okehampton in 1875. It was to be many years yet before the school which took no interest in anything behind the splinter-bar died out, but there were not wanting officers of repute ready and willing to back up the efforts of those who wished to take a lesson from foreign experience. In 1877 Captain Fox-Strangways contributed a paper to the "Proceedings" in which, after animadverting on the backwardness of the gunnery at the time, he summed up the situation in a passage that is worth quoting :—

"If opinion in the Regiment was convinced that good shooting was essential to success in war, and that it was worth while to work for it, the greater part of the difficulty would be overcome. We can do much for ourselves. Let us cease the eternal rivalry of spit and polish, and, whilst not valuing appearance less, value shooting more. For the moment at all events we can rest and be thankful for the brilliancy that we have reached, and let other needs have their turn. If it is understood that the reputation of a battery

LIEUT.-GENERAL SIR CHARLES NAIRNE, K.C.B.
Inspector General of Artillery in India 1887-1892.

From the portrait by Mr. C. W. Furse in the Royal Artillery Mess
unveiled by Lord Roberts on the 16th October, 1901.

depends in some measure on its shooting, and its readiness for war from a war stand-point, there will soon be improvements in these respects.''

Another decade was to pass, and the writer of these weighty words was to have met his death[1], while Commandant of the School of Gunnery, by an accident at experimental practice, before regimental opinion was really roused. But the leaven was working, and 1877 saw the formation of "Camps for Artillery Instruction" at Aldershot,[2] Hay and Romney, as well as at Okehampton.

From then onwards, all throught the 80's, the demand was for more and better ranges, and the grouse on many a quiet moor were disturbed by the incursions of artillery officers on the search for ground—sometimes followed by the guns themselves with even more disturbing results.[3] There were applications for the enlargement and improvement of the existing ranges, for the provision of permanent quarters for the staffs, cook-houses and drying rooms for the men, shelters for the horses. The old 6' × 6' wooden targets were soon found too cumbrous for carting about over the bogs and boulders, so came the "Hessians", familiar to many generations of range officers.[4] The first moving target followed, a skeleton roller, suggested by major R. A.

---

[1] See Chapter VIII.

[2] It was only in 1882 that batteries ceased to practice at Aldershot.

[3] The following extract from the *Shrewsbury Chronicle* might be parallelled from the files of many a local paper :—"The greatest consternation was caused on Friday in the little village . . . . by the booming of cannon, and the unwelcome arrival of shot after shot from the Royal Artillery stationed on the Church Stretton Hills. Upon this lofty eminence the guns are fixed, and incessant firing continues from morning until night. Whether the gunners miscalculated their distance is not known, but visitors were disconcerted by the whizzing of cannon balls over their heads when walking on the hills, the balls falling in the village of Minton nearly two miles off, to the great danger of that peaceful locality. The greatest damage was the destruction of a barn . . . . The women ran screaming from the houses carrying their children with them."

[4] The suggestion came from Major Hon. A. Stewart, R.H.A., whose battery used small canvas targets which could be rolled up and carried by a mounted man as early as 1877 or 1878.

Montgomery,[1] which held the field with slight modifications for many years. Wooden dummies, which could be arranged into martial formation, were issued by the thousand, dummy guns and carriages followed. At the same time the scale of ammunition was steadily increased. With the adoption of rifled guns in 1860 the annual allowance had been raised from 140 rounds a battery to 200, and then to 300. The institution of the practice camps brought another increase for batteries practising at them—336 in 1878, 510 in 1882, and 640 in 1888. It cannot be said that the War Office showed any parsimonious spirit in providing for the requirements of the new system of training.

A by-product of the extension of the practice camps which deserves mention here is the marching. Batteries had always changed station by march route, but for their annual practice those at Woolwich had gone down to the Plumstead Marshes, and those elsewhere had taken their gunners by train to Shoeburyness, or had found some convenient seaside resort near their station. Now they marched to Okehampton, Hay, or some other camp, usually a matter of weeks. And so officers and men learnt much about the important business of marching, and all that it implies for mounted troops.[2] They learnt, too, much of the charms of the English countryside, which were strangely little known to the majority before the days of motors. And they familiarised the inhabitants with the idea of an army, and greatly stimulated recruiting. For it was in the days when attention was still paid to appearance, and dress jackets or tunics were worn in marching order, while the officers always dined in the handsome mess dress of those days, whether it was at the hospitable board of some local magnate, or in the coffee room of the best Inn. All through the 80's the marching was a great feature, perhaps

---

[1] Maj.-General R. A. Montgomery, C.B., C.V.O., Col. Commandant.

[2] The "Proceedings" of the time are full of articles by the noted horse-masters of the Regiment on the way to condition horses for the march, and the various expedients for keeping them fit. The heavy neck-collar harness of those days was terribly apt to gall.

the outstanding feature, of regimental soldiering for all ranks.[1]

In India the conditions were very different. There were few stations where the batteries could not find adequate space for practice within easy reach of cantonments, if indeed they need go off their parade grounds. Year after year the Commander-in-Chief's orders were confined to the laconic announcement that "The Annual Practice of the Artillery will commence as usual on the 1st December." It can scarcely be said, however, that the artillery in India had taken advantage of their opportunities until its most distinguished member came to the head of affairs. It was indeed fortunate that Lord Roberts' tenure[2] of the chief command coincided with what was the most critical period of artillery development. He never forgot that he was a gunner, and almost his first act was greatly to extend the scope of the Inspector-General's duties. For at the great camp of exercise at Delhi in the winter of 1885-1886, which inaugurated his command, he noted the want of an Artillery Commander, and in order to meet that want, set about the re-organization of the artillery staff which has been described in Chapter IV. His view was that the Inspector-General should be an officer who in the event of war would take command of the artillery in the field,[3] and that, in order to gain practical experience, he should every winter exercise command over as large bodies of artillery as could be collected in various locations.

The man Lord Roberts had in mind was Colonel C. E. Nairne, Commandant of the School of Gunnery, whom he had known well since the days when they had been

---

[1] Good as the marching was in many ways, it kept the batteries too long away from the summer drills which were beginning to grow in importance, and it became burdensome to the towns along the more frequented routes. In 1897 a new departure was made in sending the batteries to practice by train.

[2] From 1885 to 1893.

[3] He was, however, careful, when urging some years later the appointment of brigadier-generals to command the artillery of army corps, to make it clear that he was opposed to anything which would keep the artillery separate from the army generally.

subalterns together in the Bengal Horse Artillery.   An enthusiast on the subject of gunnery, General Nairne[1] soon effected a much needed improvement in shooting, but—a fine horseman himself, and the acme of smartness—he took good care that there should be no falling off in horsemastership or turn-out.   The plan of concentrations of artillery, which Lord Roberts had had in mind when making the appointment, was put into force, and in India these artillery camps became the great feature of regimental training.   They followed, wherever possible, camps of exercise of all arms, and were much more than mere practice camps; for full advantage was taken of the possibility of obtaining in India ground which was suitable for manœuvre as well as for shooting.

The interest of the Commander-in-Chief was evinced not only by frequent visits to the camps, but by the personal appeals which he made to all ranks on such occasions.   It was his custom to address the batteries formed up on foot in a hollow square.   Sitting on his Arab "Vonolel", almost as well-known as his rider, in his own particular uniform of furred and frogged khaki jacket, just as he is represented in the statue on the Horse Guards Parade, he would speak as one gunner to another, dealing with every detail of the work as if he were familiar with it.   And he would conclude with weighty words of warning, that, even for the army in India, the next enemy might be a European one with an artillery as well armed as themselves, when the victory would lie with the batteries which could soonest find the range, and then fire with the greatest accuracy, steadiness and rapidity.

Such appeals from such a man, made face to face, backed with all the force of his great prestige and personal charm, brought an enthusiastic response.   All ranks began to take as much pride in belonging to the "best-shooting" battery as they had hitherto taken in belonging to the smartest, the best-horsed, or the best turned-out; and when he laid down the Commander-in-Chiefship in 1893, Lord

---

[1] Inspector-General of Artillery in India 1887-1892.

Roberts could well refer in his farewell order to the remarkable improvement in artillery practice, and to the share of the Inspector-General in effecting that improvement. In unveiling Sir Charles Nairne's portrait, reproduced here, in the Mess at Woolwich in 1901, his old Chief, and life-long friend, paid a well-deserved tribute to the services of one "who was better known to, and more looked up to by, his brother officers of the Regiment generally than perhaps any other officer of our time in the Royal Artillery."

The increased attention paid to shooting at home and in India is shown by the numbers of papers on various aspects of the subject which appeared in the "Proceedings" all through the 80's. It must not, however, be thought that progress was confined to matters of gunnery, although the development of the practice camps was, undoubtedly, the predominant feature of the period. The changes in the tactics of artillery brought about by rifled arms were being studied in the light of the history of the European wars of the 70's, and the artillery were being brought into closer touch with the other arms, as will be told in the next chapter, and this was re-acting upon their technical training. These various activities culminated in the issue of "Field Artillery Drill, 1889"—the first of the new type of Manual, which has held the field ever since. Instead of a handsome octavo volume, bound in scarlet cloth and enriched with coloured plates, there appeared an unadorned pocket-sized work. Terribly long-winded as this first effort was, and elementary as much of the instruction it contained must appear to a modern reader, it contained the first at all adequate chapter on the "Employment and Conduct of Artillery in the Field",[1] and so at last put into the hands of artillerymen, a work from which they might learn what would be required of their arm in war, and how they should prepare for it in peace.

CHAPTER X

India.

"Field Artillery Drill."

---

[1] The fact that the original chapter was cancelled, and an entirely fresh chapter issued as an amendment, is a sure indication of the interest aroused.

It was astonishing what progress had been made in field artillery gunnery during the 80's, more especially when it is remembered how defective was the organization for training. The practice camps had grown up haphazard, commanded by such public-spirited lieut.-colonels, usually on half-pay,[1] as were willing to undertake the hard work, considerable discomfort, and heavy expense involved in the appointment. Their staffs had to be found by temporary appointments each year, and were absurdly inadequate in number. Above all, there was no central authority to exercise any general supervision over the gunnery training. For the control of the Camp Commandants only lasted for the few months of the shooting season, and the Commandant of the School of Gunnery (to whom it might naturally be expected that this duty would be entrusted) had come to be considered as concerned only with Garrison Artillery training—in spite of the fact that the actual holders of the office during this period happened to be in the front rank of field artillerymen. The work of Fox-Strangways, of Nairne, and of Stuart Nicholson has been alluded to in the preceding chapter, the services of their Brigade-Majors had been equally conspicuous. We have seen the part taken by Captain Wolfe at the first manœuvres : the work of Major Walford nearly twenty years later was probably the chief contributory cause to the awakening of the Regiment from its long lethargy. And yet the Commandant of the School of Gunnery could not inspect the Camps— he was only "permitted to visit"! The position was ridiculous.

In 1891 the Deputy Adjutant-General drew official attention to the necessity of securing continuity in the office of Camp Commandant at Okehampton, where, in addition to the actual practice of the batteries, and the instructional

---

[1] It was necessary that the Camp Commandant should be senior to any lieut.-colonel who might come to the camp in command of a detachment, and it was to ensure this that officers who had completed their period of command as lieut.-colonels were usually chosen.

courses[1] for artillery, special classes for officers of cavalry
and infantry had now been instituted, and where all practical trials of field artillery equipment were carried out. He
proposed the addition of a second Chief Instructor to the
School of Gunnery, to be Camp Commandant at Okehampton during the summer, and to be at Shoeburyness during
the winter, where—under the Commandant, School of
Gunnery—he would deal with all questions connected with
the instruction and practice of field artillery, trials of equipment, and changes in drill. The Adjutant-General accepted the proposal at once; the Commander-in-Chief strongly
recommended it; the Financial Secretary considered it a
reasonable mode of providing for the duty; and the Secretary of State directed that it should be included in the
Estimates. It had taken just a month to pass through
all the stages, and not one dissentient voice had been raised
—surely a happy augury for the future of what has developed into the great School of Artillery at Larkhill.[2]

During the 80's the ungrudging labour of all hands—
Camp Commandants, Battery Commanders, and Gunnery
Instructors—had built up a system of Fire Discipline based
on sound principles. The battery had replaced the gun as
the fire unit, the bracket system[3] of ranging had been

CHAPTER
X

The
School of
Gunnery.

Fire Dis-
cipline.

---

[1] An "instructional battery" was sent to the camp in 1888 for the
benefit of the courses, but was not a success, and was discontinued in
1891.

[2] From the very establishment of the Horse and Field Artillery
School it had been obvious that Shoeburyness was a most unsuitable
place. But there was at the time no alternative, for none of the
Practice Camps were possible as winter stations. With the acquisition
of Salisbury Plain the opportunity came—the story of how the first
chance was missed belongs to the next volume of this History.

[3] The first mention of this system is to be found in the Manual of
1881, and is worthy of rescue from oblivion, more particularly as the
original owner of the volume has added the marginal note "This is
quite wrong".

"The following (based upon the system laid down in the German
practice regulations) will be found a quick method of ascertaining
the correct elevation. Begin with the elevation for the estimated
or measured range. If the shell falls short (or over) increase (or
reduce) the elevation by 100 yards at a time till the shell falls over
(or under). Then reduce (or increase) the last elevation by 50

adopted, and the rule by which a battery was not permitted
to change to another target until the range party had cer-
tified that it had obtained "three effective shrapnel" had
convinced all except the most recalcitrant, that batteries
"can and must be exercised in the whole system of ranging
and fire discipline as a drill" before going to practice.   The
careful analysis of practice reports first worked out by Major
Walford at Shoeburyness had shown beyond possibility of
doubt that many Nos. 1 were either incapable of consistent
laying, or were persisting in altering the elevation to suit
their own ideas instead of accepting the directions of the
battery commander; and "qualified layers" had been introduced in spite of a stout resistance on the part of many
senior officers.   Various methods of engaging a moving
target were under trial, and the use of auxiliary marks for
laying had been suggested and several systems put forward
for experiment.   The time had come when "elementary"
practice could be devoted to trying out such developments
instead of going through the solemn farce of deliberately
making such mistakes as using a damp cartridge in order
to show the result.[1]

The real blot on the practice was the "Competitive",
which had remained practically unaltered since its institution.   The Committee which carried out the historical
"Okehampton Experiments" in 1875, had pointed out that
the artillery was the only arm in which no prizes were given
for shooting; but unfortunately when these were introduced
the conditions[2] were based upon a conception of artillery

---

yards and fire a few rounds.   If another correction is required increase or reduce the elevation by 25 yards.   If half the number of
rounds fired with any given elevation falls short it shows that the
main point of inpact of the series is at the foot of the target".

---

[1] The order abolishing this procedure in 1890 gave the reason—
somewhat cruelly—"as error in judgment is sure to produce some, if
not all, of these faults during practice".

[2] The target was 6' × 6' with a 2' bulls-eye, and competitors fired
six rounds of plugged shell for "positive accuracy" at 600 yards, and
two rounds of time shrapnel at 1,500 yards.   Marks were given for direct
hits with plugged shell, and according to the position of the burst with
shrapnel.

practice which was already out of date. For the competitors (who had been selected by a written examination) fired
individually at a square target at known ranges, and
although it was usual to ask one of the subalterns—after
a somewhat embarassingly frank discussion of their respective merits—to fire the trial shots, the officers were otherwise mere spectators. Such a procedure might have had
some justification when battery commanders contented
themselves with leading their batteries well to the front,
and then letting the Nos. 1 engage the enemy in their own
way. But when the observation and direction of the fire
had been concentrated in the hands of the battery commander, and the duty of the layers had been limited to
laying every round on the same spot, with the elevation and
deflection ordered, such a competition could do nothing but
harm, for it was a direct encouragement to the generation
which had been brought up under the old ideas to adhere
to their out-of-date practice.[1]

In 1891 this extraordinary system was done away with.
The battery competition which took its place was a great
step in advance, for it brought out the idea of the battery
as an entity, in which every individual could contribute his
share to the success of the whole, and officers of the other
arms attending artillery practice camps bore unstinted
witness to "the extraordinary zeal and keenness for their
business evinced by all ranks from field officers to private
men." Under it there was developed also that high standard of fire discipline which was to prove its worth on many
a field. Consisting, however, of only one day's shooting,
and that under strictly defined conditions of range and
target, it led in many cases to a stereotyping of the practice
which greatly hindered progressive training. More serious
still it afforded no test of tactical handling, for the rigid

---

[1] Right up to the 80's the regulations had definitely directed that
"each man laying a gun is to estimate the range and deflection
of the shot, and the point of explosion of the shell, and this estimate
is to be inserted opposite his name in the Practice Report, before
the distance as measured by the Range Party is signalled to the
battery".

rules which governed it denied any freedom of action.   And
yet, "the competitive" dominated the minds of all.[1]   So
people began to ask whether, granted all the good it had
done, it had not now ceased to exercise a good influence,
whether indeed, like Frankenstein, we had not created a
monster which was getting out of control.   In 1897 it was
accordingly abolished as a separate portion and batteries
competed throughout the whole of the practice.

The trammels of the competitive shaken off, each year
saw further advances towards making the practice a true
training for service.   Battery commanders received orders
only as to what their task was, and were criticised not only
on the way the fire was conducted, but also as to whether
the battery was handled in accordance with the tactical situation.   The staffs of the various camps vied each other in
devising surprise and moving targets, and the success of
their efforts is vouched for by the evidence of an infantry
officer, who wrote in his report, after seeing the effect of
some of the more realistic of these contrivances, "the
sudden appearance of infantry demoralises artillery"!
The final stage of the continuous effort to represent service
conditions was reached in 1898 by the introduction of
"casualties".   They afforded many opportunities for the

---

[1] In 1895 General F. T. Lloyd, the last D.A.G., R.A., presented
the "Centenary Cup" for competition between batteries.   The following is the Regimental Order announcing it :

No. 118/1895.   " By permission of H.R.H. the Commander-in-
Chief a Cup will be presented to the Royal Artillery for excellence
in gun practice by the present deputy-adjutant-general in commem-
oration of the appointment of Lt.-General Sir John MacLeod,
G.C.H., as the first deputy-adjutant-general, Royal Artillery, in
1795, in which appointment he served continuously during the
Peninsular and Waterloo campaigns".

" It will be competed for in alternate years by the Horse and
Field Artillery batteries which attend the camp at Okehampton,
and by the Garrison Artillery companies which carry out their
competitive practice at stations in the United Kingdom hereafter
enumerated.   The conditions will be subject to such revision by
the Commandant, School of Gunnery, &c., &c."

It was won in 1895 by the 52nd Field Battery, in '96 by 1/Southern,
in '97 by D/R.H.A., in '98 by 31/Southern, and in '99 by 81/R.F.A.
In India, prizes were also given by the Commanders-in-Chief, and the
Inspector-General of Artillery.

wit of the scoffers, but this resolute facing of the realities of war—from which the other arms shrank—served the Regiment well when the casualties came in earnest.

With all these developments the old ranges were found quite inadequate. Some, such as Hay, were unsafe, besides affording no scope for tactical work, while others, such as Morecambe and Lydd, were so flat as to give no practice in gunnery problems. But the great blot on the gunnery training was that every year more than two dozen batteries still had to shoot at Shoeburyness, leaving their guns and horses at home. Every effort was made therefore to crowd in more batteries at Okehampton, for here alone in England at that time could the practice be conducted with proper supervision and under anything approaching service conditions. In Ireland the ranges of Glenbeigh, although better than Shoeburyness, had many defects, but the search for better ground had resulted in the discovery of Glen Imaal, and the artillery practised there for the first time in 1899—The year which saw also the first practice on Salisbury Plain.[1]

The rising influence of the School of Gunnery was not, however, to go unchallenged. At the time of the creation of the Field Artillery Branch of the School, General Sir W. J. Williams, K.C.B., an officer of distinction who had not only seen but studied war—witness his well-known *sobriquet* of "Jomini"—had just concluded a notable tenure of the command of the artillery at Aldershot. In a paper published in the "Proceedings" in October 1891, he made an attempt, as he put it :—

" to show that military virtue is more important than skill-at-arms, that in our pursuit of skill-at-arms we are sacrificing much of our military virtue, that it is better to move a brigade-division of batteries under one command than under three commands, and that our latest gun-drill is very unwarlike."

"Letters on field artillery written by a distinguished foreign officer to a compatriot . . . . have been accepted

[1] One brigade only.

without contradiction, and welcomed by the regiment
. . . . Has our respect for a distinguished officer carried us too far? Have we mistaken his meaning?
. . . . Going away in the direction which seemed to be
pointed out to us, we have come to exaggerating the
importance of gunnery.''

In a second slashing article he returned to the
charge :—

"That our gun-drill is very unwarlike will not be
allowed by the officers who made it. It is not alleged
that they designedly, to get good shooting at targets,
made a gun-drill which they knew to be unwarlike.
The drill they have made is unwarlike because . . . .
from want of knowledge, or from want of imagination,
they have failed to distinguish between what is best
for shooting at targets, and what is good for discipline
and war . . . . our gun-drill ought not to name taking
cover or hiding from the enemy. Nothing more
irrational than putting cover into field drill ever grew
upon an army . . . . The principal points of error in
our new tactics are drilling to reconnoitre and to take
the range, going into action independently by batteries, and halting in a preparatory position . . . . we
ought to drill to come into action by brigade-divisions,
without reconnaissance, against something not seen
from where we start. That would be drill in handling
for the commanding officer, and drill in gunnery for
the commanding officer and his command. Our
range-finding is skill-at-arms for domestic use only.
It is not possible to believe that any officer who has
seen the proceeding can think it warlike ; not possible to
believe that any officer will maintain that it would be
right in war for the commander of a brigade-division,
or of a battery, to put any faith in a report of range
found by a non-commissioned officer.''[1]

---

[1] The land ranges had soon shown the impossibility of "guessing"
ranges correctly, in spite of all the attention paid to the practice of that
art, and Weldon and Watkin range-finders had been in use as early as
1877.

Could reaction go further? In spite of the reputation of the writer, and his incisive style, the School of Gunnery could afford to ignore such an attack. It had almost at once, to meet more serious criticism.

In a lecture on "Experiences at Okehampton in 1891" Captain White,[1] Instructor in Gunnery, had made some remarks on "distribution" of fire which were suspected of meaning "dispersion". Lieut.-Colonel Maurice,[2] who had just returned to regimental duty at Aldershot from a professorship at the Staff College, took occasion to refer publicly to "a tendency in some quarters to speak with a certain amount of dogmatism from experiences acquired merely by practice at the butts and from ballistic theory," and to declare that "at Aldershot we are unanimous in regarding this notion of distributing fire as a rash and dangerous heresy", winding up with the fine rhetorical flourish "it will be too late for the common hangman then to burn pamphlets which it may be hoped that their writers, better instructed, will themselves now consign to the flames."

Captain White picked up the glove, and far from consigning his pamphlet to the flames launched a vigorous counter-attack; the quarrel spread from the pages of the "Proceedings" to the "United Service Magazine"; and was still raging when the protagonists met face to face at the Royal Artillery Institution. Fortunately it was discovered that both were right, and with the issue of a new "Field Artillery Training" the storm passed away.

It was only, however, to be succeeded by an even more serious one, which took on almost an international aspect. The subject in this case was the use of "direct" or "in-

The Watkin instrument was adopted for the service in 1881, range-takers were added to battery establishments, a School was established at Aldershot, monthly reports had to be sent in that range-takers had been practised at least once a week : and officers had to pass before being considered for promotion. But right up to the end of the century there was a great distaste for the whole business.

[1] Brigadier-General W. L. White, c.b., c.m.g.
[2] Major-General Sir Frederick Maurice, k.c.b., Col. Commandant, R.A.

direct" fire, and the discussion was again started in a
lecture at the Institution, but this time by an infantry
officer, Captain Pilcher.[1]   In the discussion the spokesman
of the School of Gunnery opposed some of the opinions expressed by the lecturer as regards the superiority of German methods : officers who had friends in Germany wrote
for their views, and the pages of the "Proceedings" were
opened to the criticisms of "A German General" on the
teaching of the School of Gunnery : there were replies and
counterblasts, and there was at one time a real danger of
serious dissension between Aldershot and Okehampton
which would have been disastrous to progress.

It must be remembered that there was still strenuous
opposition to the acceptance of Prince Kraft's Gospel as
containing all things necessary to salvation.   It was contended, and with reason, that his "to hit . . . . to hit
. . . . to hit" required the addition of "the right target,
at the right time, from the right place"—and there were
many who held that it was no business of the School of
Gunnery to meddle in such matters as these.

The idea that "Fire Discipline" and "Fire Tactics"
must be practised together was a novel one in the 90's.
When the combination was first attempted at practice camps
it caused intense indignation.   "We don't come to Okehampton to drill" was the cry !   But as battery commanders
became experienced in the direction of fire, movements into
position[2] were studied, and the barrier between gunnery
and tactics was broken down.   Then batteries at Okehampton manœuvred as they had learnt to do at Aldershot,
and when they came into action at manœuvres they did so
as if there had been shell in the guns.   The old fashioned
tricks with blank ammunition, which Lord Roberts had

---

[1] Major-General T. D. Pilcher, C.B.

[2] In the Instructions for Practice in 1889 it was *suggested*, quite as
a novel idea, that the method of bringing a battery into position at
practice would be found described in Field Artillery Drill !   About
the same time an order that batteries were to be brought into action
"at least once" on every drill parade was received with very general
resentment.

stigmatised as "pernicious shams", but which had been common enough in the 80's, at home as well as in India, were no longer tolerated.

As Captain Granet wrote when the controversy was at its height :—

"For many years it has been a custom of the Royal Artillery to set up for itself certain temples of knowledge, or to put it in plain English, to look upon certain stations as the headquarters of Artillery science. The first of these universities is Woolwich, and here the doctrine of smartness and "turn-out", and exactitude of parade movements is rigidly enforced. On the appearance in this country, through Major Walford's translation, of Prince Kraft zu Hohenlohe's famous Letters on Artillery, our artillerymen turned their attention to good shooting, and Shoeburyness and Okehampton took the place of Woolwich. And now, owing in a great measure to the recognition on our part of the great skill that is required to bring the guns into positions favourable for the development of their fire, the School of Gunnery has been to a certain extent supplanted in popular favour by Aldershot."

The danger of a schism between the two chief training centres was averted however, greatly owing to Sir Evelyn Wood's good offices as related in the next chapter; and any fear of its recurrence was set at rest by the appointment of Colonel G. H. Marshall, to succeed Colonel Tyler as "Chief Instructor Field," and Commandant at Okehampton. For there was no one more closely identified with Aldershot, where he had commanded the Chestnut Troop, and then the Horse Artillery Brigade, with conspicuous success.

CHAPTER XI.

"L'ARTILLERIE PREND SA PLACE".

Napoleon I.

CHAPTER XI.

The other Arms.

IT was not only in matters of controversy that the artillery filled much space in the pages of the military Journals of the 90's. In one of his speeches at artillery camps in India, Lord Roberts had expressed a hope that some officer of the Regiment would undertake the task of compiling a compendious history of artillery combats. Major May[1] accepted the task, and sent to the "Proceedings" a series of papers, afterwards brought out in book form under the title of "Achievements of Field Artillery". This account of the great deeds of their Arm came as a revelation to many artillery officers, who had never previously realised the results which had been achieved by artillery under leaders who understood how guns should be handled. It also attracted much attention outside the Regiment, and greatly stimulated the growing interest in artillery matters throughout the Army.

At Aldershot especially was this the case. It was a memorable day for the Regiment when Sir Evelyn Wood assumed the command of our chief training centre,[2] for,

---

[1] Major-General Sir Edward May, K.C.B., C.M.G. He was prominent also in the horse artillery movement (p. 251), and his lectures and articles on the subject were published under the title of "Guns and Cavalry".

[2] 1889 to 1893.

with that distinguished artilleryman Sir James Alleyne[1] as his Chief Staff Officer, he took up the study of artillery training with his accustomed energy and thoroughness, and did all in his power to ensure tactical and technical training going forward hand in hand. He started a series of "Artillery Days" at Aldershot, and invited the staff of the School of Gunnery to attend them. He went down to Okehampton, and he took Lord Wolseley—then a frank sceptic as to the effect of artillery fire—with him, and insisted on the general and staff officers from Aldershot going themselves to see what the guns could do. It was indeed the interest thus aroused which caused the critical examination at Aldershot of the work of the School of Gunnery, and so led to the controversies recounted in the last chapter. The courses for officers of the other arms at Okehampton were developed,[2] and, through these courses and the visits of the Staff College, a very considerable number of staff officers and of regimental officers of cavalry and infantry obtained an insight each year into the powers and the limitations of artillery, and at the same time exercised a valuable influence on the work of the practice camps by their advice and criticism.

The question of the vulnerability of artillery to musketry fire was naturally a frequent subject of discussion among them. The introduction of rifled small-arms in the 50's had sounded the death-knell of the case-shot tactics of the smooth-bore days, but many infantry officers held that the artillery of the 90's did not take into sufficient account the increase in the range and accuracy of infantry weapons since that period. An experiment at Hythe as long before as 1857 had shown the power of marksmen to pick off the men of a gun detachment at 800 yards. Two years later, with the Volunteer Movement, a wave of enthusiasm for

---

[1] Major-General Sir James Alleyne, K.C.B.

[2] The courses were extended to Ireland as soon as the School of Gunnery were able to supply an Instructor. In applying for the services of the Instructor, Lord Wolseley made an *amende honorable* for his previous scepticism by writing—"I know how much has been the benefit conferred upon the army by the courses at Okehampton."

rifle shooting swept over the country, and the winner of
the first Queen's Prize,[1] who had been acclaimed almost
as a national hero, had challenged the War Office to a
match between a dozen riflemen and a 12-pr. Armstrong—
which the School of Gunnery had successfully evaded!
But the Franco-German War had brought the subject to the
fore again with stories of German batteries suffering heavy
losses from French skirmishers, and these had been confirmed by the casualties constantly sustained from long
range infantry fire during the Russo-Turkish War.   In
spite of such instances, however, artillery opinion in the
90's generally supported the statement in the Drill Book
that musketry fire might be neglected at ranges over 1000
yards, though many infantry officers claimed that they
could inflict severe losses on batteries up to much greater
distance.   There were trials at Okehampton and Glenbeigh,
but for various reasons these gave no very conclusive results.   It was left for Colenso to afford proof in tragic
fashion!

It was not only the Infantry that were getting interested
in artillery matters.   The question of the part that Cavalry
should play in war was coming much to the front, and
there were those who pre-visaged an army of mounted
troops riding unopposed through Europe, just as there are
those now who predict a similar career for a mechanised
force.

The year 1890 saw the first great cavalry manœuvres at
home, and these proved a hard experience for the horse
artillery.   Armed with the same gun as the field batteries,
they found it impossible to keep with the cavalry up the
steep hills of the Berkshire Downs; and in India, where
Sir George Luck had been holding similar exercises on a
scale (both as regards the numbers engaged and the distances covered) far in excess of anything possible in England, the heavy sand and the deep *nalas* had proved equally
fatal to the guns.   The cavalry were naturally dissatisfied,

---

[1] Mr. Edward Ross at the first meeting of the National Rifle Association at Wimbledon in 1860.   The move to Bisley was made in 1890.

and began to talk of adopting machine guns if the horse artillery could not live with them.   The Press took the matter up, and Mr. Punch commenced his volume for 1894 with a cartoon of a horse artilleryman with a Maxim for a weapon.   It was fortunate that in Sir Charles,[1] and his brother General Keith Fraser, the horse artillery had staunch friends among the cavalry who could stand up for it in Parliament and at the War Office.   The latter, who became Inspector-General at the critical time after the manœuvres of 1890, was especially active in identifying the interests of the cavalry and horse artillery.   He lectured himself on their co-operation, and he did much to encourage cavalry and artillery officers to do the same, and very useful propaganda work was effected by this means.   But there was no question that the horse artillery must be re-armed if it was to fulfil its role, and with an equipment designed exclusively for its use.[2]

At the same time the suitability of the field guns for meeting some of the requirements of modern war came under review.   In the great battles of the Franco-German War field works were never of a very formidable character, so that it came to be accepted that field guns were capable of doing all that was necessary in the way of "preparation" for the infantry attack.   The Russo-Turkish War dispelled this illusion, for at Plevna up-to-date field artillery was proved powerless for the destruction of well constructed earthworks, and equally impotent against the defenders when sheltered by head cover.   There grew up in England an agitation in favour of segment or ring shell with percussion fuzes, and the abandonment of time shrapnel was even mooted.   The publication in 1877 of an exhaustive paper on "Shrapnel Fire" by Captain Stuart Nicholson[3] saved the day, but when the artillery was re-armed with the 12-pr. of 7 cwt. it was given a common shell specially

CHAPTER
XI.

Horse
Artillery
with
Cavalry.

The
abolition
of
common
shell.

---

[1] An account of his petition to the Secretary of State for War against the reductions in 1887 is given on p. 97.

[2] The 12-pr. of 6 cwt. was the result, and the whole of the batteries at home had been re-armed with it by 1898—see pp. 190-1.

[3] Major-General Stuart Nicholson, C.B., Colonel Commandant.

CHAPTER
XI.

The
abolition
of
Common
Shell.

designed for destructive effect, while an attempt was made
to render the shrapnel of more value when used with a
percussion fuze by placing its bursting charge in the head.
Experience however showed that the common had little or
no practical effect on earth-works, while the change in the
design of shrapnel had seriously reduced its effectiveness
when used with a time fuze against troops in the open—
its primary function. Once again the Balkan Peninsula
was to furnish an object lesson. A chance visit to the
battlefield of Slievnitza while the marks of the fight were
still fresh on the ground, showed conclusively how two
Bulgarian guns firing time shrapnel had completed defeated
two Servian batteries firing common, although the advantages of the ground, etc., had been all with the Ser-
vians.[1] It was probably the first occasion of the use of
time shrapnel of modern type, and the example did much
to confirm the opinion that for field guns common shell
should be relegated to the same category as solid shot.
The cry was for "one shell and one fuze", and it was
decided that the 12-pr. of 7 cwt. should be converted[2] into
a 15-pr. with shrapnel as its only shell. Nearly a century
after its first use in the Peninsula, the traditional projectile
of the Royal Artillery had ousted all rivals!

The abolition of common shell for field guns brought to
a head the demand for some form of artillery which would
give greater shell power in the field. In the smooth-bore
days all batteries had had both guns and howitzers, but
with the introduction of rifled guns the howitzers had
dropped out. A return to a mixed armament for the battery was obviously incompatible with the existing system of
fire discipline, and the use of reduced charges with guns

---

[1] "An Artillery Duel"; by Lieut.-Colonel (now Major-General Sir
Desmond) O'Callaghan, K.C.V.O., Colonel Commandant. "Proceedings," 1891.
[2] The whole of the batteries at home had been converted by 1898.
The change that had come about regarding the attitude of the other
arms to artillery matters cannot be better exemplified than by the
following extract from a letter written by Sir Evelyn Wood from Aldershot about this time :—"I think the infantry officers here are just now
more interested in the question whether you gunners are going to get a
satisfactory shell than in any question of infantry tactics."

so as to allow of curved fire, had been proved a failure.[1] **CHAPTER XI.**
The formation of field howitzer batteries was therefore
decided upon, and the first of the batteries to be given the The intro-
new equipment[2]—the 37th—practised at Lydd in 1896. duction of Field

While, however, agreement was general as to the Howitzers.
necessity for field howitzers, there was no formed opinion
as to their functions. And so when Lord Wolseley put the
pertinent query—"What I want to know as to the relative
merits of the 5-inch howitzer and the 15-pr. is—which
would for instance have done the Germans best service in
their attacks upon St. Privat?", no definite answer was
forthcoming. Rather late in the day extensive comparative
trials were ordered in order to afford material for establishing the tactical role of the new batteries, and on their
results the Commander-in-Chief approved of the field howitzer batteries being kept as a special reserve for employment against entrenched positions, etc. In accordance with
this decision the shrapnel and case were withdrawn from the
equipment, and the batteries appeared in "War Establishments, 1898", under the head of "Units possibly required
but not forming part of the Field Army".

Important as was the effect on artillery tactics of the Smokeless
changes in armament recounted in the three preceding Powder.
paragraphs, it is questionable whether any of them had
such far-reaching tactical implications as the introduction
of cordite. Unfortunately all attempts to provide a smokeless "blank" had failed, and in consequence the possibility
of concealment afforded by smokeless powder was little
realised. At manœuvres and drills it was hard to insist
upon time and trouble being expended in search for concealment, with the probability of reproach for slowness,
when the first round would inevitably give the position
away.

---

[1] Reduced charges were issued for trial with the 16-pr. in 1877, but
were given up in 1878.

[2] The new equipment was styled the 5′ B.L. Howitzer. A second
battery was converted in 1897, and a third in 1898 to complete the
brigade.

In the preceding chapters little reference has been made
to any higher formation than the battery.[1]   In the wars of
the past the English artillery had always fought by batteries; in peace the great majority had been quartered in
single battery stations; and the jealousy of Majors regarding any encroachment on their prerogative had the support
of public opinion throughout the Regiment.   The lieut.-
colonels who had been brought up in this tradition showed
little inclination to challenge the position, and for the most
part contented themselves with regimental routine.   They
did not as a rule even accompany their own batteries to
practice, but either stayed at home, or were detailed for
the command at a camp of a "detachment" of batteries
collected indiscriminately[2] from other stations.   But the
"Artillery Days" instituted by Sir Evelyn Wood[3] at
Aldershot in the early 90's changed the whole position.
For in them the brigade was the unit the action of which
was studied, and its commander was therefore the hero—
or the villain—of the piece!   It had been realised that
with the changes in the tactical rôle of the artillery a higher
organization than the battery was required, and the brigade
had been definitely adopted as the tactical unit.   But right
up to the end of the century brigade work was the weak
spot in the field artillery, both in manœuvre and practice.
Real efficiency could scarcely be hoped for until the brigade

---

[1] The first mention of brigade drill is only to be found in 1850,
when the following "addenda" to the field exercises was issued:—
"The recent organization of the R.H.A. in 4 guns per troop and existing arrangements rendering it probable that two or more troops of that
strength will be constantly exercised together at Headquarters, the
present ' instructions for the field exercises ' being limited to the manœuvres of a single troop, it has been thought advisable that a few of the
principal movements of a brigade should be laid down in order to
ensure uniformity in their execution."   Then followed 45 evolutions!

[2] The writer's first experience may be cited as an example.   Of
two field batteries at Weedon, one marched to Hay Camp, while the
other took its gunners by train to Shoeburyness, where they found
themselves in camp with those of a horse battery from Aldershot.   The
lieut.-colonel stayed at home.

[3] Writing from India to Sir Evelyn Wood about this time on the
subject of artillery training, Lord Roberts comments "Your difficulty
seems to get lieut.-colonels to learn their work and practise it."

had been made a permanent unit with a proper staff, and that was not to be conceded until forced upon the War Office by the stern logic of war.

The recognition of the brigade as the tactical unit was a necessary step towards carrying into effect the latest theory on the subject of the tactical action of artillery, namely that of its employment in masses. From the welter of controversy which had followed the awakening of interest in artillery generally, there had emerged at last a definite doctrine as regards its employment in the field—sound if not subtle. This doctrine was based upon the German use in 1870, modified by the wider knowledge of the powers and limitations of the arm since acquired by careful study and by much actual practice on the ranges. It took into special account the little damage likely to be caused to the *matériel* of the batteries in action, the time required for ranging before an effective fire could be opened upon the *personnel*, the difficulty of directing the fire of batteries in covered positions, and the necessity of concentrating batteries if concentration of fire was to be effected.[1] In order to facilitate the carrying out of this doctrine the organization, drill, and gunnery were carefully co-ordinated.

The *organization* of a field force allotted only one brigade to each division, but provided a corps artillery of three brigades under a full colonel, whose sole duty was the executive command of this large number of guns. Moreover the whole of the corps artillery and of the divisional artilleries were under the orders of the officer commanding the artillery of the corps for combined action, in which case he took command in person.

In the *drill* every effort had been made to reduce the movements[2] to those actually required to give effect to such a theory of employment, while insisting on the greatest

---

[1] The appliances available must be remembered. For instance the only means a brigade commander had of communicating with his batteries was by mounted orderlies.

[2] The 60 battery movements and 40 brigade movements of 1860 had dropped by successive stages to 20 and 10.

exactitude in their execution. The insensate repetition of
orders had been abolished, drill by signal was being introduced, and the criterion of excellence was quietness and
steadiness.

In *gunnery* the bracket system had been developed into
a methodical process in which strict adherence to the formal
procedure was insisted upon : "Show it me in the book"
became almost a catch-word at the practice camps! The
method was simple and sure, but it was desperately slow,[1]
for it depended upon the fire of single rounds by each gun
in turn, all by order of the battery commander. And the
key-note of gun-drill, as of manœuvre, was steadiness.
The definition of Fire Discipline summed up the whole
spirit of the training—"The essentials for fire discipline
are the quiet, orderly, and correct performance of all
duties under hostile fire."

Whatever efforts had been made to simplify procedure,
it was obvious that mass movements required practice if
they were to be executed with the precision on which their
success depended. It was therefore decided in 1899 to
take advantage of the recent acquisition of Salisbury Plain
to concentrate there the whole artillery of an Army Corps[2]
for exercise under Major-General G. H. Marshall, who had
recently succeeded Sir James Alleyne in command of the
artillery at Aldershot. Unfortunately there was no Captain
Wolfe[3] on his staff to tell the story of that important event
in Regimental History, but we know that, during the
first fortnight of August 1899, seventeen batteries were
gathered on West Down; that the General worked his

---

[1] The average time from "action" to the first time shrapnel during
the practice of 1899 was between five and six minutes.

[2] Corps Artillery :—

1 brigade horse artillery	... ...	2	batteries.
2 brigades field ,,	... ...	6	,,
Divisional Artillery of three Divisions :—			
3 brigades field artillery	... ...	9	,,
		17	,,

[3] See p. 225.

command as a whole, drill exercises alternating with tactical
schemes; that the weather was fine, the ground new, the
going sound; and that camaraderie and good fellowship
reigned supreme.

The Commander-in-Chief came down and expressed
himself as pleased with the instructive nature of the training, although he considered that the guns did not pay
sufficient attention to concealment, and in especial were
too ready to expose themselves when coming into action.
With his usual acumen Lord Wolseley had put his finger
on the weak spot. But the majority of gunners then held
the view that, however well it might look at manœuvres
to tuck the guns away under cover, when it came to actual
shooting—with the appliances then available—such positions would inevitably entail serious loss of effect. For
immunity from loss they placed reliance on the simul-
taneous appearance to the enemy of the long line of batteries, and on quickness in getting the horses off the
position. For protection for the gunners, once in action,
they trusted to the fire of their guns.

Difficult as it always must be to picture and allow for the
presence of the other arms during the training of artillery
alone, such a rehearsal on the grand scale of the work of
the artillery of an Army Corps on the very eve of the first
serious war since the Crimea and the Mutiny, was a worthy
climax to the long years of development which had followed
the introduction of rifled guns. And it was fitting that it
should be directed by the General who had borne so large
a part in that development, and who was to command in
war, before many months had passed, the largest force of
artillery which the nation had up till then ever put into
the field.

PART III.—TRAINING.

B. MOUNTAIN, HEAVY & SIEGE ARTILLERY.

CHAPTER XII.

MOUNTAIN ARTILLERY.

The first Mountain Batteries—Native Batteries in India—British Batteries—Progress in India—The Training Manuals—The Punjab Frontier Force—Active Service—The Practice Camps.

THE first mountain batteries in the British service appear to have been those raised in 1813 during the fighting in the Pyrenees at the close of the Peninsular War. But these were temporary formations, and mountain artillery found no place in the regular establishment[1] of the army at Home until the last decade of the nineteenth century. It is to India, therefore, that we must look for the development of this branch of the Regiment. Curiously enough the first demand for mountain guns in India came with the war against Nepal in 1814 within a twelve-month of their first use in Europe. But while the call in the Pyrenees had been met by pressing the mule into the service, in the Himalayas recourse was naturally had to the elephant. The next step was the raising of a camel battery during the Pindari-Mahratta War in 1817-1820, and although both these formations were broken up at the conclusion of hostilities, elephant and camel equipments for artillery were regular articles of store in India throughout the period

[1] Particulars of the organization and equipment of mountain batteries were, however, preserved in the "Artillery Establishments" compiled under the orders of the Duke of Wellington in his capacity as Master-General of the Ordnance.

covered by this volume, and were used on many occasions.[1]

To the mountain artillery purist of a later date the very idea of any conveyance for his guns except mule-back savoured of heresy. As one wrote in the Prize Essay of 1887 :—

> "Genuine mountain artillery has nothing to do with elephant, camel, or coolie transport . . . It is true that elephant transport is often used to carry guns in the hills, camel transport in the plains, and coolie transport in dense jungles, but batteries so organised do not come under the head of mountain artillery."

According to this definition the first "genuine" mountain battery was not formed in India until 1841. Wonderful as had been the work of the Bengal Horse Artillery in the first Afghan War, such mountain warfare was not the rôle for which the troops were intended, and so a Captain J. B. Backhouse was sent down from Kabul to raise a "Mountain Train". He had learnt the value of the mule for such work while serving in Spain with the "British Legion"[2] under Sir de Lacy Evans, and to him belongs the credit of raising the first Indian mule battery. He was back in Afghanistan with it in time to form part of Sale's "Illustrious Garrison" in Jalalabad, and to return to Kabul with Pollock's "Avenging Army". Once again, however, as soon as hostilities ended the battery was broken up. The Sikh Kingdom still lay between the Company's Territory and the Border Tribes.

On the Bombay side the conquest of Sind soon swept away such buffers, and Jacob[3] formed his mountain train. The annexation of the Punjab in 1849, brought the Bengal army in turn up against the Hills, and led to the raising

---

[1] The last and most notable instance was the equipment of the Chestnut Troop for the Tirah Campaign in 1897. The battery did not actually go into action, but the experience showed that even 12-pr. B.L. guns could be carried by elephants without difficulty.

[2] Formed of volunteers to help the Spanish Government against the Carlists in 1837 : it included a mountain battery.

[3] Brig.-General John Jacob, C.B., A.D.C., of the Bombay Artillery.

for the "Punjab Irregular Force" of three light field batteries, a garrison company, and two "mountain trains".[1]

From these units were formed the four mountain batteries and the "frontier garrison battery" of the Punjab Frontier Force, while the Sind mountain train became two Bombay mountain batteries. Thus, previous to the second Afghan War, there had been established as a regular part of the Indian Army six mountain batteries.[2] They were the first permanent mountain batteries in the British service, but they were all native batteries, and as such, strictly speaking, did not belong to the Royal Artillery until after the period covered by this volume, although they were all officered by the Regiment.

From as early as the 60's, however, garrison companies of the Royal Artillery serving in India had been temporarily equipped from time to time for mountain service, native drivers being attached with elephants and mules. But the establishment of British mountain batteries on a definite basis may be said to date from the formation at Jutogh and in the Murree Hills of two regular "mountain trains", which in this case consisted of the native driver establishment, mules and equipment for a mountain battery. Garrison companies of Royal Artillery, formed with these trains into mountain batteries, served in the second Afghan War, and it is from this war that the development of the British mountain artillery really dates. Directly after the war the Government of India pointed out in a despatch how strongly the value of mountain batteries had been exemplified, and pressed for an increase in the number

CHAPTER
XII.

Native
Batteries.
in India.

British
Batteries

---

[1] In his *Forty-one years in India* Lord Roberts tells how, in 1853, he arrived just too late for the Jowaki expedition :—"very disappointed at missing this my first chance of active service, and not accompanying the newly raised 'Mountain Train' (as it was then called) on the first occasion of its being employed in the field."

[2] Nos. 1 (Kohat), 2 (Derajat), 3 (Peshawur) and 4 (Hazara) of the P.F.F., Nos. 1 (Bombay) and 2 (Jacob's) of the Bombay Artillery.

Mention must also be made of "The Eurasian and Native Christian Company of Artillery" which was raised in Bengal immediately after the Mutiny. In 1865 it was reorganized as a Mountain Battery under the title of "The Eurasian Battery of Artillery", and as such took part in the Lushai Campaign of 1868, after which it was disbanded.

of British batteries from two to six at least, and for improvements in their organization.   The result of these
representations was that batteries were made permanent
during their tour of service in India, and were distinguished
by the word "(Mountain)" after their number.[1] Finally,
in the general Artillery Re-organization of 1889, the
Mountain Artillery was constituted a separate branch of
the Regiment, its batteries numbered from 1 to 10.

During the days of great battles on the plains of India
the horse and field had been the most important branches
of the artillery.   But with the conquest of Sind and the
Punjab, and the suppression of the Mutiny, that period had
closed, and with it the opportunities for service for those
branches.   The Afghan wars and frontier expeditions which
followed brought the mountain artillery to the front in
India, and the fact that Lord Roberts took no other artillery
with him on his famous march from Kabul to Kandahar
carried the new branch into the limelight of popular
interest at Home.   As he has related, "I was pressed to
take more and heavier guns, but . . . . I decided I would
only have mountain batteries . . . . wheeled artillery
would, in a country where there were practically no roads,
have only prevented our moving as rapidly as we might
otherwise have done."

Thus, throughout the period covered by this volume,
while in the development of horse and field artillery training the initiative came from England, where the lessons
of the great wars in Europe loomed largest in men's minds,
it is to India that we must look for progress in the mountain
artillery.

In frontier expedition after frontier expedition the new
branch soon proved its value.   As was pointed out at the
time of the Chitral Expedition of 1895, it was then ten
years since horse or field artillery had fired a round on
service, while every single mountain battery, British and
Native, had been through at least one campaign during that
time.   No wonder that the lure of active service drew to

---

[1] Regimental Order No. 13 of 1881.

the mountain batteries many of the keenest and most active officers from both field[1] and garrison artillery ; and the rank and file were also of the best—the drafts for the British batteries specially selected, the recruiting for the native batteries[2] as carefully controlled.   All the world was searched for ordnance mules, and the equipment and transport were kept on battery charge and in constant use, so that every section was capable of taking the field independently at a few hours' notice.   The mountain batteries were the admiration of all, and before the end of the century the organization of the army in India for service beyond the frontier included three such batteries in the establishment of each division.

Yet no trace can be found of any official instructions as to the part they were to play in war!   The first[3] Manual of Mountain Artillery was published in India in 1882 : it was followed in 1891 by "Mountain Artillery Drill", issued by the War Office, but, curiously enough, without the usual preface authorizing its use.   In it there is to be found a great deal about marching, but not a word about fighting. This is perhaps not so surprising when it is remembered that there had been, up to that time, no officer at home whose duty included any responsibility for the training of the mountain artillery.   But what is really astounding is that the next edition, that of 1897, although issued in India, was little better.   It included, indeed, a chapter on "The employment and conduct of mountain artillery in the field", but this was simply a reprint of the similar chapter in the field artillery drill book, with the addition of one short section on "Mountain artillery in the Hills", con-

CHAPTER
XII.

Progress
in India.

The
Training
Manuals.

---

[1] Whatever its merits or demerits in other respects, the separation of the Regiment was a serious blow to the mountain artillery in cutting off the supply of officers from the mounted branch.

[2] As the only form of artillery open to natives after the Mutiny it was much sought after.

[3] There was really an earlier one, compiled by Colonel Colquhoun who commanded the artillery of Sir de Lacy Evans' Force.   The story of its discovery—in M.S.S.—in the Royal Artillery Institution has been told by Lt.-Colonel H. C. D. Simpson in the *Proceedings* (Vol. XXIV).   Curiously enough no copy of the Manual of 1882 can now be found.

CHAPTER
XII.

The
Training
Manuals.

taining a few somewhat elementary hints as to the pre-
cautions to be observed when working in the hills, but
little to show an officer without practical experience in hill
warfare how to handle his guns. Where was such a one
to find a record of all the lessons that had been learnt
during half a century of such fighting?

This conspiracy of silence as to the tactics of mountain
warfare was not, however, peculiar to the artillery : the
cavalry and infantry text books equally omitted all reference to the subject. The explanation can perhaps be found
in the peculiar position of the Punjab Frontier Force.

The
Punjab
Frontier
Force.

This Force had been formed after the annexation of the
Punjab with the express purpose of dealing with the hill
tribes of the North-West Frontier, and nobly had it responded to the trust reposed in it. Cavalry, artillery and
infantry had learned their work together, and knew it—
and each other—thoroughly. But they were not inclined
to share the knowledge with those who had not served the
same hard apprenticeship, Mountain warfare was their
business, and not that of the army of the "plains", to which
indeed they scarcely belonged, since they owned allegiance
only to the Government of India, and were not put under
the Commander-in-Chief until 1886. What wonder then
if the lessons learnt in the rough school of the Khyber Hills
found no place in the official training manuals, but were
jealously guarded as trade secrets in the standing orders
of the regiments and batteries?[1] This did not greatly
matter so long as hostilities were on a scale with which the
Frontier Force could cope. But when the Afghan War in
1878 necessitated the employment of troops from the plains
it was found, as was to be expected, that they knew nothing

---

[1] The officers commanding native mountain batteries were only
regimental captains, but they enjoyed the title of "Commandant", and
complete independence. When the P.F.F. was put under the Commander-in-Chief, and the batteries came in consequence under the
control of the higher artillery authorities, the idea of being inspected
by these latter was by no means welcome. There are many tales of
the forms the indignation took, which it may be hoped will some day
be recorded

of mountain warfare. And twenty years later when the blaze spread from tribe to tribe along the frontier, and the army at large had to be called in, the results of a faulty system were still more apparent.[1]

The mountain artillery was an exception. The fact that the officers, whether serving in British or native batteries for the time being, all belonged to the same Regiment, precluded such exclusiveness, and the comradeship of all who serve the guns, and the close association of the frontier stations, soon communicated the spirit and the traditions of the mountain service to each new battery as it was raised. It only wanted a frontier expedition to give the practical lesson, and there was never long to wait for that. How frequent these expeditions were, and how closely British and Native batteries were associated in them, will perhaps be best realised from the following extract from the Report of the Inspector-General of Artillery in India for 1891 :—[2]

" During the past six months the following have been "on field service—

British Mountain Batteries.

No. 1 with Hazara Field Force.
,, 2 in Northern Burmah, and four guns with Manipur Field Force.
,, 3 with Miranzai Field Force.
,, 7 ,, Zhob Valley Field Force.
,, 9 ,, Hazara Field Force.

---

[1] Sir James Grierson tells how he gave a lecture on Mountain Warfare in 1888, and how, after the next campaign, a serjeant reminded him of what he had told them of the mode of fighting of the tribes, adding :—"1 told the men all about it beforehand, and wasn't it just what they did at Kot Kai? "

[2] Perhaps even more convincing is the record of service of a very well-known and highly esteemed member of the Mountain Artillery though she was but an ordnance mule ! "Kandahar" joined the 3rd Mountain Battery at Peshawar in 1879 and marched to Kabul in the following year, and from there with Roberts to Kandahar. During the next twenty years she saw service in the Zhob Valley, Burma, Sikkim, Miranzai, Isazai, Chitral and Mohmand Expeditions, finishing her active service with Tirah in 1897-8. She then went on the retired list, to live as the honoured guest of the battery—her brow-band bright with medal ribbons—until her death in 1912—at the age of 35 or thereabouts.

CHAPTER
XII.

Active
Service.

Indian Mountain Batteries.

No. 2 with Hazara Field Force, and Miranzai Field
Force.

,, 3 with Miranzai Field Force.

,, 4 ,, ,, ,,

,, 6 in Northern Burma.

,, 8 with Manipur Field Force.''

The
Practice
Camps.

If, as Lord Seaton is reputed to have said, "Fighting,
and a damned lot of it" is the best training for a soldier,
the mountain batteries should indeed have had little to
learn about their business. But it may be doubted whether
such service as the above quite fulfilled the idea of the old
Waterloo hero, who was no doubt thinking of his long years
in the Peninsula facing the French. Fine fighters as the
tribesmen were they had no artillery, while on our side the
size of the Force usually limited the artillery to one battery
—if that. The gunner therefore learnt nothing as regards
dealing with opposing guns, little of the work of anything
more than a section, and less of the combined work of
several batteries. And it may be doubted whether there
was much opportunity for the study of gunnery. With the
short-range 7-pr. guns of 150 and 200 lbs. that was not a
matter of much importance, but with the introduction in
the 80's of an accurate long-range gun such as the 2·5″[1]
gunnery came to the fore. With the inclusion of a brigade
of mountain artillery in each division of the field army, the
principles of the employment of artillery in the field, as
worked out in the field artillery camps of the 90's, had also
to be studied.

The strides made by the horse and field artillery under
Lord Roberts and Sir Charles Nairne have already been
described. These officers were at least as solicitous for the
training of the mountain artillery, but there were great
difficulties in arranging for practice camps in the hills on
the same lines. Early in the 90's, however, a start was

---

[1] See p. 178.

made, and then it was seen how necessary such training was if the batteries were to do justice to their guns. For many had never before practised at a regularly organized camp under expert supervision, while the majority had not previously worked in brigade. It was found—as was to be expected—that while in every other respect the state of the batteries left nothing to be desired, their shooting was not up to the same high standard. With such first-class *personnel* and *matériel* it was, however, only necessary to afford facilities for practice under modern conditions in order to bring the gunnery up to the mark. Before the great frontier outbreak of 1897 made the severest call yet experienced upon their services, the mountain artillery had added efficiency in the direction and application of their fire to their other accomplishments.

CHAPTER XIII.

HEAVY ARTILLERY.[1]

The Position at Home—The Position in India—The Training Manuals
The "Bail Batteries."

DURING the smooth-bore period, and indeed for some time
after the introduction of rifled guns, the lines of demarca-
tion between the different branches of the artillery were
not so clear-cut as they afterwards became. The Horse
Artillery stood apart, but in the Foot Artillery the "field"
melted almost imperceptibly through "heavy field" into
"position" and so to "siege". A company ordered "into
battery", or *vice versâ*, would find little difference in the
handling of the guns—they might be a little heavier or a
little lighter, but their drill would be much the same, and
so would be their method of employment. But with the
establishment of field batteries as permanent formations,
no longer subject to reversion to garrison, the heavy batteries either dropped out—as at home—or emerged as a
distinct branch as in India.

The possibility of such batteries being required in
war was, of course, fully realised by the War Office—it
could scarcely be otherwise after the famous exploit of the
two 18-prs. at Inkerman.[2] These guns had not, however,

---

[1] This term is used in the sense which it bore up till after the Great
War, that is as meaning "heavy field" or "position" artillery, corresponding to what is now termed "medium" artillery.

[2] *The History of the Royal Artillery (Crimean Period)*; by Colonel
Julian R. J. Jocelyn.

belonged to any particular unit, but had been kept in the
Siege Park in case they might be required, and, when the
emergency arose, had been manned by scratch detachments, and dragged into action by the gunners themselves
or by field artillery teams which happened to be passing.
It was thought sufficient, therefore, to maintain the equipment of such batteries in store, and to lay down a War
Establishment for them should their formation ever be
decided upon, although it was added—with unconscious
irony—that this establishment would "probably not be
adhered to in the event of such batteries being actually
required for field service."

The two position batteries which had been formed in
the Crimea in 1855 were accordingly allowed to revert in
1859, and the only heavy batteries seen at home during the
remainder of the century were those belonging to some
corps of Volunteer Artillery to which discarded Armstrong
40-prs. had been issued. Drawn by fine teams of cart-
horses, led by drivers in smock frocks, they made a brave
show at the great Easter Monday Volunteer Field Days at
Brighton.

The position in India had been much the same in the
days of the Company, for although elephant batteries had
done good work at Chilianwala and Gujerat, they had been
broken up at the conclusion of the war. Thus when, in the
final stages of the Mutiny, Lord Clyde directed that two
heavy guns should accompany each column for the reduction of the forts in which the mutineers took refuge, they
had to be equipped on the happy-go-lucky system which
has so often been necessitated by want of preparation.
In India, at any rate, the lesson was not lost, and after
the amalgamation heavy batteries were established on a
regular footing as part of the Royal Artillery in India.

The Afghan War of 1878-80 proved the wisdom of this
course, for the field guns could make little impression on
the thick mud walls of which houses, as well as forts, were
built. In letters from Afghanistan, in memoranda written
while in command in Madras, and in minutes and de-

spatches when Commander-in-Chief in India, Lord Roberts reiterated the opinion he had formed during the war. "I am inclined to think", he had written from Afghanistan, "that for service beyond our North-West Frontier the most useful armament would be the best gun that can be carried upon mules, and the heaviest gun that can be dragged upon wheels". From this principle he never swerved, and a dozen years later we find him writing to a high military authority at home :—"And now I want to invite your attention to an equally important matter, viz. : the rearming of heavy batteries in India. I am not sure whether you have ever seen these batteries; they are most valuable, so valuable that I consider no army in India should take the field without them.

Thus, while at Home the authorities contented themselves with keeping a certain number of guns in store for such batteries should they ever be formed, those in India pressed for the improvement of their position, of their organization, and of their armament. The four garrison companies that were equipped as heavy batteries were distinguished by the word "(Heavy)" after their number; their period of service as heavy batteries was definitely fixed as the first eight years of their tour in India; and one was allotted to each of the four divisions which then formed the Field Army for service beyond the frontier.

But what of their training? Throughout the period under consideration in this volume the artillery manuals—field, siege and garrison—were absolutely silent on the subject. Even the "Regulations for the R.A. in India" contained little beyond the details of gun drill and ceremonial. For tactical instruction they referred heavy batteries to "Field Artillery Drill" and to "The Tactics of Field Artillery" by von Schell, neither of which dealt at all with heavy artillery. The truth was that, as in the case of field howitzers,[1] no definite doctrine for their employment in war had been formulated. On one point only regarding

---

[1] See Chapter XI.

their behaviour in battle did the regulations give any
guidance. It was ordered that whenever it was probable
that the battery would come into action draught was to be
changed from elephant to bullock. The reasons for this
precaution are interesting.

In ordinary course the gun teams consisted of two
elephants, harnessed tandem fashion, while the wagons
were drawn by bullocks. It was not only their strength
which had earned the elephants their pride of place, it was
their combination of intelligence with power. Experience in
Afghanistan had shown their value in getting a heavy gun
out of difficulties in cramped or steep ground where there
was no space available for a "team" to exert their power.
But the sagacity of the elephants had its drawbacks, for
while it taught them how to get a gun out of danger, it
taught them also how to avoid this for themselves! They
had a particular objection to being shot at, and at Sobraon
a whole battery had bolted as soon as fire opened, not to
be stopped until they had got half-way back to camp.[1]
To take the guns into action, therefore, teams of bullocks
had to be provided, as well as for the ammunition and other
wagons which were normally drawn by them. Such a mass
of animals naturally required a great number of attend-
ants—mahouts, bullock drivers, and so forth—so that in
addition to the European personnel of a garrison company,
a heavy battery included a native establishment of 213,
with 18 elephants and 262 bullocks, besides the ponies for
the staff serjeants, farrier, and trumpeters. The elephants
gaily caparisoned in scarlet, the mahouts and drivers gor-
geous in crimson and blue, it might well be said that "the
Indian Heavy Battery provided a spectacle that was at
once impressive, martial and many coloured."

But gradually, as the century drew towards its close,
the elephant lost favour in the eyes of the military author-

CHAPTER
XIII.

The
Training
Manuals.

The "Bail
Batteries".

---

[1] It was recommended in the Regulations that, in addition to hob-
bling the elephants' forelegs in action, a long chain should be attached
with drag ropes to their hind legs—to be manned by the detachment
when necessary !

ities.   The era of jungle fighting was over, and all efforts
were concentrated on fitting the army in India for war in
Central Asia.   Wonderful hill climber as the elephant was
acknowledged to be, it was said that his feet were too
soft for stony roads, that his constitution was as weak
as his nerves, that his appetite was as delicate as it was
voracious, and that such a mass of animals was quite unsuited for campaigning in the country beyond the North
West Frontier, where the cultivation was sparse and the
climate rigorous.   Thus when, towards the end of the 90's,
the re-armament of the heavy batteries with B.L. guns
and howitzers was decided upon, it was also decided to do
away with both bullocks and elephants in favour of horses.
The actual change did not take place until the beginning
of the next century, but the last year of the nineteenth
saw the trial in India of a battery armed with B.L. guns
and howitzers drawn by teams of eight heavy horses.   It
was the writing on the wall!   And so passed the last relic
of the oriental pageantry that once lent a charm to soldiering in the East.   "Bail Batteries" were an anachronism,
and they had to go, but fortunately not before they had
found their Laureates![1]

---

[1] Lieut.-Colonel H. P. P. Leigh, C.I.E., d. 1928 (3355) and Lieut.-
Colonel A. B. Stopford, d. 1892 (3137) wrote "I love to see the Sepoys,
with their noble martial tread" for a Christy Minstrel Entertainment
at Mhow in 1873.   The authorship of "I was born in sweet Ballinasloe"
is unknown.

CHAPTER XIV.

SIEGE ARTILLERY.

The first rifled Siege Train—The Franco-German War—The Lydd experiments—The Bucharest experiments—The attack of Armoured Defences—The gun v. howitzer Controversy—The first Siege Batteries—"Siege Artillery Drill"—Observation of fire—Organization—India—Conclusion.

THE greatest Siege Train which this country ever put into the field had returned in triumph from Sebastopol but three years before the opening of the period recorded here. They had been welcomed at Woolwich by their comrades, and reviewed by their Sovereign, with all the honour due to their services.[1] But splendid as these had been, it must be admitted that the siege of Sebastopol, like its famous fore-runners of the Peninsula, had shown how protracted and costly such operations become unless the artillery *matériel* is ready when required, and the *personnel* is trained in its use. At last, however, it seemed as if the lesson had been learnt, for no sooner had rifled guns been introduced into the service than they were put to the test against a siege work constructed in the Plumstead Marshes and a Martello Tower on the beach near Eastbourne. The result was that the unwieldy mass of over a hundred pieces of every size and shape, requiring 26 companies of

CHAPTER
XIV.

The first
rifled
Siege
Train.

---

[1] *The History of the Royal Artillery (Crimean Period)*; by Col. Julian R. J. Jocelyn, p. 441.

artillery to man them, which had constituted the smooth-bore siege train[1] dropped out of the Regulations. In its place a certain number of Armstrong R.B.L. guns, together with the S.B. mortars, were kept ready for use.

The first examples of the use of rifled guns in siege operations are to be found in the American Civil War (1862-65), but, full of interest as these were, they received little attention in Europe at the time. The Schleswig-Holstein campaign of 1864 brought only the Prussian attack on the Düppel Redoubts, which may be summed up in the words of Prince Kraft,[2] "the effect of our rifled siege guns surprised not only the enemy but also our-selves". The war with Austria two years later gave even less guidance; but that of 1870-71 was as fruitful as those of the 60's had been barren. In six months some two dozen French fortresses fell before the Prussian siege train, while only one—Belfort—held out to the end. Such an object lesson as to the possible fate of the fortresses with which their frontiers were studded forced all the great Powers to turn their attention to the new problems con-nected with their attack and defence. The experiences of the Prussian Siege Artillery[3] superseded those of Todleben and Niel; Brialmont[4] dethroned Vauban; while extensive and costly experiments were conducted in Germany and in Russia. In England a special Committee was set up, under whose auspices a siege work was constructed in 1874 on the beach near Eastbourne, against which to test the accuracy and the power of the new R.M.L. guns and howitzers which it was proposed to substitute for the R.B.L. guns and S.B. mortars of the 60's.

---

[1] It consisted of:—

45 —	24 pr.	iron guns.
30 —	8 in.	iron shell guns.
15 —	10 in.	iron mortars.
15 —	5¼ in.	brass mortars.

105

[2] *Notes on Sieges;* Prince Kraft zu Hohenlohe-Ingelfingen.
[3] *Prussian Fortress and Siege Artillery;* Major Müller.
[4] *Traité de Fortification Polygonale;* General Brialmont.

The results of these various experiments were compared with the experiences of the Franco-German War,[1] and analysed by a host of writers abroad and at home. On many points opinion remained unsettled for years, but it was generally agreed that the breaching of unseen revetments by simple demolition with curved fire would take the place of the elaborate cutting of vertical and horizontal cannelures in the masonry by direct fire. Such a conclusion caused serious searchings of heart in England, for breaching by curved fire had not been seriously practised since some experiments in 1822—more than half a century earlier—and the more far-seeing artillery officers were pointing to the fact that the success of the Prussian breaching batteries at Strasbourg had been largely due to their having been directed by an officer who had learnt the way to use curved fire at experimental practice only the year before.

This was an argument which could not be gainsaid, and it was decided to undertake a thorough series of experiments. Year by year, from 1880 to 1884, these were continued at Dungeness and Lydd, under the direction of the "Siege Operations" and "Ordnance" Committees, the various problems requiring solution being methodically approached, and practically worked out.

The first thing to ascertain was the lowest limit of effective striking velocity, and the greatest obliquity of fire permissible. These preliminaries settled, the more difficult problems of breaching presented by narrow deep ditches with well-covered escarps and detached walls were tackled. Then came trials to ascertain the penetration and disruptive effect of shells, followed by others to discover the value of howitzer fire against both *personnel* and *matériel*, followed in their turn by comparative trials between guns and howitzers in the dismounting or silencing of guns. Finally the effect of position and field guns, and of 6-pr. quick-

---

[1] The Russo-Turkish war of 1877 gave little guidance, for although the Russians brought up siege guns against Plevna the method of their employment was so faulty that little or no value attached to their experiences.

CHAPTER
XIV.

The
Lydd ex-
periments.

The
Bucharest
experi-
ments.

firers and 1″ machine guns, was tested on parallels and approaches.

The above gives but a bare outline of the experiments, which included also tests of the searching effect of high-angle shrapnel with the new time fuzes against *personnel*, and of delay-action fuzes against overhead cover, of the use of reduced charges with siege guns, and of countless questions connected with the engineering rather than the artillery side of the subject. For not the least valuable feature of the Lydd experiments was the bringing together of the two services who must be so intimately connected in siege operations, but who heretofore had seen little of each other either in training or experiments.

Meanwhile Europe was being fortified to an extent, and at a cost, undreamed of in the past, and continental military literature was being flooded with ingenious, and, in many cases, fantastic proposals. The divergence of views was bewildering, but one feature which had not come within the purview of the Lydd experiments, was common to the majority. This was the use of armour for the protection of the guns of the defence. As early as the 70's there had been experiments, but it was not until the 80's that the subject came into prominence, owing to the fact that General Brialmont had introduced such armoured defences into the designs of the Belgian fortresses, and was advocating their use on a large scale in the projected fortification of Bucharest. The Rumanian Government decided to carry out an extensive series of trials during the winter of 1885-86, and representatives of all the nations were invited to attend.[1] There were many points to be decided; the best form for the shields—cupola or turret; the best material—cast-iron, wrought iron, or steel; and the best

---

[1] The War Office representatives were Major D. O'Callaghan, R.A., and Capt. G. S. Clarke, R.E.—Now Major-General Sir Desmond O'Callaghan, K.C.V.O., and Lord Sydenham of Combe. Interesting accounts of their experiences will be found in the former's *Guns, Gunners and Others*, and in papers contributed to the *Proceedings* by the latter. These were published in book form in 1890 under the title of *Fortification, its past achievement, recent development and future progress*.

mounting for the guns.[1] It was a great gathering, but for various reasons the experiments did little to solve these technical problems, or the tactical one which was agitating the siege artillery—the best method of attacking such armoured defences.

On this latter point, the official view, as expressed in the siege artillery manual, was that armoured defences should be dealt with by armour-piercing shell from high velocity guns. The guns of the siege train were, however, at that time mounted on over-bank carriages,[2] which had been introduced to save the detachments when embrasures became death-traps, but which could scarcely be expected to stand up against the shielded guns. In this dilemma the siege artillery turned to the disappearing principle, and there was added to the siege train of the 80's the 6·6″ gun on hydro-pneumatic mounting. But there were not wanting those who maintained that, even if this complicated device proved workable in practice, and enabled the siege guns to maintain their position, their fire could scarcely be expected to prevail against the cupolas, whose strength could be increased indefinitely. There was also the possibility of the disappearing principle being applied to the cupolas themselves, and gun, cupola and all, dropping out of view.[3] Another solution must be sought.

The introduction of rifled guns in 1860 had naturally been followed by endeavours to devise a rifled substitute for the smooth-bore mortars which still kept their place in all siege trains long after the smooth-bore guns had disappeared. In the Report of a "Professional Tour"[4] of

---

[1] The great object was to reduce as far as possible the size of the port. In 1879 Krupp had carried out trials with a 6″ gun where this object was completely assured by the gun itself, the muzzle of which was formed into a ball which pivoted in a socket in the shield. There was no recoil, and the layer sat, somewhat uneasily one would imagine, in a saddle on the chase.

[2] See p. 171.

[3] Trials of a disappearing cupola had taken place in Germany in 1890.

[4] The Department of Artillery Studies at Woolwich was given occasional grants for such tours by a party of selected officers. They visited European battlefields, fortifications, arsenals, etc., and their reports are of considerable interest.

artillery officers in 1868 there is a reference to these early efforts which is perhaps worth quoting in illustration :— "The most remarkable novelty in Ordnance consisted in large rifled muzzle-loading howitzers manufactured specially for Verona, and the other fortresses of the Quadrilateral. They would also be used with a besieging force. The howitzer possesses certain advantages over mortars which it will probably supersede."

The success of the Prussians at Strasbourg with $15^{c/m}$ "short" rifled guns gave impetus to the movement, and all through the 90's the controversy between the "gun" and "howitzer" enthusiasts bore witness to the awakened interest in siege artillery matters, just as had those which divided field artillerymen at the same period, as told in Chapter X. And the case for the howitzers daily gained in strength. Driven from their place in the breaching batteries by the success of curved fire, the supremacy of the guns for dealing with the fortress armament had been still unquestioned when the adoption of armour by the defence introduced a new element. It is not necessary to repeat the familiar arguments, but one point of considerable importance at the time may be mentioned since it has long ceased to apply, namely the possibility of using *high-explosive* bursting charges—established about this period for howitzers, but long doubtful for high-velocity guns. Here at last was a method of dealing with the cupolas. These might be immune from the glancing blows of armour-piercing shell—they might even be made strong enough to withstand the shock of heavy high-explosive shell dropping upon their roofs—but they must remain vulnerable to the effect of such shell attacking their foundations through the surrounding concrete. "Siege Artillery Drill 1891" had been cautious in its attitude, but by the time of the introduction of the 6″ B.L. howitzer[1] in 1898 the battle was over. The long list of pieces which had been a feature of the R.M.L. as of the S.B. Siege Train had given place to but one!

[1] See p. 203.

In the preceding paragraphs some account has been given of the most notable of the series of experiments which were such a feature of siege artillery progress during the period under review. But while on the Continent, and especially in Russia at the instigation of the great Todleben, siege exercises for artillery and engineers had been instituted, at home no serious steps for the training of the *personnel* appear to have been taken. There were still not a few of the older officers who were sceptical as to the value of rifled guns for siege work, and who remembered that Sebastopol had been crushed by a siege train which had received little training for their task. The necessity of sending a siege train to Egypt in 1882, however, forced the necessity upon the War Office, and a Regimental Order announced that six garrison batteries were to "proceed to Chatham for instruction in siege operations, and thence to Dungeness[1] for annual, including competitive practice."

Like the establishment of the field artillery practice camp at Okehampton seven years before, it was the turning point in the development of Siege Artillery. At last it had been recognized that the attack and defence of a modern fortress was primarily a contest between the two artilleries, and that, other things being equal, success would lie with that which displayed the greater skill and energy in the establishment of its batteries, and the greater accuracy in their fire. But it had not been recognized that continuity of training was necessary. During the first eight years of the existence of the camp at Lydd it was under six Camp Commandants, and nearly fifty companies were put through the siege course, but (with one exception) no company attended twice. Under such a system real progress was out of the question.

This serious defect in the system inaugurated in 1882 had not, however, escaped notice, and the Regimental Orders of January 1889 contained the welcome announce-

---

[1] Regimental Order, No. 16 of 1882. Next year's order substituted "Lydd" for "Dungeness".

ment that it had been decided "to organize a Siege Train unit with a view to batteries of Garrison Artillery being thoroughly instructed in the use and service of the ordnance etc., in connection therewith"; and that four companies[1] low down on the roster had been selected to form this Siege Train until required for service abroad.

At the same time the position of Camp Commandant at Lydd was recognized as being no longer one which could be filled by an appointment for the practice season only. More fortunate than their comrades of the field artillery, the siege artillery had a Commandant for their camp ready to hand in the Superintendent of the Royal Military Repository at Woolwich. This oldest of gunnery schools had long been the nominal headquarters of siege artillery work, but instruction had been concentrated rather on the shifts and expedients which might be required than on the shooting of the guns—it could scarcely have been otherwise since Woolwich Common had ceased to be available as a practice range.[2]

The first result of these changes was the appearance of "Siege Artillery Drill 1891." It was not indeed the first siege manual, for, previous even to the first institution of the siege course at Lydd, all those portions of the "Artillery Exercises" relating to siege artillery had been republished—slightly expanded—in a separate volume entitled "Instructions for the service of the Siege Artillery engaged in Active Operations together with the details of stores to be supplied in connection therewith." It can hardly be said that an officer appointed to command a siege train, or even a siege battery, would find in these "Instructions" at all adequate guidance; that could scarcely be expected at the stage then reached. But he would find every detail connected with the establishment

---

[1] Regimental Order No. 8, of 1889—5/1 Northern, 7/1 South Irish, 10/1 London, 10/1 Scottish. They were each provided with four "pieces"—one of each nature, 25-pr., and 40-pr. R.M.L. guns, and 6·6″ and 8″ howitzers.

[2] It was only well on in the 60's that practice on the Common was discontinued.

and equipment of his command, and full directions as to
the whole procedure, from the building of the jetties for the
landing of his guns to the arming of the batteries, with
every conceivable "shift". It was all that the Repository
could practice. Even "Siege Artillery Drill 1891," although a great advance on its predecessors, and dealing
fully with the various methods of attacking a fortress and
the general duties of the siege train, gave little help as
regards the direction of fire.

The service of the gun, and the duties of the No. 1,
had been worked out, and were fully detailed, but the
battery commander was scarcely mentioned; indeed a
battery—or as it was then termed, a "group"—was only
defined as consisting of "such pieces of the same nature as
fire at the same objective, and can be conveniently worked
by one officer." Until 1891 there had been no attempt
to work more than two guns together, and the distinctive
feature of the practice of that year was the introduction of
a series fired from four guns instead of from only one
or two as hitherto. This naturally proved a much more
difficult task than had been anticipated, requiring careful
organization, and a stricter fire discipline than had, up to
that time, been deemed necessary. The problem, however,
was resolutely tackled, a method of ranging worked out,
battery gun drill elaborated, the nomenclature of commanders of all ranks changed from the unsuitable system
of coast defence, and the battery of four pieces established
as the "fire unit" for siege artillery. The result appeared
as a supplement to the drill book in 1895, and marks
another stage in the progress of siege artillery training.

While still almost ignoring the battery and its organization, the manuals had devoted some attention to the division of the artillery in a siege into "Sections", each under
a lieut.-colonel, and to some description of the duties of
these officers. It was obvious therefore that as soon as
the work of the battery had been systematized, that of the
section must be taken up. But here the siege artillery
was even worse off than the field. Lieut.-colonels of the

latter branch had at least commanded field batteries as
majors : in the siege artillery there had been no batteries
for them to command.   They had thus had no previous
experience of siege work until they found themselves in
command of a "division" at Lydd.   Thanks, however, to
the fact that large amounts of obsolete ammunition became
available in the later 90's considerable progress was made
in the trying out of various systems for the control of the
fire of their batteries by lieut.-colonels.   But it cannot be
said that the problem had been solved before the century
closed.   One thing only was clear—if success was to be
achieved lieut.-colonels with previous experience in siege
work must be selected for the command of siege brigades.

The story of the long struggle between gun and howitzer has been told above.   It must not, however, be
supposed that the triumph of the howitzer was entirely due
to improvements in the *matériel* : important as these were
they would have been of little avail had it not been that
the *personnel* had learnt how to take full advantage of
them.

The siege artillery can justly lay claim to having been
far in advance of both the field and the coast artillery in
laying.   As early as the 70's a system of sighting invented
by Captain G. A. French[1] had been adopted, by means of
which "the reverse method of laying is made applicable
under all circumstances".[2]   Even more important was
their discovery of the great truth that capacity for command
does not necessarily involve skill in laying, and the adoption of the system of "selected layers" a dozen years before
they had been heard of in the other branches.

But however accurate the laying of the guns, good
results could not be expected unless the effect of each
round was carefully watched and noted.   This had ever
been the maxim of siege artillery, but how was it to be
effected under modern conditions?   The "Instructions for
the Service of Siege Artillery 1880" still placed reliance

---

[1] See footnote p. 134.
[2] *Manual of Siege and Garrison Artillery Exercises,* 1879.

on the sound of the shell striking, the colour and form of
the smoke, and the appearance of the fragments thrown up;
and only advocated the establishment of an observing
station if it was impossible to observe from the immediate
neighbourhood of the battery. It was not until 1887 that
observation from a flank was really tried, but by 1891
"Instrumental Observation" was established as the service
system. It was another step, but it was to be some years
yet before the system had been rendered practicable for
service. The theodolites employed were neither capable of
standing the ordinary trials of active service, nor were
they suitable for use by the rank and file. The need once
recognized, however, the ingenuity of artillery officers was
to be trusted to find a way, and by 1895 all observation
was carried out by non-commissioned-officers or men, using
the "Watkin"[1] observation of fire instruments and the
"Hickman"[2] plotter. An accurate and businesslike system
had been introduced, though subsequent experience might
lead to such simplifications as the use of the slide rule for
calculations, and less delicate instruments—notably the
"Tancred"[3]—for emergencies when the observation instruments were not available.

And then, when all seemed clear, the introduction of
smokeless powder came as a bolt from the blue to threaten
the whole theory of instrumental observation. For this
system was based on the possibility of observing the discharge of the enemy's guns, and trials appeared to indicate
that with smokeless powder this would be extremely difficult
by day. The only conclusion seemed to be that such a
necessary preliminary to opening fire as the location of the
enemy's guns must be undertaken at night. So at any
rate the question stood when the century closed.

The subject of organization has been dealt with in
Part I, but some reference must be made to it again here,
since in the siege artillery the organization finally adopted
was definitely based on the requirements of training.

---

[1] Colonel H. S. S. Watkin, c.b., d. 1905.
[2] Major-General H. P. Hickman, c.b., d. 1930.
[3] Major-General T. A. Tancred, c.b., c.m.g., d.s.o.

From the year 1889, when for the first time certain companies were set aside for siege work, as already mentioned, until 1894 the organization had provided for the training annually at Lydd of three siege batteries, and also of three garrison companies to form a kind of reserve from which new siege batteries could be formed in rotation. It was held, however, as of the utmost importance that the siege batteries should have regained their efficiency in coast defence work before proceeding abroad, and to ensure this they had to become ordinary garrison companies again for two years before reaching the top of the roster. Thus, taking eight years as a normal term of home service, a company would go to Lydd as a garrison company in its second year at home, become a siege battery in its third year, revert to garrison in its sixth, and go abroad again in its eighth. By the time that the officers and men had become efficient at their siege work, the shadow of reversion came over them, and the system was therefore naturally intensely unpopular in the siege batteries. It was almost equally so in the coast artillery, for the garrison companies undergoing reserve training in siege artillery were taken away from their ordinary duties. In the interests of all a change was essential, and in 1895, as a provisional arrangement, the number of garrison companies under training was reduced from three to one. In 1899 a new organization was approved, under which the number of siege batteries was raised to four, and these were given an establishment under which each half-battery contained the full number of specialists required for the fighting of a four-gun battery. On mobilization, therefore, it should only be necessary to post untrained gunners or reservists to allow of each battery expanding into two.

At the same time it was proposed that these four batteries, with the three siege batteries and four heavy batteries in India, should be formed into a permanent "Siege and Fortress" branch on the same footing as Mountain Artillery. The negotiations with India dragged on, and no definite conclusion had been arrived at before the end of the century, so that no more need be said of the proposal in this volume.

If, so far, mention has only been made of siege artillery activities at home, it must not be thought that the subject had escaped attention in India. Far from it. All through the long years of peace in Europe that had followed Waterloo, the Indian armies had been continually confronted with walled cities, or isolated forts, whose reduction taxed their skill to the utmost; and after the Mutiny many companies of garrison artillery found themselves garrisoning those same works. Moreover Lord Roberts, on assuming the chief command in 1885, had insisted upon the fortification of the frontier in preparation for the war with Russia which appeared imminent. In the works which were constructed in the 90's round Quetta and Rawalpindi and at Attock, the siege artillery were thus provided with an object lesson in the latest types of permanent fortification. He insisted also on supplementing the "R.M.L." siege trains, the equipments of which were maintained in the great arsenals, by the creation of a "B.L." siege train manned and trained ready to accompany the army into Afghanistan. Rurki was selected to be the Lydd of India, and it possessed certain undeniable advantages. The ordinary soil of the country allowed of siege works being carried out which could not be attempted in the shingle at Lydd; the three siege batteries were permanently stationed there; and it was also the headquarters of the Bengal Sappers and Miners, and was within easy reach of other military stations. The result was that the siege operations which were regularly conducted at Rurki throughout the 90's, were far more realistic than those at Lydd. They comprised not only the construction of batteries, parallels, approaches, and saps, by engineers and infantry, but also such incidents of siege warfare as the driving in of outposts preparatory to the establishment of a first artillery position, sorties for the capture of the siege batteries, and the final assault of the target position, a

couple of thousand troops or more being engaged from time
to time.   And it was not only at Rurki that such exercises
took place : at Kirkee, on more than one occasion, they
were a feature of the annual manœuvres of the three arms.
India was ahead in bringing home to the army at large the
importance of siege warfare, and in training the siege
artillery to work with other troops.   Thus when the new
armament of B.L. guns and howitzers was received in 1898,
the three batteries were well prepared to put it to good use.

The first step towards the creation of a siege artillery
trained to the standard required by rifled guns had been
the issue of the Regimental Order of 1882 establishing the
Chatham and Lydd course.   The second was the definite
allotment of certain companies—if only temporarily—as
siege batteries in 1889, and the combination of the appointments of Superintendent of the Royal Military Repository
and Camp Commandant at Lydd.   Thenceforward all
through the 90's the progress was steady.   Siege artillery
training had begun with the attempts to get accurate shooting from one or two howitzers.   The development of the
battery of four as the fire unit, and of a system of instrumental observation suitable for service were the problems
of the early 90's.   In the last few years of the century
the working out of a method for the control of the fire of
a brigade by its lieut.-colonel had been resolutely tackled.
As was natural when all was in the experimental stage,
technical conditions changing and authoritative guidance
lacking, the work during the first years had been somewhat
tentative.   New gun-drills, new systems of ranging, new
appliances for the observation of fire, were all under trial,
and with so many new things to see and talk about, the
habit crept in—it indeed became the rule—for all not
otherwise employed to gather round the guns at work.   But
with the adoption in 1894 of the battery of four pieces as
the fire unit it was obvious that the time for such free and
easy methods had passed.   From that time until 1899 there
was no change in the Commandant—Colonel Rainsford-

Hannay[1]—nor in the batteries, and progress was rapid. Finally in 1899 an organization was adopted which did much to ensure that the effects of the training were not lost. The great siege train of 1860 with its 105 pieces had dwindled to 32 howitzers, but at home as well as in India, there was a trained *personnel* to handle them.

---

[1] Not so fortunate as Sir George Marshall, who had the privilege of commanding in South Africa the field artillery he had done so much to prepare for war, Colonel Rainsford-Hannay's fruitful term of command at Lydd came to an end in 1898; and it was his successor, Colonel Perrott, who took into the field the siege batteries which had been trained at the Siege School.

PART III.—TRAINING.

C. COAST ARTILLERY.

CHAPTER XV.

THE DARK AGES.

The last of the Smooth-Bores—The Royal Commission of 1859-60—
Repository exercises—The Armament charge—Practice—The Dark
ness before the Dawn.

CHAPTER
XV.

The last
of the
Smooth-
Bores.

ALTHOUGH the wars of the nineteenth century had brought
no achievements in Coast Defence to compare with the ever
memorable defence of Gibraltar against the fleets and
armies of France and Spain, the coast artilleryman of 1860
could point to the signal failure of the naval attack on
Sebastopol as proof of the supremacy of his arm. The
cannonade of the Allied Fleets, anchored in long array
almost under the eyes of the Allied Armies,[1] had proved
powerless against the casemated batteries which guarded
the harbour mouth; while half-a-dozen guns in an earthen
work on the cliff top had grievously mauled an English
squadron. Coast artillery was at its zenith. Gibraltar
mounted seven hundred pieces, manned by a whole brigade
of artillery,[2] and the garrisons and armaments of other
fortresses were on the same generous scale. But far-
reaching changes were imminent.

---

[1] "The most powerful cannonade ever seen on the ocean." Letter
from Admiral Dundas to Lord Raglan. The allied fleets brought
over 1100 guns to play.

[2] *Shot Guns*: 68-pr.—40, 42-pr.—9, 32-pr.—310, 24-pr.—103,

12-pr.—11, 9-pr.—4, 6-pr.—10	487
Shell Guns: 8″—72	72
Howitzers: 10″—26, 8″—30	56
Carronades: 68-pr.—5, 24-pr.—47, 12-pr.—2	54
Mortars: 13″—23, 10″—4	27
	696

In the first year of the period under review (1860) Lt.-General C. J.
Dalton—Col. Commandant, R.A.—raised the 1st Brigade at Woolwich,
and took it out to Gibraltar in the following year, where he commanded
it until 1866. His son, Major-General J. C. Dalton—Col. Commandant, R.A.—followed in 1870, and has given many interesting reminis-
cences of life on the Rock in the Jubilee Number of the *Proceedings*.
The armament was much the same as that taken over by his father in
1861, and the gunners still drilled with red hot shot, and had the furnaces in the batteries.

CHAPTER
XV.

The
Royal
Commis-
sion of
1859-60.
In 1859 Sir John Burgoyne, Inspector-General of Fortifications, had pointed out that one probable effect of the
introduction of rifled guns would be to reduce in an enormous degree the power of resistance of existing fortresses.
The subject was examined by a Committee under the Duke
of Cambridge, and their report led to the appointment of
the famous Royal Commission on the Defence of the Dockyards and Naval Stations. The next year (1860) saw not
only the adoption of rifled guns by the Artillery, but also
the launching of the first armoured ship,[1] in the Navy.
The never-ending duel between guns and armour had
begun! Under the influence of such momentous changes
it is perhaps not to be wondered at that the Royal Commission demanded the expenditure of eleven millions on
forts and other defences round the coasts. This is not
the place to discuss the wisdom or otherwise of the Commission's recommendations. Fiercely attacked in later
years, they were accepted at the time without demur, and
the money voted for carrying them into effect.[2] So vast
an outlay on fixed defences could not but profoundly affect
the Coast Artillery. As regards Training it unfortunately
completely over-shadowed the advent of rifled guns and
armoured ships.

Repository
exercises.
It was not only that the new batteries had to be armed,
they had to be re-armed with each change in gun construction, so that for nearly a quarter of a century the energies
of the artillery were absorbed in this gigantic task. The
"Instructions and Regulations for the Service of Heavy
Ordnance" in force up to 1860 had devoted more than three
quarters of its pages to what had come to be known as
"Repository Exercises" from their being compiled at the
Royal Military Repository at Woolwich. They comprised
every conceivable operation in connection with embarking,
disembarking, moving, mounting, and dismounting, ordnance, and the "Warde" Committee[3] of 1870-71 had laid

---

[1] The "Warrior".
[2] Only seven millions were actually spent. One of the recommendations was that "Shooters Hill should be permanently fortified".
[3] On the education of Artillery Officers—the work of this Committee
is dealt with in Vol. II.

it down that "no officer can be considered as qualified to command artillerymen until he can direct with intelligence these various and difficult operations." With the increase in the size and weight of the guns and of their mountings the work became much more serious, for to get these monsters into their places in works designed long before they were dreamt of, often with very inadequate appliances, required no mean engineering skill as well as nerve. It was fine training in which some young officers—to rise later to fame in other ways—developed an uncanny skill, and old volumes of the "Proceedings" contain many interesting accounts of the feats they performed.[1]

The Artillery had not only to mount, but to look after this great mass of weapons. The armament charge was overwhelming. Company officers instead of training their men to fight their guns were absorbed in looking after the immense mass of stores connected with them. As a contemporary writer put it:—"If the system had been extended to the field artillery, each battery would have had charge of the equipment of half-a-dozen volunteer batteries, not all collected in one gun-park but distributed over a distance of several miles, and standing in the open; and even then the field battery would have had an advantage over the garrison company for the officers could ride!" And when company officers could tear themselves away from their ledgers, they could find no men to teach. To quote the bitter cry of another sufferer:—"The garrison gunner is employed in a score of ways from his battery upon duties which have no connection with artillery work—he is lent to this Department and to that as a labourer—he

Margin notes:

CHAPTER XV.

Repository exercises.

The Armament charge.

---

[1] The following is perhaps worth preserving. "At Malta in or about 1870, a subaltern was told off to hoist a 12-ton gun out of a lighter on to a battery on top of the cliff. Sheers were erected, but when the word was given to take the weight, their feet slipped, and the tackle flew back, seriously injuring several of the detachment, one at least being killed. The subaltern was aghast, but the serjeant-major kept his head, and in a stentorian voice gave the word of command 'Prepare to remove d-e-e briss'"—which included the wounded and the dying!

CHAPTER
XV.

The
Armament
charge.

Practice.

is used in fatigues of all kinds—he is prostituted to heavy porter, fancy sailor, and general military odd-job man, and when he is available for drill a great part of his time is taken up in learning to drill as an infantry soldier and to handle a carbine!"

The annual practice itself did little to suggest that its primary object was to instruct all ranks in the art of shooting, rather than in drilling with a multiplicity of weapons, for the allowance of ammunition was split up, a few rounds for each nature.[1] The following table, which shows the actual number of rounds of each nature fired by the garrison artillery at Home and in the Colonies during 1877—a year taken at random about the middle of the period under discussion—will show more strikingly than any general description the way training suffered from the complexity of the armament :—

	Nature of Ordnance.	Number of Rounds.		Nature of Ordnance.	Number of Rounds.
R.M.L.	12″	5	S.B.	8″	249
	10″	190		68-pr.	65
	9″	765		32-pr.	289
	7″	1010		24-pr.	135
	64-pr.	1730		18-pr.	35
	80-pr.	650		24-pr. (How :)	20
R.B.L.	7″	1727	Mortars	13″	215
	40-pr.	550		10″	203
	20-pr.	270		8″	270
	9-pr.	90			
	6-pr.	100			

[1] The normal allowance of a company was :—

12″, 11″ or 10″ R.M.L.	...	5 rounds.
9″ „	...	10 „
7″ „	...	35 „
68-pr. or 80-pr. „	...	40 „
7″ R.B.L.	...	20 „
40-pr. „	...	15 „
Mortars	...	25 „
		150 „

All through the 60's and 70's, and right on into the 80's, the practice of the garrison artillery was of the most elementary description. Whatever the regulations might say it was carried out under the very reverse of service conditions—the target an anchored barrel—the range party reporting every round—the Nos. 1 correcting their fire at discretion. Such shooting had been all very well in the smooth-bore days, when the target was a three-decker only a few hundred yards away,[1] and all that the regulations had to say about direction of fire was "when the gun is to be fired the No. 1 places himself to windward of it in order to ascertain, by watching the effect of the projectile, whether any alteration is necessary for the next round." It may well be asked, however, how it came about that such methods were persisted in long after the advent of steam and armour and rifled guns : how it was that while the gun-makers had kept pace with the shipbuilders, the gunners lagged so far behind?

To a certain extent the answer is no doubt to be found in the amount of other, and apparently more pressing work in connection with the armament as explained above. And the study of contemporary warfare had done nothing to stimulate interest. The European wars of the 60's and 70's had afforded no single example of attacks by ships on forts, while those which had taken place in the Civil War in America had been for the most part in inland waters. Such as were known about, as for instance the attack on Fort Fisher, in which the Federal fleet fired 45,000 rounds with comparatively trifling effect, indicated the invulnerability of forts of the poorest description to naval attack. Even the bombardment of Alexandria in 1882 seemed to show that the finest ships must anchor, or at least come back to known ranges, if they were to deliver an effective fire, thus delivering themselves an easy prey

---

[1] It must be remembered that in the days of wooden ships long range gave immunity to the forts but not to the ships, and the latter therefore liked to run in as close as possible. The inshore squadron at Sebastopol engaged the forts at from 600 to 800 yards.

to the guns on shore.   But there was a darker side to the
picture.   Moral causes, infinitely more serious, were at
work.   For reasons which have been given in Part I, the
popularity of the old "Foot Artillery" had been gradually
declining until the object of all was to avoid service in it,
or if posted to escape as quickly as possible.   Among
officers it had come to be treated as a penal service, with
its well-known "Alsatias", and such a state of affairs could
not but re-act disastrously upon the training.   It had, in
fact, by the beginning of the 80's resulted in a state of inefficiency which was causing the gravest concern to those
in authority.   The Garrison Artillery was passing through
the darkest hour of its existence.   But it was the Darkness
before the Dawn.

CHAPTER XVI.

THE RENAISSANCE.

The Dawn—The Moving Target—The Depression Range-Finder—The Position-Finder—The Chain of Command—Communications— Annual Practice—The School of Gunnery—The Branch Schools— Practice Batteries—The Annual Reports.

IN the last chapter the designation of the "Dark Ages" CHAPTER XVI. was applied to the quarter of a century from 1860 to 1885 which followed the advent of rifled guns and armoured The Dawn. ships. If such a description was justified, the succeeding period deserves as surely the title of the "Renaissance." For during the early 80's certain technical inventions had paved the way to a change in the whole spirit of coast artillery practice. And these were closely followed by the various reorganizations related in Part I, which were introduced with the avowed object of obtaining "greater efficiency in the duties of Coast Defence and increased means of instruction in the higher and more technical duties connected with the heavy armament now in use." Real progress had been made in relieving company officers of the burden of excessive store-keeping, and in combating the blight of employments and fatigues which had defeated all efforts to raise the standard of training for the men. Finally an amendment to Queen's Regulations had definitely ordered that the garrison artillery was only to be called on to parade as a battalion for inspection, and that their instruction to this end was to be confined to ordinary parade movements. No more were to be seen such ludicrous spectacles as gunners skirmishing against their own iron-

CHAPTER
XVI.

The Dawn.

clad forts, which had taken the heart out of earnest officers for a generation![1] The new spirit was soon manifested in the steps taken to infuse greater life into the annual practice.

The
Moving
Target.

Probably the most potent factor in restoring this part of the training to its proper place in general estimation was the introduction of moving targets. Whether the first of such targets took the water in Cork Harbour or at Hong Kong seems doubtful, but certain it is that the year was 1882, and that the idea "took on" at once. There was some sport in firing at a target that moved, and the pages of the "Proceedings" bear witness to the interest aroused. More elaborate patterns were designed; the School of Gunnery gave its blessing—although somewhat grudgingly; a clause in Army Circulars gave official sanction; and the Instructions for Practice of 1886 told how the firing was to be carried out. Service patterns of targets were authorized—the "Hong Kong" and the "Portsmouth" first, soon to be followed by the "Richardson" and the "Record" series, designed to give some suggestion at any rate of the size of the target presented by a warship. The pace was the difficulty, for the tugs pressed into the service had been designed for other purposes—taking rations to isolated forts, relieving detachments, and so forth—and were naturally not built for speed. It took many years of bitter struggle to convince the War Office that suitable steamers for towing targets were essential to the training of coast artillery. Indeed right up to the end of the century the laborious procession of targets presented a sorry contrast to the movements of the actual warships that passed under the eyes of the gunners.

The De-
pression
Range-
Finder.

Without a range-finder practice at moving targets would have been of little interest. The Manual of 1860 had indeed dismissed the idea of any long-range engagement

---

[1] These performances were deservedly pilloried by the mordant pen and facile pencil of Major-General J. B. Richardson, Col. Commandant, R.A., who did so much about this time to bring the training of both siege and coast artillery into line with service conditions. He died in 1923.

CHAPTER
XVI.

The De-
pression
Range-
Finder.

by coast batteries owing to the "practical difficulty in
estimating the true distance of a ship in motion." But
with the advent of rifled long-range guns such a *non
possumus* attitude could not be maintained, and as early
as 1862 a Regimental Order had suggested that something
might be done with a table of the angles subtended by the
height of a battery above the sea at every hundred yards
of distance, used in conjunction with a spirit-level. There
is no trace of any further official action for nearly twenty
years, but the suggestion had borne fruit, and an ingenious
young officer, whose inventions were to revolutionize coast
artillery practice, was busy at Gibraltar putting it into
practical shape. During the 70's Captain H. S. Watkin
brought out his "Range-Finder for Elevated Batteries",
and the Equipment Regulations of 1881 authorized the
issue of an instrument for all those armed with heavy
R.M.L. guns having an elevation of 100' and upwards.
The "D.R.F.", as it soon began to be called, at once
assumed an importance in the training of coast artillery
which was in marked contrast to the cold welcome given
to its inventor's corresponding instrument by the field
artillery.   While in the mounted branch range-finding
lingered on for many years on sufferance, insisted on by
the authorities, but exercising little or no influence on the
actual fire discipline of a battery, in the coast artillery the
whole system of command and communications might
almost be said to have been built up round it.

The mechanical genius of Captain Watkin was not,
however, satisfied with supplying the artillery with the
means of ascertaining the range.   Even with this assistance the task of engaging a moving target had been found
to present unexpected difficulties, for corrections had to
be made for target travel, tide level, displacement, strength
of powder, error of the day, and so forth, all involving
calculations far beyond anything to which officers had been
accustomed.   It was about the middle of the 70's that
rumours began to circulate regarding a mysterious con-
trivance which, unaided, would solve such problems.   It

sounded too good to be true!   But, after official trials in
1879, the "position-finder" was adopted for the service,
and within the next ten years the more important of our
fortresses had been equipped with this new adjunct in coast
defence.   In telling, however briefly, the story of an
instrument about which controversy raged so fiercely, it
is perhaps as well to commence by a statement of its claims
in the words of its inventor.   Speaking at the Institution
in 1886, Major Watkin said :—

> "With recruits and men not expert it was hopeless
> to follow a ship going at any speed—so now the
> position-finder traces the course of the ship, and when
> the guns are ready to lay, predicts the position the
> ship will occupy half a minute or more in advance.
> The dials on the gun floor automatically indicate the
> range and training to hit that predicted position.
> When the guns are laid an electric tube is inserted,
> and a signal goes up to the observing station that all
> is ready for firing.   The non-commissioned officer in
> charge of the position-finder watches for the appear-
> ance of the ship in the field of view of his telescope,
> and when she arrives at the cross wires presses a
> button, and the guns are fired.   Thus, if we have a
> small body of men well acquainted with the peculiar-
> ities of a fort and the working of the position-finder,
> the rest of the work could be efficiently done by the
> militia or volunteers."

Such a promise naturally fascinated his hearers who
were struggling with the new problems presented by practice at a moving target.   But when put to the test of
practice under the severer conditions of the 90's, the performance scarcely came up to the promise of the 80's.
The nervous strain on the observer alone in his cell, feeling
that the entire fire of the battery depended on his unaided
judgment, acutely conscious that the great guns miles away
would be actually fired by the touch of his finger on the
button, was found too much for men who, after all, were
electricians rather than artillerymen.   At the same time

the situation was intolerable to artillery commanders, who found themselves, when nominally in discharge of their most important and responsible duty, actually in the hands of the electricians in their cells. To make matters worse these latter were in no way under the control of regimental officers even when working their instruments in conjunction with the guns at practice.

And the mystery in which everything connected with it was shrouded when it was first introduced into the service, did much to intensify this dislike. The instrument itself, the principle on which it was based, and even the mode of working it, were kept jealously guarded from the knowledge of regimental officers—with the exception of a limited number who were admitted by the inventor into the secret, which they were solemnly engaged not to divulge.[1] Gradually, however, the cloak was dropped, and the procedure in the use of the instrument greatly modified. "Predicted firing" was relegated to cases in which local conditions made laying the guns over the sights impossible, as in casemated batteries where all view was obscured by the smoke,[2] or with high-angle-fire guns from under cover. For normal use the P.F. became an improved D.R.F.,[3] with the additional advantage of doing away with the correction for displacement. Too much had been expected of it to begin with, but by the end of the century it had found its place as a familiar and trusted adjunct.[4] Perhaps,

---

[1] "Like the mysteries of Isis, position-finders and submarine mines required a special priesthood with which the uninitiated might not intermingle"—Major G. S. Clarke, R.E. (Lord Sydenham of Combe).

[2] By placing guns and instruments at different levels, mists, peculiar to certain ports, were prevented from interfering with the shooting. Major-General Sir Desmond O'Callaghan tells how Admiral Fisher sang out to him one day in Malta—"I say, Desmond, one of my captains has brought a wonderful yarn from Gib. He tells me that he has seen some wonderful practice carried out there from guns at the top of the Rock, although being in the thick of the Levanter cloud they were quite invisible".

[3] The horizontal position-finder was introduced with the intention of solving the difficulty of range-finding for low site batteries where a D.R.F. could not be used, but was not at first successful in practice.

[4] 330 instruments and 644 specialists in 1899.

CHAPTER
XVI.

The
Position-
Finder.

The
Chain of
Command.

however, its greatest service was that it brought home to
the coast artillery the value of electrical communication.
At the time of its introduction the common facts of electricity were little understood by garrison artillery officers
generally; under the influence of the position-finder
electricity entered the syllabus of their ordinary training.

It has been said above that the whole system of command came to centre round the range-finder, and this is
scarcely an exaggeration. For the coast artillery laboured
under the grave disadvantage of having no organic connection between the units and the guns they fought.
Whereas in a field or siege battery every detail of organization could be referred back to the six or four guns, of which
all were the servants, a coast company had no such firm
framework. The works they had to man presented every
variety of construction and armament : they might consist
of any number of guns, possibly of several different natures,
collected in a fort or battery, closed or open, or scattered
in separate emplacements. Under such conditions it is
little wonder that right on through the 80's the only unit
really firmly established was the gun detachment. The
subaltern's command, acknowledged to be the backbone of
the mounted branches, had no *raison d'être*, and the company command had little more justification. It was but
an arbitrary arrangement for convenience of administration. The direction of fire was in the hands of the Nos. 1.

The introduction of practice at a moving target soon
showed the inadequacy of such a system, and in 1889 it
was laid down in the Regulations for Station Practice that
each fort or battery was to be divided into "groups" of
guns, the grouping to be determined generally according
to the bearing of the guns, and their number and position.

The next link in the chain was the battery, and that
presented greater difficulties. It had generally been
possible to find from two to four guns of the same nature
firing over the same water area, and sufficiently near
together to be commanded by one officer, and so form a
group. But there were no definite limits to the command

of the officer entrusted with fire direction, beyond the fact
that, broadly speaking, it must be the number of "groups"
which could be efficiently commanded by one officer, and
the range-finding instruments and means of communication
dealing with them.   The difficulty of the task is indicated
by the changes in the title given to the office of "fire
director" : he was in turn—"Fort Commander"—"Fire
Commander" [1]—"Battery Commander."

For the control of the fire of several batteries in accordance with the tactical situation it was obvious that another
link was necessary.   But lieut.-colonels were at least as
reluctant as those of the mounted branch to assume any
responsibility for the training of the companies under their
command—and with more excuse.   The choice of objectives,
the transmission of orders to the battery commanders, and
the decision as to the right moment for relinquishing control to them, could not be learnt without practice, and
there were few places where such practice could be obtained.   The regulations had recognized this, but with
the opening of the school in the Isle of Wight the opportunity came, and the reins began to tighten.   Lieut.-
colonels had first to attend, and then to criticize, the
practice of their companies ; finally to take executive command at "combined" practice.   By the middle 90's the
concluding day's practice of each division was devoted to
the combined working of three or four forts.   The chain
was complete.

A chain of command was however of little value without
means of communication between its several links.   In
open batteries this was comparatively simple, although
even there the enormous volume of smoke given off by the
heavy guns was a difficulty.   But a large proportion of
the heaviest guns were at that time in casemates, sometimes in double tiers.   "Communication" was one of the
chief problems of the period.   At first the only means provided was the battery commander's voice in an open work,

---

[1] This title was subsequently given to the lieut.-colonel.

or speaking tubes in a casemated one, although these
latter were practically useless once the firing commenced!
Clock-face dials, megaphones, whistles, boatswains pipes,
trumpets and bugles, all had their advocates, until the
improvements in electrical contrivances brought these
latter to the front, and there remained only the question
whether the telegraph, the telephone, or order dials were
the most suitable form. The improvements in the telephone carried the day, and before the end of the period
it had become the standard system of communication.

Allusion has already been made to the revival of
interest in the annual practice due to the introduction of
moving targets and range-finders. These soon showed
the necessity of drilling detachments to the watch, for,
unless the guns were ready to the moment, the prediction
would be lost. Nos. 1 had to learn that their business
was to lay their guns exactly as ordered, and to reload as
quickly as possible, instead of falling out to observe the
effect of their fire. This pleasant habit had not indeed
been confined to them, and its very general adoption had
contributed to the painful slowness of fire which had come
in with rifled guns. Once started the reaction against the
go-as-you-please style made rapid strides. Many minor
measures were taken to quicken up the drill, such as
sandals for the men on the gun floors, benches for the
detachments, etc., and the coast artillery showed once
more that smartness in the service of their guns which had
been their boast in the smooth-bore days.

The allowance of ammunition for company practice,
instead of being divided up a few rounds to each nature,
was computed in terms of 64-pr. (140 rounds), and company commanders were given wide discretion in the way
of commutation. By utilizing these powers, and the
rounds allowed for recruits, they were able to obtain sufficient ammunition to make the practice instructive to all
ranks from a "shooting" point of view. Moreover, with
the mounting of the new armament of heavy R.M.L. guns
on traversing platforms, there had been added in 1876 to

the company allowance a special allowance for "station" practice, in which all the heavy guns fired three rounds every other year to test the efficiency of the guns and their mountings. In 1889 a further addition was made by the institution of "regimental" practice, consisting of six rounds for 6″ and upwards, and a larger number for the smaller natures; the object of the practice being to familiarize all ranks with every nature of gun and mounting in the district. Before the end of the century all these allowances had been merged in a block grant of money to the station, its expenditure being left to C.R.A's—subject to the necessity for carrying out the provisions of the Equipment Regulations as regards the testing of the mountings of heavy guns.

In 1876 the system of competitive practice in force in the horse and field artillery had been extended to the garrison brigades, and all through the 80's this individual prize-firing, wrong though it was in principle, and extravagant in ammunition, held the field. In 1891 its place was taken by company competitive, which was at once welcomed as it had been in the mounted branch, and, as with them, aroused keen interest by giving every man a share in the result. The presentation of the Centenary Cup[1] in 1896 still further stimulated this interest, although the competition had to be confined to the companies quartered at the principal stations at home, who alone could shoot under approximately similar conditions.

The introduction of casualties to men and material not only drew attention to the fact that the training was for war, but also led to the inclusion of drill with reduced numbers, a contingency which does not appear even to have been contemplated until well on in the 90's. It led also to a realization of the exposed position of command

[1] For the presentation of this cup by Major-General F. T. Lloyd, D.A.G., R.A., see p. 242.

posts, range-finders, etc., and their danger under the storm of fire which might be anticipated from the great increase in the number of quick-firing guns which were beginning to be carried by warships in the 80's.

The progress of gunnery training between 1885 and 1895 had indeed been beyond belief. In that decade the gunner had learnt to use his new guns, and all the complicated adjuncts which science had brought to their service, for simple target shooting in the *group*. A system of fire discipline had then been evolved which enabled a company of garrison artillery to man the guns of a fort or battery, and its commander to direct the fire of the several groups. The manning and fighting of a *battery* was thus the second step. Finally, tactical control of the fire was secured by the institution of the *fire command* under the lieutenant-colonel.

In this progress the School of Gunnery had played the leading part. Throughout the period covered by previous volumes of Regimental History the only gunnery school was the Royal Military Repository at Woolwich. But its value had declined as guns outgrew the possibilities of Woolwich Common as a practice range, and the creation of a new school at Shoeburyness had been authorized by a general order of 1st April 1859.[1] Henceforward, as laid down in Regimental Standing Orders, the School of Gunnery was to consist of two branches, "of which that at Shoeburyness provides for the instruction of Horse, Field, Mountain, and Garrison Artillery, while that at Woolwich is in addition intended to train the Militia and Volunteer Artillery."

The ample ranges at Shoeburyness were of incalculable value, and for the first fifteen to twenty years of its existence, the new school was able to fulfil the duties for which it had been created, in that it dealt with the gunnery

---

[1] The first entry in the War Office Register under the heading "S of G" is dated 5th January 1858 and reads "Establishment of a school recommended".

instruction of the Regiment at large. But as gunnery
developed, and the breach between the mounted and dismounted branches widened, the field artillery insisted on
land ranges, and the direction of their gunnery fell more
and more into the hands of the Commandants of these
practice camps, who were quite independent of the School
of Gunnery. Events followed almost an identical course
in the case of the siege artillery with the establishment of
the practice camp at Lydd. The result was that the sphere
of the Chief Instructor at Shoeburyness became gradually
narrowed down to coast artillery. Shoeburyness, however,
possessed no facilities for working out the problems connected with the gunnery of that branch which were crop-
ping up so fast with the "Renaissance" in the 80's, and
so the coast artillery, finding the old home inadequate,
followed the example of the field and the siege, and set
out to find a practice camp.

The locality selected was in the Isle of Wight, and it
had marked advantages. It was in the immediate neighbourhood of the greatest of the naval ports. The series of
works known as "The Western Forts" afforded excellent
examples of high-sited open batteries, while across the
channel lay the most powerful armoured fort in the
country, and the armament of all these works consisted of
the heavy R.M.L. guns[1] with which the coast defences
everywhere were in process of being re-armed. The new
position-finder had been installed—and was at its most
dramatic when the great 38-ton guns in the casemates at
Hurst Castle answered to the touch of an observer in his
cell above the Needles—three miles across the Solent.
There were submarine mining defences, and the "Brennan" torpedo—almost as mysterious as the position-finder.
More important still a comparatively clear range could
generally be counted on. Not to be despised, moreover,
were the amenities of the Isle of Wight—in marked contrast to the "bogs and boulders" of Dartmoor or the "flat
and featureless plain" of Romney Marsh.

[1] See p. 175.

CHAPTER
XVI.

The
School of
Gunnery.

The
Branch
Schools.

In due course a Regimental Order[1] accordingly announced "the formation of a Camp at Golden Hill, Isle of
Wight, for instruction in the defence of a Coast Fortress
and Channel in connection with position-finders." The
establishment of the practice camps at Okehampton in
1875, at Lydd in 1882, and in the Isle of Wight in 1888
are landmarks in the history of artillery training.

The coast artillery responded with alacrity to the
opportunity at last offered of working out the problems con-
fronting them under something approaching service conditions. "It gave zeal and hope to those who had toiled so
often without much hope that facilities for instruction in
war tactics would ever be given to the coast artillery. The
turning out of the lane has come at last, and we can but
rejoice". There was an immediate demand for further decentralization of instruction. Gunnery Instructors were
appointed to the principal garrison artillery stations—
Dover, Portsmouth, Plymouth, Cork, Gibraltar, Malta,
Bermuda—and it was recommended that the system of
branch schools inaugurated in the Isle of Wight should be
extended to all the great garrison artillery stations at home
and in the Mediterranean. The first of these was opened at
Plymouth in 1893, but it was sadly deficient in many of
the most important attributes which had contributed to
the success of its forerunner, especially that of a clear
range. Although, therefore, much useful work was done
by the School, particularly in connection with the Auxiliary
Artillery, no great advance was possible until steps had
been taken to counteract these drawbacks.[2]

---

[1] Regimental Order 38 of 1888. "Golden Hill" was one of the
Western Forts, but inland and obsolete as a defence. It was used
merely for quarters, offices, mess, etc., and the camp was sometimes
spoken of as "Golden Hill" and sometimes as "Western Forts", but
there was no distinction; it was all one establishment.

[2] The work done at the Branch Schools must not be allowed to
obscure that still carried out at Shoeburyness. The various courses
which formed so large and so valuable a part of the work of the School
of Gunnery spent most of their time there, and there were other
activities which will be recorded when dealing with Educational Establishments in Volume II.

It was not only at Plymouth that "foul ranges" had proved the greatest obstacle to coast artillery progress. The very fact that coast batteries were built to protect the entrance to important harbours implied that the water before them would usually be crowded with shipping. And with the increase in the power of guns, and the consequent enlargement of the danger zone for ricochets, the trouble grew ever greater. It had been bad enough in the days of the moored barrel, for the constant delays took the heart out of all ranks, and induced a general lassitude which was hard to eradicate. But when the moving target appeared upon the scene the conditions became hopeless— almost ridiculous. All that could be looked for was an occasional shot, and officers and men, wearied out with waiting, lost all interest.

So arose the cry for "Practice Batteries" situated where clear ranges could be counted on. And their advocates soon found that other advantages could be claimed for them. With the development of practice under a tactical idea, and the necessity for giving the many specialists frequent employment if full value was to be got out of the costly instruments they manipulated, the maintenance of a *sustained* fire was essential. This, however, required a considerable number of rounds, the cost of which, if fired from the heavy guns now mounted in the defences, would be prohibitive.[1] But 64-prs. on naval slides, discarded by the ships, were to be had for the asking, and their ammunition was cheap. A practice battery armed with such guns was accordingly constructed at Whitsand Bay for the use of the Plymouth School, and proved of such value that there was an immediate demand for the extension of the system even to places where little difficulty had been occasioned by foul ranges. To this there was strenuous opposition from those who maintained that the true principle of training consisted in companies practising from the batteries they would man in war, and that the remedy for foul

---

[1] For example, companies practising with 10″ R.M.L. guns would only get an average of about 60 rounds

CHAPTER
XVI.

Practice
Batteries.

The
Annual
Reports.

ranges lay in the acquisition of further powers of control over shipping under the Artillery Ranges Act, rather than in the construction of practice batteries.   So the matter stood when the period closed.

The annual "Instructions for Practice over Sea Ranges", compiled at the School of Gunnery, and first published in pamphlet form in 1891, contained a mass of useful lessons on the conduct of practice, methods of ranging, and so forth, which were of great value in those days even if to a modern reader they have rather the character of spoonfeeding.   More valuable still were the annual reports of the Commandant.   In the 70's these had been but a collection of bald statistics as to the number of companies that practised, the guns they used, and so forth.   With the 80's came a remarkable increase in fulness and interest. It was demonstrated how much could be learnt by careful systematic analysis of the practice reports, how the errors of layers as well as of battery commanders could be detected.   But it was only in 1892 that they took on their most useful form with the incorporation of the reports of the branch schools or camps, the Commandants of which, following the example of Okehampton and Lydd, had become Chief Instructors of the School of Gunnery. Their annual conference provided for expert scrutiny of all new ideas, and ensured progress on practical lines.   The reports, with their elaborate tables of times and results, and accounts of such experiments as might be described, formed not only a very complete record of the work done, but an invaluable basis for comparison and estimation of the progress made.   Above all they gave the views of the leading authorities on all the questions of the day—gunnery, drill, equipment—and thus kept the Regiment at large *au courant* with what was being done.   There can be little doubt that, at such a time of transition at any rate, this plan of taking officers generally into the confidence of the authorities did much to stimulate interest, and thereby greatly assisted in the remarkable renaissance in gunnery, which is the distinguishing characteristic of the period.

CHAPTER XVII.

THE FORTRESS.

The Garrison—Defence Schemes—Ships v. Forts—Forts v. Ships—
Form of Naval attack—Artillery action—Q.F. Guns—India and the
Dominions and Colonies—Conclusion.

IN the preceding chapters the training of the garrison artillery in coast defence work has been considered from the regimental and technical point of view. It was necessary that the coast artillery should first work out its own salvation, and during the decade (1885—1895) of the "Renaissance" it was fully occupied in finding the solution to the various purely artillery problems. The Milford Haven Experiment of 1886 had, however, opened the eyes of all to the fact that the defence of a coast fortress was not a matter for the artillery alone, or even for the army alone. It had shown the naval guard boats rushing to and fro across the mine-field which the batteries were supposed to be sweeping with their fire—the electric lights working irrespective of the guns they were supposed to assist—and similar scenes of confusion in every part of the defence. It was obvious that action must be taken to prevent a repetition of such chaos, and since the garrison must in almost all cases consist of a mixed force of sailors, marines, gunners, sappers and infantry, means must be found to secure the co-operation of all these heterogeneous elements.

The first step towards co-ordination of effort appears to have been the issue shortly after the Milford Haven fiasco of a memorandum to general officers, instructing them to draw up Schemes of Defence for the Fortresses under their command. But so very secret was this kept that its existence was not suspected, even by the School of Gunnery, for some years after its issue. It is not therefore perhaps uncharitable to suspect that nothing very practical had been done in the matter. When Colonel Walford first ventilated the subject at the United Service Institution in 1889 he had to premise that there was no literature on the tactics of coast defence in existence, English or foreign!

The hands of the War Office were fortunately strengthened by the popular interest aroused by the Naval Manœuvres of 1887, 88, and 89; especially by a failure of the "English" Fleet to keep the quasi-enemy blockaded in Berehaven. The escaped vessels raided the commercial ports along the English coast, and there was an immediate outcry. The newspapers declared that from Portland Bill to the Tweed there was not a modern gun; there were "scare" debates in Parliament; and three millions were voted for the fortification of ports and coaling stations. But the Naval Estimates were cut close. There was counter-agitation, this time to persuade the nation that money spent on forts and guns was wasted, and that ships were the only true defence. The challenge was taken up. Admirals and Generals wrote to *The Times*; Professors to the *Morning Post*; and Lord Charles Beresford to the *XIX Century*. During the twelve months that followed, the theatre of the United Service Institution was the scene of four important debates[1] on the subject, in which the highest authorities— statesmen and historians as well as soldiers and sailors— argued with such vehemence that on each occasion the discussion occupied a second afternoon.

The result was the issue of a "Provisional Manual of the Tactical Working of Coast Artillery" in 1891, to be incor-

---

[1] The Naval Prize Essay of the year also dealt with Maritime Defence.

porated in "Garrison Artillery Drill" of the following year.

It was long-winded and involved, and admittedly tentative but the ice was broken, and Colonel Jocelyn,[1] lecturing in 1894 in the same theatre, could justly claim that the subject was no longer an unfamiliar one. It was not, however, until the issue of the drill book of 1895 that the tactics of the defence of a Coast Fortress took practical form.

From that date to the end of the century the order books of those districts in which fortresses were situated are full of the subject. Problems connected with coast defence took the place of "Reconnaissance" for officers of garrison artillery going up for promotion, and these problems included all that was involved in securing the combined action of all the elements of the defence. There were rehearsals and manning parades by day and by night, and mobilizations partial or complete. And in all this the garrison artillery took pride of place. Here, at any rate, there could be no question of "conforming" to the other arms as had been the lot of the field artillery for so many years. And if, as was too often the case, considerations of safety prevented actual practice with the guns of the forts, much could be learnt with blank. This was especially the case in regard to night firing, which was then thought to be generally impossible over water without a risk that it would have been unwise to incur. What lights were required in the gunfloors and magazines—how ranges were to be found, and guns laid, on targets lit up by electric lights—whether these lights should be fixed beams or searchlights—how they should be sited and by whom controlled—could all be worked out, to a considerable extent at any rate, with blank. The first lesson was that until proper arrangements had been made, special lamps and other equipment provided, and money allowed for running the lights, the forts would be practically helpless after dark.

Exercises such as the above were all for the good so long as they were based on sure foundations. But at first, at any rate, they suffered from the want of definite ideas as

---

[1] Colonel Julian R. J. Jocelyn, c.b., d. 1929.

to the nature of attack to which the defences were exposed. The positions which it was necessary to defend had been established in 1880 by the Royal Commission on the Defence of Colonial Ports and Coaling Stations under Lord Carnarvon, and during the next few years rearmament committees[1] and deputations had toured the sea ports at home and abroad.   Naval tactics had, however, been little studied, although the Committee on Naval and Military Defence issued from time to time confidential documents dealing with such matters, and the interest in coast defence was bringing the Army into closer touch with the Navy. This was particularly the case with the coast artillery where the two services had so much in common.   The Navy could not be ignorant of the great change which had come over the whole spirit of artillery practice when they saw at their very door the batteries on the Isle of Wight at work.   Between the two schools of gunnery an *entente cordiale* was established; Naval officers lectured at Shoeburyness, and Artillery officers were shown the latest types of ship under construction and in commission at Portsmouth.   Above all Admirals sent ships to simulate an enemy, and so gave verisimilitude to the defence rehearsals.   From such interchanges there resulted far-reaching changes in coast artillery.   In the domain of fortification it was learnt how guns should be protected from naval attack; in the domain of gunnery where ships were most vulnerable to shells; in the domain of tactics what form of attack to be prepared for.   As usual the technical preceded the tactical.

In coast defence, where no movement of guns is possible, their siting and protection, and the arrangements for the direction of their fire, may almost claim to be the controlling factors in the tactics of the defence.   As far as the actual protection of the guns was concerned attention had been paid from the first to naval progress.   Ironclad forts had answered ironclad ships; the imitation of naval construction had even gone as far as an actual

---

[1] Notably Mr. Stanhope's Committee of 1887 on the "Fortification and Armament of Military and Mercantile Ports"—p. 193.

turret on Dover pier; and experiments had been carried out with the massive cupolas of the Grüson system adopted by Germany on her Baltic and North-sea coasts. The many inconveniences of the casemated batteries, and the enormous cost of turrets and cupolas, if they were to be strong enough to justify their existence, brought the barbette mounting into favour, especially as the increased range of the B.L. guns coming into use in the 90's allowed of their being sited back from the sea and on high ground.[1] Where the lie of the land did not allow of such disposition open mountings were rendered impossible by the increased power and accuracy of ships' guns, and especially by the development of their secondary armament of quick-firing and machine guns. In this dilemma the coast artillery, like the siege, turned to the disappearing principle with which the name of Moncrieff is generally associated. Experiments at Inchkeith in 1884 in the attack from the sea of a barbette gun, were followed next year at Portland by a similar attack on a disappearing mounting, and it seemed at one time as if lines of pits would take the place of the great granite castles at the entrance to our harbours. Wiser counsels fortunately prevailed, as told in Chapter VIII, but before the end of the century the mounting of guns for coast defence had been reduced to two types— barbette and disappearing.

How were these guns to deal with a naval attack? "It is not much use going out to shoot an elephant unless you know where to hit him" as some artillery officer appositely remarked when discussing the duel between guns and ships. Ever since the setting up of the so-called "Warrior" targets at Shoeburyness in 1864,[2] much atten-

---

[1] The controversy between high and low sites showed a curious disregard of the plain teaching of the Telegraph and Wasp batteries at Sebastopol.

[2] It is of some interest to note that these trials led to a serious suggestion that the coast artillery should go back to smooth-bore guns in order to deal effectively with armoured ships. The proposal was dealt with—in characteristic style—by Lieutenant Noble, R.A., then an officer in the experimental branch, afterwards so well-known as Sir Andrew Noble.

tion had been paid to the subject of armour and its attack by artillery, thanks, largely, to the masterly papers and lectures of Captain C. Orde Browne[1]; and it had been accepted without cavil that the chief duty of coast batteries was to penetrate the armour of attacking ships, shrapnel being used against their ports, barbettes, and fighting tops, and common only against unarmoured ships. The study of Brassey's "Naval Annual", Jane's "Fighting Ships", and similar works led at first to further nicety. The theory was that familiarity with the appearance of every individual foreign warship would enable artillery commanders to identify those of an attacking force, and from their knowledge of the arrangement, the thickness, and the quality of their armour, to decide what part of each to attack, with what guns and what projectiles. This was the procedure followed when a tactical idea was first introduced at practice, but unfortunately the best pace of the targets was only ten knots, and so there crept in a deplorable slowness of fire. It was not until the study of naval tactics had been taken up in the last five years of the century, and attention had been directed rather to the form of attack to be expected than to the details of naval construction, that the training of the coast artillery became really practical.

The most important conclusion arrived at was that a deliberate attack by a naval force on a coast fortress need not be anticipated unless command of the sea had been lost. It was therefore no longer the form of attack to be chiefly prepared for, as coast artillery training had hitherto regarded it. The possibility of a temporary reverse, or of the absence of the fleet, which might expose some portion of the coast or a coaling station could not, however, be ignored.[2] Bombardment—possibly py a swift steamer with one long-range heavy gun—had also to be reckoned with.

---

[1] "Armour and its attack by artillery"; Captain C. Orde Browne, R.A., d. 1900.

[2] This question formed the subject of very important debates in the House of Lords in February 1897.

In the important memorandum quoted in Chapter XV,
Sir John Burgoyne had suggested that the most important
effect of the adoption of rifled guns would be the exposure
of our great naval arsenals to this danger, and his prediction had been borne out by the experiences of the war
between Chili and Peru in 1879-80. It was obvious that
with the increase in the size of naval guns this danger was
a growing one, and must be guarded against. Following
once more the example of the siege artillery, the coast
artillery fell back upon the howitzer. However proof the
sides of ironclads might be against the heaviest guns on
shore, their decks were extremely vulnerable, and before
the end of the 90's there had been added to the defences
of the principal naval ports batteries of 9″ and 10″ "high-
angle-fire guns." For these accuracy rather than rapidity
was the essential, and the position-finder proved invaluable,
with the additional advantage of allowing of a completely
covered position for the batteries.

As regards deliberate attack by a fleet, it was certain
that if such an attack were ever made it would not take
the form of the leisurely procession of ships delivering a
deliberate fire from a few heavy guns as they steamed
slowly past the batteries as at Alexandria, the idea on which
the accepted system of practice had been laboriously built
up. What was to be expected was something very different—an advance at full speed without warning, covered
by a hail of shells from the large armament of both heavy
and light guns now carried by ships.

Moreover, if serious attacks by fleets were unlikely so
long as the navy held the supremacy of the sea, it was
clearly established that no practical naval supremacy could
ensure immunity against the action of ships which might
escape the blockading squadrons. Such "raiders" might
be expected to attempt the penetration of the defences with
a view to the destruction of shipping in the harbour or
under construction, docks, coal, stores, etc. Their raids
might be attempted at any time, but were most probable
immediately after, or even before the declaration of war.

And when the enemy's ports were within striking distance
they would in all probability be carried out by fast torpedo
craft.

How were such forms of attack to be dealt with by the
coast artillery? Certainly not with a position-finder pre-
dicting, or with the over-elaboration that had gradually
gathered round the recognized method of engaging a moving target, and led to a painful slowness of fire. The cry
was for simplification—"Here's a ship, let's hit her"—
"Common sense and common shell"! The need once recognized the rate of fire was soon increased. Better equipment of all sorts, especially improvements in sights and
mountings, did much : practical methods of command and
training did more : and in combination resulted in a general
access of all round smartness in the service of the guns,
and an enormous increase in the rate of fire of all. It was
a return to the methods which had distinguished the action
of the smooth-bores against the three-deckers before the
changes brought about by rifled guns, steam and armour.[1]

To stem the sudden and continuous rush of torpedo
craft was a far more difficult problem, and yet it was the
one which the forts guarding the approaches to naval road-
steads must be prepared to face from the very commencement of hostilities, or even before the declaration of war.
It was obviously futile to go on devoting all attention to the
training with the heavy armament, and remain unprepared
for what was becoming by far the most probable form of
attack.

The first suggestions for dealing with such targets
envisaged the use of shrapnel, or even of case from the
heavy guns, but as late as 1894 the leaders of coast artillery opinion had to admit that no satisfactory scheme for

---

[1] "When land batteries are constructed to oppose ships they require
to be armed with guns which can be loaded and laid with great rapidity.
Length of range has not its usual importance, because there is so much
practical difficulty in estimating the true distance of a ship in motion,
but large calibres are especially desirable, because the explosion of a
single 8″ or 10″ shell between decks is enough to inflict a terrible loss
. . . . Of late years the 10″ and 8″ shell guns which are far more effective than howitzers, and are more manageable than the heavy shot guns,
have been constructed particularly for coastal service and brought into
very general use". (Equipment Regulations, 1860).

stopping torpedo craft by artillery fire had been devised, and seemed almost ready to surrender the task to the Navy. The advent of the quick-firing gun changed the situation, for it put into the hands of the artillery an adequate weapon, and in 1897 Parliament voted the money for the provision of medium and quick-firing armament against torpedo-boat and destroyer attack.

Thus there was opened up in the closing years of the century an entirely new vista in coast artillery training. There was no time here for eloborate calculations or for waiting for orders : a cool head and a quick decision, with hand and eye working together was what was required. But the necessary training presented great difficulties. A suitable target for practice was the first desideratum, and the problem appeared at first insoluble. Even if a target could be invented which would represent at all adequately a torpedo-boat moving at speed, the guns in the defences were for the most part mounted for the protection of land-locked waters where firing by day was rarely safe, and where practice at night was considered out of the question. And yet torpedo craft would always attack at night, and no amount of shooting by day could make up for actual practice by night. Observation of fire; estimation of speed, range and direction of the target; indication of which of many should be engaged; blinding effect of cordite flash; all had to be learnt by experience; and the sands at Shoeburyness were in those days the only place where that experience could be gained.

Thus it was to Shoeburyness that the coast artillery had' to return for their final training. The installation there of an ingenious winding apparatus[1] made practice possible at targets moving in varying directions at a speed fairly approximating to that of torpedo craft, and the last year of the century saw the inauguration of a special quick-firing course, which soon raised the rate of fire with the 12-pr. Q.F.[2] from a couple of rounds a minute to a dozen or more.

[1] Shortly afterwards extended to the launches at the branch schools.
[2] See p. 196.

The working out of a system of fire-discipline for a
battery of quick-firing guns appeared at first to present
insuperable difficulties; it was the very antithesis of all
that had gone before. Telephones, dials, range-finders,
correction cards were all obviously out of place. It seemed
that nothing could be hoped for better than the establishment of a succession of shell-swept zones through which
the target must pass. And then came the automatic sight.
There was natural hesitation in accepting all that was urged
in favour of the new device—like the position-finder it
sounded too good to be true. There were those also who
objected to the direction of fire being taken out of the
hands of the battery commander. The controversy filled
the pages of the "Proceedings", and by the end of the
century the automatic sight, though it had made good
experimentally, had not yet been generally accepted.[1]

India
and the
Dominions
and
Colonies.

In India and the colonies and overseas coaling stations
the progress had followed the same lines as at home, but
mention may be made of some of the local experiences
which affected the training. While in command at Madras
Lord Roberts had been impressed with the vulnerability of
the Indian ports to bombardment, and his representations
had led the Government of India to place orders in the 80's
for large numbers of heavy B.L. guns (10$''$ and 6$''$). The
artillery at Aden and Bombay were thus practising with
these modern weapons while the School of Instruction in the
Isle of Wight was still confined to the 9$''$ and 10$''$ R.M.L.
There were also to be seen at Bombay actual examples
of the "Floating Defences" which had been so much
discussed at home, in the shape of the the the turret-ships
"Abyssinia" and "Magdala" of the Royal Indian Marine.[2]

---

[1] Automatic sights were not available for Q.F. practice even in
1899.

[2] Their guns were in the first instance manned by the Royal Artillery, and there is a tradition that this dual control nearly led to disaster.
On one occasion the Captain R.I.M. commanding the ship, and the
Major R.A. commanding the gunners, had an argument. The Captain
wanted to alter course and told the Major he was not to fire until he
had done so. The Major replied that he had already said that he

Many of the Dominions had also devoted large sums to the defences of their ports, and the armament of heavy B.L. guns on disappearing mountings, as well as of Q.F. guns, was ahead of that of the old country.

CHAPTER
XVII.

India
and the
Dominions
and
Colonies.

At foreign stations elsewhere, while the garrison companies were better off as regards men than those at home, the armament was apt to be terribly old-fashioned. This does not, however, apply to the Mediterranean, where both at Malta and Gibraltar the armament was a very fine one and well up-to-date. At these great fortresses large artillery garrisons under a general officer kept the Regiment to the fore, and the competition among the companies brought the shooting up to a very high standard.

In conclusion it may be said with confidence that at the close of the nineteenth century the men, the material, and the methods of the coast artillery were in a fair way to becoming meet for the requirements of war. The scares of the bombardment of coast towns had made coast defence a subject of popular interest, and this interest had been stimulated by the controversies regarding the Navy, and such sensational developments as the 80-ton gun turret on Dover pier, and the position-finder.

Conclusion.

There was indeed a time when technical considerations were allowed to outweigh tactical principles in the training. But the mistake was realized, and a closer study of the true principles of coast defence, in co-operation with the navy, led to modifications in method to meet the most probable form of attack. A gradual shifting of the centre of gravity from the heavier to the lighter natures ensued, hastened by the coming of the torpedo-boat and the quick-firer. Practice with the latter, with its revolutionary simplicity and return to elementary methods, brought about a realiza-

---

was going to fire, and that the Captain was not to alter course until he had done so. After an exchange of compliments, each did what he said he would, with the result that a 10″ shell went hurtling up amongst the shipping in Bombay Harbour, instead of proceeding out to sea! Happily no damage was done, but the Royal Artillery soon relinquished their nautical duties.

tion of the value of rapidity as well as accuracy of fire for the heavier natures also, and of the fact that the great obstacle to its attainment was the elaborate centralized system of finding and communicating ranges, and of directing the fire. The automatic sight hastened the movement, and before the century was out it was being freely mooted whether fire direction could not in the majority of cases be carried out in the group rather than in the battery even in the case of the big guns, while with the quick-firers it was giving back to the subaltern and the serjeant the initiative and the responsibility which they had lost with the passing of the smooth-bores.

And then came the separation. It was the most important change in the organization of the Regiment during the two centuries of its existence, and the steps leading up to it have therefore been dealt with at length in Part I of this volume, while its results will be further examined in the corresponding portion of Volume II. But no record of the progress of coast artillery training during the closing decade of the nineteenth century would be complete without reference to the profound effect of the measures leading up to separation on the efficiency of that branch. They brought back to all ranks that spirit of contentment and pride in their service without which all other steps to improve its efficiency must have proved unavailing. Without them the "Renaissance" would have been impossible.

There had been a time when many garrison artillerymen openly welcomed the "smartening up" which a company received from the posting of a captain or major on promotion from a horse or field battery—however little such an officer might know, or condescend to learn, of coast artillery work. At the same time a constant flow of subalterns of any standing to the more fashionable branch was depriving the companies of their best officers just as they had learnt their duties. No service could stand such a strain.

The special Regimental Order of 1891 which paved the way for separation was issued with the definitely de-

clared object of securing greater efficiency in the duties **CHAPTER**
XVII.
of coast defence, by restricting such transfers.   Thence-
forward the garrison artillery must stand alone.   Officers Conclusion.
realized that their regimental career was to be spent in
the dismounted branch, and the unsettling influence of
a desire for change—often only at the beck of fashion—
thus removed, they threw themselves heart and soul into
the task of making their branch worthy of the great traditions of the Royal Garrison Artillery—with the success
which has been recorded.

APPENDIX A.—THE AMALGAMATION.

GENERAL REGIMENTAL ORDER.

Horse Guards, S.W.
19th February, 1862.

Her Majesty having been pleased to approve of the amalgamation with the Royal Artillery of the Artilleries of the three Presidencies in India, and to sanction an augmentation to the Royal Artillery of 4 Brigades of Horse Artillery, and 10 Brigades of Field and Garrison Artillery, His Royal Highness The General Commanding-in-Chief has directed that the following General Order published in India, should be circulated for the information and guidance of the Regiment at large, viz. :—

GENERAL ORDER.

By His Excellency The Governor-General of India
in Council.

Fort William, 12th October, 1861.

No 924 of 1861.   In accordance with the instructions of Her Majesty's Government, the Bengal, Madras, and Bombay Regiments of Artillery will be formed into the 2nd, 3rd, 4th, and 5th Royal Horse Brigades, and the 16th, 17th, 18th, 19th, 20th, 21st, 22nd, 23rd, 24th, and 25th Brigades of Royal Artillery.

The Batteries of the new Royal Artillery Brigades will be composed of the soldiers of the existing Troops and Companies of the Bengal, Madras, and Bombay Regiments of Artillery who have volunteered for the Royal Artillery.

The Artillery men who have elected for local service will be formed into separate Indian (European) Batteries.

The 2nd Royal Horse Brigade will be formed of seven Troops of Bengal Horse Artillery, the 3rd Brigade of the

four Troops of Madras Horse Artillery, the 4th Brigade of
the four Troops of Bombay Horse Artillery, and the 5th
Brigade of six Troops of Bengal Horse Artillery.

The Brigades of Royal Artillery will be formed :—

16th	of 5	Companies	of Bengal	Artillery.
17th	of 6	,,	Madras	,,
18th	of 6	,,	Bombay	,,
19th	of 5	,,	Bengal	,,
20th	of 5	,,	Madras	,,
21st	of 6	,,	Bombay	,,
22nd	of 5	,,	Bengal	,,
23rd	of 5	,,	Madras	,,
24th	of 5	,,	Bengal	,,
25th	of 4	,,	Bengal	,,

Additional Field and Garrison Batteries will be formed
as soon as Artillerymen are available, and will be attached
to the several Brigades, in such proportions as may hereafter be determined.

.   .   .   .   .

*(Here follows a table of batteries and companies which
it has not been thought necessary to reproduce.)*

All Batteries will remain at their present Stations, and
their Artillerymen who have elected for Indian Service,
will continue to do duty with their former Troops and
Companies until the weather permits of their being
collected and formed into separate Batteries.

Consequent upon the foregoing formation of the Brigades and Battalions of Bengal, Madras, and Bombay
Artillery, into Brigades and Batteries of Royal Artillery,
all Reports and returns required by Her Majesty's Regulations will be forwarded by these Brigades and Batteries
through the Commandants of Artillery at each Presidency
to the Adjutant-General's Department, British Forces.

All Correspondence, Returns and Reports relating to
the interior Economy of the several new Brigades, as well

as those of purely a Regimental nature, will be forwarded to the Adjutant-General's Office, Horse Guards, direct by Commanding Officers in the same manner in all respects as now obtains in the Royal Artillery.

The names of the Officers of the late Indian Artilleries, and their posting to the several Brigades and Batteries will be published in a future General Regimental Order.

By command of

His Royal Highness The Duke of Cambridge,

Colonel of the Royal Artillery;

(Sd.)   Chas. Bingham,

Deputy Adjutant General.

APPENDIX B.—THE SEPARATION.

ARMY ORDER 96 OF JUNE, 1899.

ROYAL REGIMENT OF ARTILLERY.

WHEREAS WE deem it expedient to rearrange Our Royal Regiment of Artillery;

OUR WILL AND PLEASURE IS that from the 1st June, 1899, the mounted and dismounted branches of Our Royal Regiment of Artillery shall be separated into two corps, under the general title of the Royal Regiment of Artillery, to be named respectively—

(a.) The Royal Horse Artillery and the Royal Field Artillery.

(b.) The Royal Garrison Artillery.

Our Warrant dated the 28th January, 1899, defining "Corps" for the purposes of the Army Act, shall be amended accordingly.

The honours and distinctions now borne by the regiment, shall be borne by each of the above-named corps.

The names of the officers who have elected, or who have been selected, to serve with either corps shall be published in the Monthly Army List, and they shall then be considered as having been duly gazetted to their respective corps.

Enlistments shall in future be for service in Our Royal Regiment of Artillery (Royal Horse and Royal Field Artillery), or Our Royal Regiment of Artillery (Royal Garrison Artillery). Men for the mountain artillery will be enlisted for Our Royal Regiment of Artillery (Royal Garrison Artillery).

The service of officers in Our Royal Regiment of Artillery shall be subject to the following conditions :—

1. The selection of officers for promotion shall in future

be made from the list of officers of the corps in which the vacancy has occurred.

2. Exchanges between officers of the two corps may in certain cases be permitted under regulations to be published hereafter.

3. Officers now serving with the garrison artillery, whose names have already been noted for transfer to the mounted branch, shall be considered for such transfer as opportunities offer.

4. Officers appointed to either corps after the 1st June, 1899 shall have no claim to be considered for transfer.

5. Appointments to the Royal Horse Artillery shall be made exclusively from the Royal Field Artillery.

6. Appointments to the mountain artillery (both European and Native) shall be made exclusively from the Royal Garrison Artillery.

> Given at Our Court at Balmoral, this 29th day of May, 1899, in the 62nd year of Our Reign.

> By Her Majesty's Command,

> LANSDOWNE.

APPENDIX C.

Table showing the number of horse and field batteries armed with each nature of gun in use on five dates between 1860 and 1899.

Year	Home or Indian Establishment.	Horse or Field Battery.	S.B.	6 pr.	9 pr.	12 pr.	7 pr.	9 pr.	9 pr.	16 pr.	13 pr.	12 pr. 7 cwt.	12 pr. 6 cwt.	15 pr.	5" How.	Remarks.
				R.B.L. (Armstrong).			R.M.L. (Bronze)		R.M.L.			B.L.				
1863	Home ...	Horse		1*		10										*In New Zealand.
		Field				25										
	Indian ..	Horse	21													
		Field	46			1										
1872	Home ...	Horse					1†		16							†In South Africa.
		Field				30			10							
	Indian ...	Horse	8			7										
		Field	29			9		5								
1881	Home ...	Horse							18		1					
		Field							9	22						
	Indian ...	Horse				2			15							
		Field							47							
1890	Home ...	Horse									1	8				
		Field								2	12	24				
	Indian ...	Horse							5			6	10			
		Field							36			6				
1899	Home ...	Horse										11				
		Field												48	3	
	Indian ...	Horse														
		Field										40		1		

NOTE.—The figures show the position on the 1st January of each year. The year 1863 has been taken as the first year because by the beginning of that year the amalgamation of the Indian Artilleries with the Royal Artillery had been completed. Intervals of nine years carry the record up to the last year of the period covered by this volume. Depôt batteries are not shown.

APPENDIX D.

Table showing the main particulars of each nature of gun and howitzer with which horse and field batteries were armed between 1860 and 1899.

Nature.	Weight of Shell.		Muzzle Velocity.	Weight behind splinter bar.						Number of rounds carried.		Remarks
				Gun & Limber.			Wagon & Limber.			Gun & Limber.	Wagon & Limber.	
	lbs.	ozs.	f.s.	cwts.	qrs.	lbs.	cwts.	qrs.	lbs.			
9 pr. R.B.L.	8	11	1055	31	1	—	40	1	—	34	90	
12 pr. R.B.L.	10	11	1239	37	—	—	41	1	—	34	90	
9 pr. R.M.L.	9	12	1380	34	3	20	41	1	25	40	60	
16 pr. R.M.L.	17	14½	1310	43	0	19	43	2	7	28	72	
13 pr. R.M.L.	13	10½	1595	38	3	25	48	0	6	36	106	
12 pr. B.L. (7 cwt.) ...	12	8	1710	36	3	9	36	3	21	36	74	
12 pr. B.L. (6 cwt.) ...	12	8	1523	32	3	20	33	1	0	48	92	
15 pr. B.L.	14	0	1581	37	0	20	38	2	25	44	104	
5" Howitzer	50	0	782	46	2	8	46	1	8	21	45	

NOTE.—In order to avoid unnecessary complication the details have only been given for the first "Mark" of each nature. The weights are without personal equipment or detachments.

APPENDIX E.

Table showing the various natures of guns, howitzers, mortars, etc., in the service at the beginning and end of the period covered.

Iron Smooth-Bore.	Home.	Abroad.	Total.		R.B.L.	R.M.L.	B.L.	Q.F.
Guns.				*Guns.*				
10″	80	81	161		7″	64 pr.*	12″	4·7″
8″ of 65 cwt ...	336	213	549		40 pr.	80 pr.*	10″	12 pr.
8″ of 52 „	60	39	99		20 pr.		9·2″	6 pr.
68 pr. of 112 cwt....	24	11	35		12 pr.	17·72″	8″	3 pr.
68 pr. of 95 „ ...	271	107	378		9 pr.	16″	6″	
32 pr. of 56/58 cwt.	588	595	1183			12·5″	5″	
32 pr. of 32 „	29	30	59			12″	4″	
32 pr. of ? „	—	23	23			11″	15 pr.	
24 pr. of 50 cwt. ...	388	694	1082			10·4″	12 pr. 7 cwt.	
24 pr. of 41 „ ...	—	5	5			10″	12 pr. 6 cwt.	
24 pr. of 20 „ ...	107	117	224			9″		
24 pr. of ? „ ...	—	53	53			8″		
18 pr. of 42 cwt. ...	178	128	306			7″		
18 pr. of 22 „	—	2	2			6·6″		
18 pr. of 20 „ ...	18	3	21			64 pr.		
18 pr. of 15 „ ...	11	—	11			40 pr.		
18 pr. of ? „ ...	—	108	108			25 pr.		
12 pr. 21 to 34 cwt.	132	85	217			16 pr.		
12 pr. of ? „	—	44	44			15 pr. jointed		
9 pr. of 28½ cwt....	25	13	38			13 pr.		
6 pr. of 17 „ ...	15	8	23			9 pr. 8 cwt.		
6 pr. of ? „ ...	—	20	20			9 pr. 6 cwt.		
						2·5″ jointed		
Howitzers.						7 pr. 200 lbs.		
10″ of 40/42 cwt. ...	21	40	61			7 pr. 150 lbs.		
8″ of 20/22 „ ...	73	70	143					
5¼″ of 15½ „ ...	24	13	37	*Howitzers.*		10″ †	8″	
						9″ †	6″	
Mortars.						8″ 70 cwt.	5·4″ (India)	
13″ of 36 cwt. ...	20	87	107			8″ 46 cwt.	5″	
10″ of 18 „ ...	23	70	93			6·6″		
8″ of 8 „ ...	12	32	44			6·3″		
						4″ jointed		
Carronades.								
68 pr. of 36½ cwt....	3	16	19					
32 pr. of 17 „ ...	4	46	50					
24 pr. of 13 „ ...	78	371	449					
18 pr. of 10 „ ...	40	40	80					
12 pr. of 7 „ ...	67	30	97					
Totals ...	2625	3143	5768					

The above are all "Iron"—there were also the following natures of "Bronze" guns in considerable numbers :—

Guns. 12 pr., 9 pr., 6 pr., 3 pr.
Howitzers. 32 pr., 24 pr., 12 pr., 4 ⅖″
Mortars. 5½″ and Coëhorn.

* Converted smooth-bores.

† High-angle-fire guns.

INDEX.